E

From
African
to
Yankee

From
African
to
Yankee

Narratives of
Slavery and Freedom
in Antebellum
New England

Robert J. Cottrol

M.E. Sharpe
Armonk, New York
London, England

Library of Congress Cataloging-in-Publication Data

From African to Yankee : narratives of slavery and freedom in antebellum New England /
edited with an introduction by Robert J. Cottrol.
p. cm.
Includes bibliographical references (p.) and index.
ISBN 0-7656-0110-9 (hardcover : alk. paper).
ISBN 0-7656-0111-7 (paperback : alk. paper)
1. Slaves—New England—Biography. 2. Slavery—New England—History.
3. New England—Race relations. 4. New England—History—Colonial period,
ca. 1600–1775. 5. New England—History—1775–1865.
6. Afro-Americans—History—to 1863.   I. Cottrol, Robert J.
E445.N5F76 1998
974′.00496′002922
[B]—dc21   97-41904
CIP

Printed in the United States of America

The paper used in this publication meets the minimum requirements of the
American National Standard for Information Sciences—
Permanence of Paper for Printed Library Materials,
ANSI Z 39.48-1984.

MV (c)   10   9   8   7   6   5   4   3   2   1
MV (p)   10   9   8   7   6   5   4   3   2   1

To Sue, Dora and to John Marshall Cottrol II who was not named
after the Chief Justice.

TABLE OF CONTENTS

ACKNOWLEDGMENTS

A number of people were quite generous with their assistance during the completion of this project, and I would like to express my gratitude to them. Paul Butler, Raymond T. Diamond, Paul Finkelman, Don Kates, and Katie Harrington-McBride all made helpful editorial suggestions. George Washington University Law School librarian Scott Pagel provided superb bibliographic support. My research assistant Jeffrey Harrington greatly assisted the project. The tedious work of physically preparing the text was done by Padmaja Balakrishnan, Teresa A. Bush, and especially by Rahaf Keylani. Finally I would like to thank Jack Friedenthal, Dean of George Washington University Law School, for a summer research grant, which greatly aided in the completion of this project.

INTRODUCTION

The narratives in this volume are part of a rich, important and yet often overlooked chapter in American history. There has been a widening interest in Afro-American history since the 1960s. An outpouring of scholarly and popular writings, historical dramatizations like *Roots*, *Glory*, and *Amistad* and the long overdue integration of textbooks on American history have made such topics as antebellum southern slavery, Reconstruction, Jim Crow, and the civil rights movement at least superficially familiar to most Americans. This new interest is certainly welcome. It represents a vast improvement over a time, not too long ago, when most Americans could go through secondary school and even receive a university education, indeed even specialize in American history, without seriously examining the problem of race or the role of Americans of African descent in the nation's past.[1]

Yet as important as the recent interest in black history has been, it has often suffered from too narrow a focus. Most Americans still view the story of blacks in America's past, or at least the past before the Second World War, as an almost exclusively southern story. That is natural. Until quite recently the overwhelming majority of African Americans lived in the South. That region was the site of the most dramatic events in this nation's troubled racial history. The black experience in the South has left indelible marks in the country's history, profoundly influencing even the development of the nation's fundamental charter—the Constitution.

What is often absent from the consciousness of most Americans is that the story of black life in the North has a history at least as long as the more familiar and more dramatic southern history. The history of New England, the home of the authors of the narratives in this volume, provides reminders of the longevity of the black experience in the North and of how that history has been forgotten by many Americans. Africans were first brought to New England in the early part of the seventeenth century. Indeed legislation in the New England colonies explicitly permitted African slavery several decades before slavery was given formal legal sanction in Virginia.[2] Still our image of historic New England is, despite the occasional reference to Tituba at the Salem witch trials or Crispus Attucks at the Boston Massacre, a white one. Our historical and literary texts relate and rerelate familiar stories of the Calvinistic Puritans and their flinty Yankee descendants. To the extent that issues of slavery and race relations tend to be linked to the New England of the eighteenth or nineteenth century, they tend to be associated with New England's impact on the national antislavery and equal rights struggles, Garrisonian abolitionism, or perhaps Charles Sumner's role in fighting for the fourteenth amendment.[3]

Despite its relegation to the periphery of the consciousness of many Americans, the history of African slaves and their free Afro-American descendants in New England is a fascinating one in many ways similar and in many ways quite different from the larger national story with which we are generally familiar. Slavery lasted for about a century and a half in New England. It formally commenced in the 1640s with the passage of statutes permitting English settlers to enslave captives taken in "just wars," despite the fact that slavery was not recognized at common law and despite the fact that it was regarded by the Puritans as sin against Biblical Law. New England slavery would end with the close of the eighteenth century, a reflection of the influence of the antislavery idealism that prevailed in that region in the wake of the American Revolution. Few slaves were brought to New England, and the overall slave population in that region was small in both absolute and relative terms. New England slaves worked at a variety of occupations. Some were house servants, others permanent apprentices to skilled artisans, still others worked in that region's maritime industry as stevedores or as sailors on merchant or fishing vessels. Some were farmhands. Most lived in small households with the master's family and maybe one or two other slaves or indentured servants or apprentices.

The major exception to the prevailing pattern of small-household slavery occurred in southern Rhode Island. Rhode Island was something of an anomaly in colonial New England. In the mid-eighteenth century colonial Rhode Island had a significant slave presence, approximately 10 percent of the total population. This was far greater than elsewhere in New England. In the southern part of the state large livestock farms employed the closest thing the region had to plantation labor. Slaves were employed in these farms sometimes in crews as large as forty or fifty laborers. These crews were generally combined groups of black slaves and white and Narraganset Indian indentured servants. These crews husbanded dairy cattle, horses and sheep. Colonial Rhode Island's extensive involvement with the African slave trade helped bring a relatively large, by New England standards, black population to the colony.[4]

Venture Smith

Four of our narratives provide important insights into the often hidden world of the New England slave, his relationships with other blacks and with the white and native Indian peoples who also inhabited early New England. Venture Smith's autobiography, *A Narrative of the Life and Adventures of Venture: A Native of Africa,* is the remarkable story of a man born in West Africa, probably in what is now the modern nation of Mali, who was kidnapped and ultimately transported to southern Rhode Island at age eight and who would live out the remainder of his life in eastern Connecticut, first as a slave and later a free man. Smith's autobiography is especially interesting because it is one of a relatively small number of surviving accounts of an American slave who spent his early years with an African people, the Dukandarra; later lived a full life in America; and left an autobiography detailing his often remarkable life on two continents and in two very different cultures.[5]

Smith's recollections of his Dukandarra childhood provide a rich if brief account of his early life. The Dukandarra world of the early 1730s in which Smith spent his early childhood was quite different from the world of eighteenth century New England in which Smith would spend the balance of his life. As Smith remembered, polygamy was common as was a pattern of intertribal warfare that helped feed people into the transatlantic slave trade. One activity that Venture Smith would find common to both sides of the Atlantic was livestock raising. The Dukandarra and neighboring peoples had extensive experience raising cattle and goats, a major activity in the southern part of Rhode Island where Smith spent the remainder of his childhood and youth.

It is in the discussions of his life as a slave, his efforts to secure his manumission, and his later life as a free man that Venture Smith's autobiography sheds an invaluable light on what would otherwise be a greatly obscured chapter in the social history of eighteenth century New England. We see Smith the child slave put to work in his first owner's household. He seems, at least from the narrative, to have adjusted rather rapidly to life in New England. The autobiography makes no mention of language difficulties or culture shock, but we must remember that Smith's narrative was dictated to his probable amanuensis Elisha Niles some sixty years or so after his arrival in Rhode Island. The Dukandarra boy of the 1730s was clearly a Yankee as an old man in 1798 when the narrative was set down. His transition was doubtless aided by both his young age when he arrived in America and his long association with the predominant white population.[6]

Smith's narrative tells us a good deal about the life of a New England slave. Many slaves in eighteenth century New England worked alongside others who were enduring some form of temporary servitude. It is significant that Smith's first bid for freedom was an attempt to run away with a group of other slaves and an Irish indentured servant. Another interesting aspect of New England slavery detailed in Smith's narrative is his relative freedom of movement, a freedom Smith used to earn money to ultimately purchase his manumission.

There is cruelty in the New England slave experience, and Smith's narrative certainly speaks of harsh and often arbitrary physical punishments and the threat that always hung over the head of the New England slave, the threat of sale to the far harsher slave regimes of the West Indies or the southern colonies. Smith's narrative also informs us of another kind of cruelty, that of the master who promised a slave manumission in return for an agreed upon sum of money and then failed to honor the bargain. These evils were common features of American slavery. Venture Smith's autobiography acquaints us with some aspects of slave life that were considerably less common elsewhere in the American slave experience. Among these were Smith's ability to complain of his master's mistreatment to a justice of the peace.

It is Smith's perseverance, his willingness to continue toiling extra hours to purchase his freedom despite being cheated, sold, and discouraged and despite the long hours that he had to work without compensation in his owners' service that make Venture Smith's narrative at once compelling and inspirational. Had he simply managed to purchase his own freedom under such conditions, that would have been remarkable enough, but his subsequent purchase of the freedom of his family—his wife and three children—and, as he indicated, of the freedom of an additional three other slaves was truly extraordinary. Smith's discussion of his later life, his acquisition of a considerable amount of property and prosperity toward the end of his life add to the remarkable nature of Smith's life odyssey.

A narrative is often as interesting for what it does not discuss as for what it does. Mock elections known as the African Governor or Negro Governor elections were held among the slave and later the free Negro populations of New England. They were by all accounts quite well attended and popular with both the white and black populations, yet Smith gives no indication of any participation or even interest in those events. The Revolutionary War occurred during Smith's lifetime, and one of Smith's sons, Cuff, served with the Patriot forces. And although we can assume that Smith, like parents almost everywhere when faced with those circumstances, viewed his son's wartime service with a mixture of anxiety and perhaps pride, no mention is made of this in the narrative. We learn about it instead in an appendix written almost a century later in the 1897 edition of the autobiography. That appendix, written to further memorialize Smith whose life story had become something of a legend in eastern Connecticut, indicates that

Smith was intensely disappointed in his son Cuff, and perhaps that accounts for the lack of discussion of Cuff and his Revolutionary War service. Similarly, Connecticut enacted a gradual emancipation statute in 1784, a development that was unlikely to have escaped Smith's notice, yet no mention is made of the event in his autobiography. These omissions are curious, but ultimately little can be made of them one way or the other.[7]

One omission is significant. Smith went out of his way to help free and employ other blacks. Yet it is interesting no mention is made of any African ethnic affiliation of the blacks, slave and free, with whom he came in contact. Certainly Smith the adult does not seem to be seeking out the Dukandarra or neighboring peoples of his childhood memories. By the end of his life, and probably considerably before that, Smith had acquired a new ethnic identity different from the one to which he had been born. He was a Negro. It was another Negro, a free Negro, to whom he turned while he was enslaved in order to help ensure that his last owner kept the manumission bargain, and it was other Negroes that he set about freeing and employing once he was free. The previous African ethnic identities, even if they were remembered by some like Venture Smith, had, under the circumstances of New England slavery, yielded to a new identity.[8]

Elleanor Eldridge

If Smith, who spent nearly three decades as a slave in eighteenth century New England, left some gaps concerning slave life in New England, these gaps are partially filled by three of our narratives—those of Elleanor Eldridge, James Mars, and William Brown—detailing the lives of individuals who would live most of their lives as free people in the nineteenth century. The second, third, and fourth chapters of Elleanor Eldridge's biography *Memoirs of Elleanor Eldridge* illustrate this. Eldridge, whose biography was written by her white friend and patron Frances McDougall in 1839, was born free, the daughter of a former slave who had gained his freedom, like many other black men in New England, through Revolutionary War service with the Patriot forces. Her recollections, set down when she was well into middle age, preserve the oral traditions of her family, of her Rhode Island childhood, and of the receding eighteenth century world of African slavery that was, in her early years, yielding to the approaching world of the free Negro of nineteenth-century New England. Much of what is said and, perhaps, particularly much of what is interesting to those of us who are late-twentieth-century readers are mentioned in passing, as if the intended audience of the day was probably already familiar with much of the social and cultural background, as they probably were. Thus, the

Eldridge biography tells of her grandfather's life in the Congo. It mentions in passing that her grandmother was a Narragansett Indian. There was little need for extensive commentary on this; it was well known in the Rhode Island of the day that there had been extensive intermixture between black slaves and the Narragansetts. We also learn, again in passing, of the role of the American Revolution in helping to free black men in New England. This was especially true in Rhode Island, which raised a large number of black troops for the cause of independence.[9]

Eldridge's biography tells us a bit about the day-to-day working life of a young black woman in early nineteenth century Rhode Island. Eleanor Eldridge worked in domestic service and as a milkmaid, occupations not dissimilar to the kinds of tasks slave women would have performed in Rhode Island less than a generation earlier. The Eldridge biography also gives us a glimpse into the world of the African elections, a practice that began during slavery and continued into the first few decades after Rhode Island's emancipation. We learn from Eldridge, as filtered through Frances McDougall's writing, that the election of Eldridge's brother, George, was an event that seemed to enhance her social status among blacks.

James Mars

Like the Eldridge narrative, James Mars's autobiography, *Life of James Mars, Slave Born and Sold in Connecticut,* begins in the waning days of New England slavery and points us toward the concerns of the free Negro community that would emerge in nineteenth-century New England. Mars published his autobiography in his adopted state of Massachusetts in 1868. It was, perhaps, a peculiarly appropriate time to do so. There were, by then, few surviving people with firsthand memories of northern slavery, particularly slavery in New England. Mars himself, one of the last of the surviving former New England slaves, was an old man having been born some seventy-eight years earlier in 1790. As Mars began writing, the nation had just finished a bitter Civil War. And although the white North may have initially fought the war simply to preserve the Union, the events of that conflict had transformed the War of the Rebellion into one of the great chapters in the history of human liberation. Nowhere was this more true than in New England, a region that would, not altogether unjustifiably, come to celebrate its role in the antislavery struggle and the emancipation of the southern Negro. The region would also come to forget some of the darker aspects of its own racial past, as Mars noted in his introduction: ". . . many of the people now on the stage of life do not know that slavery ever lived in Connecticut."

There are many interesting nuggets that might be gleaned from the Mars narrative. It is perhaps most valuable in describing the perilous circumstances of the northern slave freed by gradual-emancipation statutes. Slavery ended in the North in two ways. In a minority of states—Massachusetts and Vermont are examples—slavery was simply ended by judicial decision. The Massachusetts Supreme Judicial Court proclaimed slavery incompatible with the clause in the newly adopted state constitution, which proclaimed all men to be free and equal. The court did this in the case of *Commonwealth v. Jennison,* popularly known as the "Quock Walker" case. Such decisions freed all slaves, instantly, or almost instantly, terminating the master–slave relationship.[10]

But the more common method of general emancipation in the North was the legislative enactment of a gradual emancipation statute. This was the case in the Connecticut of Mars's childhood. Such statutes freed the children of slaves born after a specified date. Such children, although not slaves, were held to a term of labor until they reached a specified age. As Mars's narrative informs us, black parents often had to struggle quite hard to ensure that their families were not sold into slavery in the South by masters anxious to avoid the ultimate emancipation of black children held in temporary bondage under gradual-emancipation statutes.

Mars, writing from Massachusetts, ends his narrative expressing the hope that equal rights would be granted to blacks in Connecticut. Unlike Connecticut, Massachusetts had had a fairly good history of extending at least *de jure* equal rights to blacks after slavery. The Massachusetts constitution of 1780 made no reference to race as a requirement for suffrage, and black men were generally voting in the state in reasonably large numbers by the 1790s. Antebellum Boston was the scene of a vigorous antebellum civil rights movement, which, by the eve of the Civil War, had succeeded in eliminating Massachusetts statutory ban on interracial marriage and legally segregated schools in the state.[11]

William J. Brown

It was the struggle for equal rights in the often harsh racial climate of antebellum New England that would come to occupy the attention of the first generation of black men and women born in freedom in the early years of the nineteenth century. Few told the story of this struggle, while also providing a compelling look at everyday life in antebellum black New England, better than Providence shoemaker William J. Brown. Brown's autobiography, *The Life of William J. Brown, of Providence, Rhode Island with Personal Recollections of Incidents in Rhode Island,* was published in 1883. It provides a comprehensive recollection of his life and the events in which he participated; Brown's narrative also supplies one of the rare glimpses that we have into that multicultural crucible that was the world of New England slavery that preceded Brown's birth in 1814. Brown, through his recounting of his family's history, introduces us to one possible explanation for the great amount of intermarriage between black men and Narragansett women in eighteenth-century Rhode Island. We are told Narragansett women married black men, often purchasing them from their white masters, in an effort to improve upon their traditional role in Narragansett society. Brown informs us that Narragansett men preferred hunting and fishing to more steady agricultural labor. Black men were more accustomed to animal husbandry and other kinds of agricultural labor that might allow a family a modest degree of comfort. Some Indian women saw African husbands as a way to possibly improve their living conditions. This pattern of marriage, Brown tells us, also created some tension between Negro and Narragansett men. This is the kind of ethnographic insight that might otherwise be lost to historians but for Brown's fortuitous preservation of his family traditions.

Brown also tells us about Rhode Island's tradition of African elections, which began during slavery in the eighteenth century and persisted among the free Negro population in that state well into the 1830s. Still the principal importance of Brown's narrative lies not in the light that it sheds on the eighteenth-century world of the Rhode Island of Brown's parents and grandparents. Brown's autobiography instead is one of the more compelling accounts of the emergence of free black New England society in the nineteenth century. Few sources have portrayed the efforts of the first and second generation of free Afro-Yankees to secure their families, educate their children, establish independent black churches and fraternal institutions, and earn a livelihood in the face of persistent discrimination as vividly and as well as Brown's narrative.

Brown was a keen observer of life in his antebellum city of Providence, Rhode Island. Because of this his biography tells us far more than the simple story of one man's life. Much of the world of race and racial attitudes as it existed in the antebellum North is reflected in the Brown narrative. Brown informs us, for example, of the support Providence's black community received from Moses Brown, heir to wealth based largely on slaveholding and slave trading in eighteenth-century Rhode Island. Brown also tells us of the day-to-day insults and threats that Providence's black residents often endured.

And Brown is an excellent eyewitness to the deterioration that occurred in race relations in the 1820s and 1830s. For those of us who are perhaps accustomed to thinking of race relations as proceeding in a linear manner—

constantly improving even if at an intolerably slow pace—the history of
race relations in those northern states that, like Rhode Island, abolished
slavery after the Revolution provides a strong challenge to our assumptions.
The period immediately after the American Revolution should be seen as a
time of relative racial tolerance and enlightenment in the North. Genuine
antislavery sentiment brought forth judicial and legislative measures that
spelled the doom of northern slavery. Black men were not barred by statute
or constitutional provision from voting, and a small number actually exer-
cised the franchise in northern states.[12]

That postrevolutionary era of relative racial enlightenment would give
way to a period of much harsher, more openly confrontational race relations
after the War of 1812. Racially motivated physical violence directed
against free Negroes became more common. A wave of vicious antiblack
riots swept a number of northern cities in the 1820s and 1830s. Two such
riots hit Providence blacks especially hard, as Brown notes in his vivid
discussions of the Hardscrabble Riot of 1824 and the Olney Street Riot of
1831.[13]

The antiblack reaction that would develop after 1812 also took a form
that would have more enduring consequences. It was in this period that
northern states increased legal discrimination against their free black populations. Blacks were disenfranchised in most states. Rhode Island restricted
the franchise to white men in 1822. In most states in areas where there was
a significant black population, black children were restricted to segregated
schools, as Brown's autobiography makes clear.[14]

These legal restrictions were important not only because they reflected
the changed and increasingly hostile racial climate that prevailed in New
England and other northern states in the 1820s and 1830s, they were also
important because these new restrictions helped shape and define an antebellum equal rights struggle that ultimately would have far reaching consequences not only for the relatively small number of free Negroes who lived
in New England and other parts of the North before the Civil War but later
for the nation as a whole. Many concepts later adopted nationally concerning what constituted unfair discrimination on the one hand or equal treatment of the races under the law on the other were initially forged in the
antebellum equal rights movement in New England and the struggle against
formal legal discrimination in that region.[15]

Brown's narrative is important for its detailing of one aspect of the
antebellum equal rights struggle, the successful effort on the part of Rhode
Island blacks to regain the franchise lost in 1822. Rhode Island was unique
of all the states that had disenfranchised black men in that it was the only
state in which black suffrage was fully recovered before the Civil War.

Brown's autobiography gives an important look at black participation in Rhode Island's "Dorr Rebellion" and how their support for the winning side led to reenfranchisement.

The Life of William J. Brown is unique in its discussion of actual black electoral behavior in antebellum Rhode Island. We learn, through Brown's memory, of the strong degree of support for the Whig Party among black men in the Providence of the 1840s. The Whigs had been instrumental in reenfranchising black men in 1842 and Providence's free Negro voters repaid the Whigs with an almost unswerving loyalty to their party during the 1840s. That support was so strong that, as Brown tells us, even the party's nomination of slaveholder Zachary Taylor in 1848 could not break the Negro–Whig alliance. The strength of this partisan affiliation and the motivations that brought it about are the kind of historical details that again might be all but invisible to us but for Brown's remarkable memoirs.

George Henry

Our last narrative, chapters 14, 15, and 16 of George Henry's *Life of George Henry: Together with a Brief History of the Colored People in America,* provides another view of black life in nineteenth-century Providence. Henry's narrative is especially valuable for its brief discussion of the effort to integrate Rhode Island's schools that began in 1855. By that year the legislature in the neighboring state of Massachusetts had passed legislation abolishing the system of separate schools for black children. Many blacks in Rhode Island were eager for their state to follow suit. But Henry tells us something quite interesting: There was a considerable division of opinion among blacks in Providence concerning the advisability of the school integration effort. Henry's account of that political conflict within the Providence black community serves as a valuable reminder of the dangers of approaching the study of any community without a realization that communities are not monoliths. There was a range of different views concerning the abolition of the all-black schools in Providence. Some members of the Providence Negro community favored straightforward legislation abolishing what they termed "caste schools." Others opposed the elimination of the Pond and Meeting Street schools for colored children, fearing that integration would mean the discharging of the black teachers in those schools. Still others were threatened with loss of jobs by white employers if they supported school integration. These community divisions are reflected in the Henry narrative.[16]

Interestingly enough, the Henry narrative also provides us another occasion to ask questions concerning silence in a text. As able a chronicler as

Brown was of the political struggle to regain and use the franchise in the 1840s, his narrative is silent on the school integration struggle of the 1850s that Henry recorded. Was Brown one of those who had opposed school integration in the 1850s but believed it imprudent to mention or no longer worth discussing when he was writing his autobiography in 1883? The effort to eliminate school segregation did triumph in Rhode island after the Civil War. Did Brown refrain from discussing his sentiments and actions concerning the school struggle because he had been on the losing side? Or was it omitted because Brown saw it as a minor event in comparison to his political activities during the 1840s? Again narrative silence can raise critical questions.

These narratives are remarkable and valuable precisely because they tell us about the lives of rather ordinary people in a time now past. None of our authors was a great statesman like Frederick Douglass or a literary figure like Phillis Wheatly or a significant political essayist like William C. Nell. They were instead people who pursued rather common occupations: Smith was a fisherman, Eldridge a laundress, Brown a shoemaker, and Henry a laborer at a variety of odd jobs. All told their stories, in part for personal reasons, in the hopes that their books might make them a little money or preserve their memory for their children. They also told their stories because they recognized that their world, the world of the New England Negro of the eighteenth and early nineteenth centuries, was in many ways a fascinating one that should not be allowed to be forgotten. In this way they demonstrated that they were indeed Yankees with all the tendency that people from the New England region have traditionally had of wanting to preserve their historical record. Finally they told their stories, in part, because they hoped that their narratives would help present Afro-Yankee culture and society in a positive light, thus furthering the cause of equal rights. Whatever the many reasons for their having written their narratives, they have left us a window from which we might view a people now gone and a time only dimly remembered.

Notes

1. August Meier and Elliot Rudwick have provided good discussions of the development of Afro-American history as a scholarly field and the reluctance of most members of the historical profession to take the field seriously until quite recently. See August Meier and Elliot Rudwick, *Black History and the Historical Profession, 1915–1980* (Urbana: University of Illinois Press, 1986) and "J. Franklin Jameson, Carter G. Wood-

son, and the Foundation of Black Historiography," *American Historical Review* 89 (October 1984): 1005.

2. Massachusetts legalized slavery in 1641, Connecticut in 1646. See Lorenzo Johnston Greene, *The Negro in Colonial New England* (New York: Atheneum Press, 1968) 18–19, 63–64. Africans were brought into Virginia and held in bondage as early as 1619. Some of the earliest captives were held for a term of years similar to the status of indentured servants. It was not until the 1660s that Virginia statutes began to give formal recognition to slave status; see A. Leon Higginbotham, *In the Matter of Color: Race and the American Legal Process: The Colonial Period* (New York: Oxford University Press, 1978) 34–36.

3. There is a significant body of literature discussing the black experience in colonial and nineteenth-century New England. This literature has addressed such topics as slavery, emancipation, race relations, black socioeconomic status, black politics, and the retention and dissolution of African culture in New England. Although generally known to specialists in African American history, this literature has been slow in reaching the consciousness of students of American history and the wider educated public. The preeminent discussion of slavery in New England remains Lorenzo Johnston Greene's 1942 classic, *The Negro in Colonial New England* (New York: Atheneum). Other works that examine black life in colonial and nineteenth-century New England include Robert J. Cottrol, *The Afro-Yankees: Providence's Black Community in the Antebellum Era,* (Westport, CT: Greenwood Press, 1982); James Oliver Horton and Lois E. Horton, *Black Bostonians: Family Life and Community Struggle in the Antebellum North* (New York: Holmes and Meir, 1979); George A. Levesque, *Black Boston, African American Life and Culture in Urban America, 1750–1860* (New York: Garland, 1994); William D. Piersen, *Black Yankees: the Development of an Afro-American Subculture in Eighteenth-Century New England* (Amherst: University of Massachusetts Press, 1988); Elizabeth Hafkin Pleck, *Black Migration and Poverty: Boston, 1865–1900* (New York: Academic Press, 1979); Robert Austin Warner, *New Haven Negroes: A Social History* (New York: Arno Press, 1969).

4. Cottrol, *The Afro-Yankees,* 15–17.

5. For a valuable discussion of Venture Smith's autobiography and its larger significance to those interested in interpreting black life in early national New England see Robert F. Desrochers Jr., "'Not Fade Away': The Narrative of Venture Smith, an African American in the Early Republic," *Journal of American History* 84 (June 1997): 40–66.

6. Local tradition maintains that Smith's amanuensis was Connecticut schoolteacher Elisha Niles, who had served in the Revolutionary War with Venture Smith's son, Cuff. For a discussion of Niles as antislavery and equal rights activist see Desrochers, "Not Fade Away," 45–49.

7. For discussions of the African Governor's elections see: Orville H. Platt, "Negro Governors," *New Haven Colony Historical Society Papers* 6 (1900): 315–335; Joseph P. Reidy, "Negro Election Day and Black Community Life in New England, 1750–1860," *Marxist Perspectives* 1, no. 3 (Fall 1978): 106–110; and Pierson, *Black Yankees,* pp. 117–140. I have argued that among the other significances of the African or Negro Governors' elections, they were important because they helped introduce Africans and their Afro-American descendants to the role of patron-client relations in Anglo-American electoral culture. This may have proven to be significant in those New England states and New York, which permitted black suffrage in the antebellum era. See Cottrol, *The Afro-Yankees,* 102–104.

8. The subject of the retention or dissolution of African culture in the New World is a long and complex one, too much so to be discussed at great length here. Much of the

debate and discussion in this area still owes much to the insights of Melville Herskovits in his pioneering study *The Myth of the Negro Past* (New York: Harper and Bros., 1941). I think specific African ethnic identities tended to be best preserved in those New World settings where there was a majority African population and where one African ethnic group tended to predominate. This tended to be the case in large portions of the Caribbean and northeastern Brazil, to name two examples. African culture also tended to be preserved among maroon communities in relative isolation, even in New World societies that were not predominately black. One interesting example of this was discovered by Mexican anthropologist Gonzalo Aguirre Beltrán in his ethnographic portrait of Afro-Mexican life in the Pacific Coast state of Guerrero. See Gonzalo Aguirre Beltrán, *Cuijla Esbozo Etnográfico de un Pueblo Negro* (México, D. F.: Fondo de Cultura Economica, 1989). Neither condition, it should be added, prevailed in eighteenth-century New England.

9. Cottrol, *The Afro-Yankees,* 30–33.

10. *Commonwealth v. Jennison,* (Ma., 1783).

11. Robert J. Cottrol, "Law, Politics and Race in Urban America: Towards a New Synthesis," *Rutgers Law Journal* 17 (Spring and Summer 1996): 483–596, 517–527.

12. Cottrol, "Law, Politics and Race," 505–508.

13. Cottrol, *The Afro-Yankees,* 53–57; Leonard Curry, *The Free Black in Urban America, 1800–1850: The Shadow of the Dream* (Chicago: University of Chicago Press, 1981) 96–111.

14. Cottrol, "Law, Politics and Race," 508–513.

15. The best example of this occurred in the 1848 Boston school desegregation case *Roberts v. City of Boston,* 59 Ma. (5 Cush.) 198 (1848). The basic argument made on behalf of the plaintiff that school segregation was inherently stigmatizing regardless of the tangible resources of the black school framed the issue for civil rights advocates even before the nation's adoption of the fourteenth amendment. The argument, which was rejected by Massachusetts' Supreme Judicial Court, would later be repeated and rejected by the United States Supreme Court in the 1896 case of *Plessy v. Ferguson,* 163 U.S. 537 (1896). It would ultimately triumph more than a century later before the United States Supreme Court in the landmark case *Brown v. Board of Education of Topeka Kansas* 347 U.S. 483 (1954).

16. Cottrol, *The Afro-Yankees,* 90–101.

A NARRATIVE

—OF THE—

LIFE AND ADVENTURES

—OF—

VENTURE

A NATIVE OF AFRICA,

But Resident Above Sixty Years in
the United States Of America.

RELATED BY HIMSELF

*New London: Printed in 1798. Reprinted A.D. 1835, and
Published by a Descendant of Venture.*

Revised and Republished with Traditions by H. M. SELDEN,
Haddam, Conn., 1896.

MIDDLETOWN, CONN.:
J. S. STEWART, PRINTER AND BOOKBINDER.
1897.

This copy of A Narrative of the Life and Adventures of Venture, a Native of Africa *is taken from the 1897 edition of Venture Smith's autobiography. The first edition was published in 1798. The 1897 edition includes a short addendum titled "Traditions of Venture! Known as Venture Smith." It was compiled by H.M. Selden, who published the 1897 edition. The "Traditions" preserve much of the local lore concerning Venture Smith including the fact that he evidently had considerable physical strength in his prime. The "Traditions" are most important for identifying Elisha Niles as Smith's probable amanuensis and for the brief discussions of Smith's children. In this, as in the other narratives in the book, most of the original spelling and punctuation have been preserved.*

PREFACE.

THE following account of the life of VENTURE is a relation of simple facts, in which nothing is added in substance to what he related himself. Many other interesting and curious passages of his life might have been inserted, but on account of the bulk to which they must necessarily have swelled this narrative, they were omitted. If any should suspect the truth of what is here related, they are referred to people now living who are acquainted with most of the facts mentioned in the narrative.

The reader is here presented with an account, not of a renowned politician or warrior, but of an untutored slave, brought into this Christian country at eight years of age, wholly destitute of all education but what he received in common with domesticated animals, enjoying no advantages that could lead him to suppose himself superior to the beasts, his fellow-servants. And, if he shall derive no other advantage from perusing this narrative, he may experience those sensations of shame and indignation that will prove him to be not wholly destitute of every noble and generous feeling.

The subject of the following pages, had he received only a common education, might have been a man of high respectability and usefulness; and had his education been suited to his genius, he might have been an ornament and an honor to human nature. It may, perhaps, not be unpleasing to see the efforts of a great mind wholly uncultivated, enfeebled and depressed by slavery, and struggling under every disadvantage. The reader may here see a Franklin and a Washington, in a state of nature, or, rather, in a state of slavery. Destitute as he is of all education, and broken by hardships and infirmities of age, he still exhibits striking traces of native ingenuity and good sense. This narrative exhibits a pattern of honesty, prudence and industry to people of his own color; and perhaps some white people would not find themselves degraded by imitating such an example.

The following account is published in compliance with the earnest desire of the subject of it, and likewise a number of respectable persons who are acquainted with him.

NARRATIVE OF LIFE OF VENTURE.

CHAPTER I.

CONTAINING AN ACCOUNT OF HIS LIFE, FROM HIS BIRTH TO THE TIME OF HIS LEAVING HIS NATIVE COUNTRY.

I WAS born at Dukandarra, in Guinea, about the year 1729. My father's name was Saungm Furro, Prince of the tribe of Dukandarra. My father had three wives. Polygamy was not uncommon in that country, especially among the rich, as every man was allowed to keep as many wives as he could maintain. By his first wife he had three children. The eldest of them was myself, named by my father, Broteer. The other two were named Cundazo and Soozaduka. My father had two children by his second wife, and one by his third. I descended from a very large, tall and stout race of beings, much larger than the generality of people in other parts of the globe, being commonly considerable above six feet in height, and every way well proportioned.

The first thing worthy of notice which I remember, was a contention between my father and mother, on account of my father marrying his third wife without the consent of his first and eldest, which was contrary to the custom generally observed among my countrymen. In consequence of this rupture, my mother left her husband and country, and travelled away with her three children to the eastward. I was then five years old. She took not the least sustenance along with her, to support either herself or children. I was able to travel along by her side; the other two of her offspring she carried, one on her back, the other, being a sucking child, in her arms. When we became hungry, our mother used to set us down on the ground and gather some of the fruits that grew spontaneously in that climate. These served us for food on the way. At night we all lay down together in the most secure place we could find and reposed ourselves until morning. Though there were many noxious animals there, yet so kind was our Almighty protector that none of them were ever permitted to hurt or molest us.

Thus we went on our journey until the second day after our departure from Dukandarra, when we came to the entrance of a great desert. During our travel in that, we were often affrighted with the doleful howlings and yellings of wolves, lions and other animals. After five days' travel we came to the end of this desert, and immediately entered into a beautiful and extensive interval country. Here my mother was pleased to stop and seek a refuge for me. She left me at the house of a very rich farmer. I was then, as I should judge, not less than one hundred and forty miles from my native place, separated from all my relatives and acquaintances. At this place, my mother took her farewell of me and set out for her own country. My new guardian, as I shall call the man with whom I was left, put me into the business of tending sheep immediately after I was left with him. The flock, which I kept with the assistance of a boy, consisted of about forty. We drove them every morning between two and three miles to pasture, into the wide and delightful plains. When night drew on, we drove them home and secured them in the cote. In this round I continued during my stay here. One incident which befel me when I was driving my flock from pasture, was so dreadful to me at that age, and is to this time so fresh in my memory, that I cannot help noticing it in this place. Two large dogs sallied out of a certain house and set upon me. One of them took me by the arm and the other by the thigh, and before their master could come and relieve me, they lacerated my flesh to such a degree that the scars are very visible to the present day. My master was immediately sent for. He came and carried me home, as I was unable to go myself on account of my wounds. Nothing remarkable happened afterwards until my father sent for me to return home.

Before I dismiss this country, I must first inform my reader what I remember concerning this place. A large river runs through this country in a westerly course. The land for a great way on each side is flat and level, hedged in by a considerable rise in the country at a great distance from it. It scarce ever rains there, yet the land is fertile; great dews fall in the night which refresh the soil. About the latter end of June or first of July, the river begins to rise, and gradually increases until it has inundated the country for a great distance, to the height of seven or eight feet. This brings on a slime which enriches the land surprisingly. When the river has subsided, the natives begin to sow and plant, and the vegetation is exceeding rapid. Near this rich river my guardian's land lay. He possessed, I cannot exactly tell how much, yet this I am certain of respecting it, that he owned an immense tract. He possessed likewise a great many cattle and goats. During my stay with him I was kindly used, and with as much tenderness, for what I saw, as his only son, although I was an entire stranger to him, remote from friends and relatives. The principal occupations of the inhabitants there were the cultivation of the soil and the care of their flocks. They were a people pretty similar in every respect to that of mine, except in their persons, which were not so tall and stout. They appeared to be very kind and friendly. I will now return to my departure from that place.

My father sent a man and horse after me. After settling with my guardian for keeping me, he took me away and went for home. It was then about one year since my mother brought me here. Nothing remarkable occurred to us on our journey until we arrived safe home. I found then that the difference between my parents had been made up previous to their sending for me. On my return, I was received both by my father and mother with great joy and affection, and was once more restored to my paternal dwelling in peace and happiness. I was then about six years old.

Not more than six weeks had passed after my return, before a message was brought by an inhabitant of the place where I lived the preceding year to my father, that that place had been invaded by a numerous army, from a nation not far distant, furnished with musical instruments, and all kinds of arms then in use; that they were instigated by some white nation who equipped and sent them to subdue and possess the country; that his nation had made no preparation for war, having been for a long time in profound peace; that they could not defend themselves against such a formidable train of invaders, and must, therefore, necessarily evacuate their lands to the fierce enemy, and fly to the protection of some chief; and that if he would permit them they would come under his rule and protection when they had to retreat from their own possessions. He was a kind and merciful prince, and therefore consented to these proposals.

He had scarcely returned to his nation with the message before the whole of his people were obligated to retreat from their country and come to my father's dominions. He gave them every privilege and all the protection his government could afford. But they had not been there longer than four days before news came to them that the invaders had laid waste their country, and were coming speedily to destroy them in my father's territories. This affrighted them, and therefore they immediately pushed off to the southward, into the unknown countries there, and were never more heard of.

Two days after their retreat, the report turned out to be but too true. A detachment from the enemy came to my father and informed him that the whole army was encamped not far from his dominions, and would invade the territory and deprive his people of their liberties and rights, if he did not comply with the following terms. These were, to pay them a large sum of money, three hundred fat cattle, and a great number of goats, sheep, asses, etc.

My father told the messenger he would comply rather than that his subjects should be deprived of their rights and privileges, which he was not then in circumstances to defend from so sudden an invasion. Upon turning out those articles, the enemy pledged their faith and honor that they would not attack him. On these he relied, and therefore thought it unnecessary to be on his guard against the enemy. But their pledges of faith and honor proved no better than those of other unprincipled hostile nations, for a few days after, a certain relation of the king came and informed him that the enemy who sent terms of accommodation to him, and received tribute to their satisfaction, yet meditated an attack upon his subjects by surprise, and that probably they would commence their attack in less than one day, and concluded with advising him, as he was not prepared for war, to order a speedy retreat of his family and subjects. He complied with this advice.

The same night which was fixed upon to retreat, my father and his family set off about the break of day. The king and his two younger wives went in one company, and my mother and her children in another. We left our dwellings in succession, and my father's company went on first. We directed our course for a large shrub plain, some distance off, where we intended to conceal ourselves from the approaching enemy, until we could refresh ourselves a little. But we presently found that our retreat was not secure. For having struck up a little fire for the purpose of cooking victuals, the enemy, who happened to be encamped a little distance off, had sent out a scouting party who discovered us by the smoke of the fire, just as we were extinguishing it and about to eat. As soon as we had finished eating, my father discovered the party and immediately began to discharge arrows at them. This was what I first saw, and it alarmed both me and the women, who, being unable to make any resistance immediately betook ourselves to the tall, thick reeds not far off, and left the old king to fight alone. For some time I beheld him from the reeds defending himself with great courage and firmness, till at last he was obliged to surrender himself into their hands.

They then came to us in the reeds, and the very first salute I had from them was a violent blow on the head with the fore part of a gun, and at the same time a grasp around the neck. I then had a rope put about my neck, as all the women in the thicket with me, and were immediately led to my father, who was likewise pinioned and haltered for leading. In this condition we were all led to the camp. The women and myself, being submissive, had tolerable treatment from the enemy, while my father was closely interrogated respecting his money, which they knew he must have. But as he gave them no account of it, he was instantly cut and pounded on his body with great inhumanity, that he might be induced by the torture he suffered to make the discovery. All this availed not in the least to make him give up his money, but he despised all the tortures which they inflicted, until the continued exercise and increase of torment obliged him to sink and expire. He thus died without informing his enemies where his money lay. I saw him while he was thus tortured to death. The shocking scene is to this day fresh in my memory, and I have often been overcome while thinking on it. He was a man of remarkable stature. I should judge as much as six feet and six or seven inches high, two feet across the shoulders, and every way well proportioned. He was a man of remarkable strength and resolution, affable, kind and gentle, ruling with equity and moderation.

The army of the enemy was large, I should suppose consisting of about six thousand men. Their leader was called Baukurre. After destroying the old prince, they decamped and immediately marched towards the sea, lying to the west, taking with them myself and the women prisoners. In the march, a scouting party was detached from the main army. To the leader of this party I was made waiter, having to carry his gun, etc. As we were a-scouting, we came across a herd of fat cattle consisting of about thirty in number. These we set upon and immediately wrested from their keepers, and afterwards converted them into food for the army. The enemy had remarkable success in destroying the country wherever they went. For as far as they had penetrated they laid the habitations waste and captured the people. The distance they had now brought me was about four hundred miles. All the march I had very hard tasks imposed on me, which I must perform on pain of punishment. I was obliged to carry on my head a large flat stone used for grinding our corn, weighing, as I should suppose, as much as twenty-five pounds; besides victuals, mat and cooking utensils. Though I was pretty large and stout of my age, yet these burdens were very grievous to me, being only six years and a half old.

We were then come to a place called Malagasco. When we entered the place, we could not see the least appearance of either house or inhabitants, but on stricter search found that instead of houses above ground they had dens in the sides of hillocks, contiguous to ponds and streams of water. In these we perceived they had all hid themselves, as I suppose they usually did on such occasions. In order to compel them to surrender, the enemy contrived to smoke them out with faggots. These they put to the entrance of the caves and set them on fire. While they were engaged in this business, to their great surprise some of them were desperately wounded with arrows which fell from above on them. This mystery they soon found out. They perceived that the enemy discharged these arrows through holes on the top of the dens directly into the air. Their weight brought them back, point downwards, on their enemies heads, whilst they were smoking the inhabitants out. The points of their arrows were poisoned, but their enemy had an antidote for it which they instantly applied to the wounded part. The smoke at last obliged the people to give themselves up. They came out of their caves, first spatting the palms of their hands together, and immediately after extended their arms, crossed at their wrists, ready to be bound and pinioned. I should judge that the dens above mentioned were extended about eight feet horizontally into the earth, six feet in height, and as many wide. They were arched overhead and lined with earth, which was of the clay kind and made the surface of their walls firm and smooth.

The invaders then pinioned the prisoners of all ages and sexes indiscriminately, took their flocks and all their effects, and moved on their way towards the sea. On the march, the prisoners were treated with clemency, on account of their being submissive and humble. Having come to the next tribe, the enemy laid siege and immediately took men, women, children, flocks, and all their valuable effects. They then went on to the next district, which was contiguous to the sea, called in Africa, Anamaboo. The enemies' provisions were then almost spent, as well as their strength. The inhabitants, knowing what conduct they had pursued, and what were their present intentions, improved the favorable opportunity, attacked them, and took enemy, prisoners, flocks and all their effects. I was then taken a second time. All of us were then put into the castle and kept for market. On a certain time, I and other prisoners were put on board a canoe, under our master, and rowed away to a vessel belonging to Rhode Island, commanded by Captain Collingwood, and the mate, Thomas Mumford. While we were going to the vessel, our master told us to appear to the best possible advantage for sale. I was bought on board by one Robertson Mumford, a steward of said vessel, for four gallons of rum and a piece of calico, and called VENTURE on account of his having purchased me with his own private venture. Thus I came by my name. All the slaves that were bought for that vessel's cargo were two hundred and sixty.

CHAPTER II.

CONTAINING AN ACCOUNT OF HIS LIFE FROM THE TIME OF HIS LEAVING AFRICA TO THAT OF HIS BECOMING FREE.

AFTER all the business was ended on the coast of Africa, the ship sailed from thence to Barbadoes. After an ordinary passage, except great mortality by the small pox, which broke out on board, we arrived at the island of Barbadoes; but when we reached it, there were found, out of the two hundred and sixty that sailed from Africa, not more than two hundred alive. These were all sold, except myself and three more, to the planters there.

The vessel then sailed for Rhose Island, and arrived there after a comfortable passage. Here my master sent me to live with one of his sisters until he could carry me to Fisher's Island, the place of his residence. I had then completed my eighth year. After staying with his sister some time, I was taken to my master's place to live.

When we arrived at Narraganset, my master went ashore in order to return a part of the way by land, and gave me the charge of the keys of his trunks on board of the vessel, and charged me not to deliver them up to anybody, not even to his father, without his orders. To his directions I promised faithfully to conform. When I arrived with my master's articles at his house, my master's father asked me for his son's keys, as he wanted to see what his trunks contained. I told him that my master intrusted me with the care of them until he should return, and that I had given him my word to be faithful to the trust, and could not, therefore, give him, or any other man, the keys without my master's directions. He insisted that I should deliver to him the keys on pain of punishment. But I let him know that he should not have them, let him say what he would. He then laid aside trying to get them. But notwithstanding he appeared to give up trying to obtain them from me, yet I mistrusted that he would take some time when I was off my guard, either in the daytime or at night, to get them, therefore, I slung them round my neck, and in the daytime concealed them in my bosom, and at night I always slept with them under me, that no person might take them from me without my being apprized of it. Thus I kept the keys from everybody until my master came home. When he returned he asked where VENTURE was. As I was within hearing, I came and said, "Here, sir, at your service." He asked for his keys, and I immediately took them off my neck and reached them out to him. He took them, stroked my hair, and commended me, saying in presence of his father that his young VENTURE was so faithful that he never would have been able to have taken the keys from him but by violence; that he should not fear to trust him with his whole fortune, for that he had been in his native place so habituated to keeping his word, that he would sacrifice even his life to maintain it.

The first of the time of living at my master's own place, I was pretty much employed in the house, carding wool and other household business. In this situation I continued for some years, after which my master put me to work out of doors. After many proofs of my faithfulness and honesty, my master began to put great confidence in me. My behavior had as yet been submissive and obedient. I then began to have hard tasks imposed on me. Some of these were to pound four bushels of ears of corn every night in a barrel for the poultry, or be rigorously punished. At other seasons of the year, I had to card wool until a very late hour. These tasks I had to perform when only about nine years old. Some time after, I had another difficulty and oppression which was greater than any I had ever experienced since I came into this country. This was to serve two masters. James Mumford, my master's son, when his father had gone from home in the morning and given me a stint to perform that day, would order me to do *this* and *that* business different from what my master had directed me. One day in particular, the authority which my master's son had set up had like to have produced melancholy effects. For my master having set me off my business to perform that day and then left me to perform it, his son came up to me in the course of the day, big with authority, and commanded me very arrogantly to quit my present business and go directly about what he should order me. I replied to him that my master had given me so much to perform that day, and that I must faithfully complete it in that time. He then broke out into a great rage, snatched a pitchfork and went to lay me over the head therewith, but I as soon got another and defended myself with it, or otherwise he might have murdered me in his outrage. He immediately called some people who were within hearing at work for him, and ordered them to take his hair rope and come and bind me with it. They all tried to bind me, but in vain, though there were three assistants in number. My upstart master then desisted, put his pocket handkerchief before his eyes and went home with a design to tell his mother of the struggle with young VENTURE. He told that their young VENTURE had become so stubborn that he could not control him, and asked her what he should do with him. In the meantime I recovered my temper, voluntarily caused myself to be bound by the same men who tried in vain before, and carried before my young master, that he might do what he pleased with me. He took me to a gallows made for the purpose of hanging cattle on, and suspended me on it. Afterwards he ordered one of his hands to go to the peach orchard and cut him three dozen of whips to punish me with. These were brought to him, and that was all that was done with them, as I was released and went to work after hanging on the gallows about an hour.

After I had lived with my master thirteen years, being then about twenty-two years old, I married Meg, a slave of his who was about my own age. My master owned a certain Irishman, named Heddy, who about that time formed a plan of secretly leaving his master. After he had long had this plan in meditation, he suggested it to me. At first I cast a deaf ear to it, and rebuked Heddy for harboring in his mind such a rash undertaking. But after he had persuaded and much enchanted me with the prospect of gaining my freedom by such a method, I at length agreed to accompany him. Heddy next inveigled two of his fellow-servants to accompany us. The place to which we designed to go was the Mississippi. Our next business was to lay in a sufficient store of provisions for our voyage. We privately collected out of our master's store, six great old cheeses, two firkins of butter, and one batch of new bread. When we had gathered all our own clothes and some more, we took them all about midnight and went to the water side. We stole our master's boat, embarked, and then directed our course for the Mississippi River.

We mutually confederated not to betray or desert one another on pain of death. We first steered our course for Montauk Point, the east end of Long Island. After our arrival there, we landed, and Heddy and I made an incursion into the island after fresh water, while our two comrades were left a little distance from the boat, employed in cooking. When Heddy and I had sought some time for water, he returned to our companions and I continued on looking for my object. When Heddy had performed his business with our companions who were engaged in cooking, he went directly to the boat, stole all the clothes in it, and then travelled away for East Hampton, as I was informed. I returned to my fellows not long after. They informed me that our clothes were stolen, but could not determine who was the thief, yet they suspected Heddy, as he was missing. After reproving my comrades for not taking care of our things which were in the boat, I advertised Heddy and sent two men in search of him. They pursued and overtook him at Southampton and returned him to the boat. I then thought it might afford some chance for my freedom, or at least be a palliation for my running away, to return Heddy immediately to his master, and inform him that I was induced to go away by Heddy's address. Accordingly, I set off with him and the rest of my companions for my master's, and arrived there without any difficulty. I informed my master that Heddy was the ringleader of our revolt, and that he had used us ill. He immediately put Heddy into custody, and myself and companions were well received and went to work as usual.

Not a long time passed after that before Heddy was sent by my master to New London gaol. At the close of that year I was sold to a Thomas Stanton, and had to be separated from my wife and one daughter, who was about one month old. He resided at Stonington Point. To this place I brought with me from my late master's, two johannes, three old Spanish dollars, and two thousand of coppers, besides five pounds of my wife's money. This money I got by cleaning gentlemen's shoes and drawingboots, by catching muskrats and minks, raising potatoes and carrots, etc., and by fishing in the night, and at odd spells.

All this money, amounting to near twenty-one pounds York currency, my master's brother, Robert Stanton, hired of me, for which he gave me his note. About a year and a half after that time, my master purchased my wife and her child for seven hundred pounds old tenor. One time my master sent me two miles after a barrel of molasses, and ordered me to carry it on my shoulders. I made out to carry it all the way to my master's house. When I lived with Capt. George Mumford, only to try my strength I took upon my knees a tierce of salt containing seven bushels, and carried it two or three rods. Of this fact there are several eye witnesses now living.

Towards the close of the time I resided with this master, I had a falling out with my mistress. This happened one time when my master was gone to Long Island a-gunning. At first the quarrel began between my wife and her mistress. I was then at work in the barn, and hearing a racket in the house, induced me to run there and see what had broken out. When I entered the house, I found my mistress in a violent passion with my wife, for what she informed me was a mere trifle—such a small affair that I forbear to put my mistress to the shame of having it known. I earnestly requested my wife to beg pardon of her mistress for the sake of peace, even if she had given no just occasion for offence. But whilst I was thus saying, my mistress turned the blows which she was repeating on my wife to me. She took down her horse whip, and while she was glutting her fury with it, I reached out my great black hand, raised it up and received the blows of the whip on it which were designed for my head. Then I immediately committed the whip to the devouring fire.

When my master returned from the island, his wife told him of the affair, but for the present he seemed to take no notice of it, and mentioned not a word of it to me. Some days after his return, in the morning as I was putting on a log in the fireplace, not suspecting harm from any one, I received a most violent stroke on the crown of my head with a club two feet long and as large around as a chair post. This blow very badly wounded my head, and the scar of it remains to this day. The first blow made me have my wits about me as you may suppose, for as soon as he went to renew it I snatched the club out of his hands and dragged him out of the door. He then sent for his brother to come and assist him, but I presently left my master, took the club he wounded me with, carried it to a neighboring justice of the peace, and complained of my master. He finally advised me to return to my master and live contented with him till he abused me again, and then complain. I consented to do accordingly. But before I set out for my master's, up he came and his brother Robert after me. The Justice improved this convenient opportunity to caution my master. He asked him for what he treated his slave thus hastily and unjustly, and told him what would be the consequence if he continued the same treatment towards me. After the justice had ended his discourse with my master, he and his brother set out with me for home, one before and the other behind me. When they had come to a by-place, they both dismounted their respective horses and fell to beating me with great violence. I became enraged at this and immediately turned them both under me, laid one of them across the other, and stamped them both with my feet what I would.

This occasioned my master's brother to advise him to put me off. A short time after this, I was taken by a constable and two men. They carried me to a blacksmith's shop and had me handcuffed. When I returned home my mistress enquired much of her waiters whether VENTURE was handcuffed. When she was informed that I was, she appeared to be very contented and was much transported with the news. In the midst of this content and joy, I presented myself before my mistress, showed her my handcuffs, and gave her thanks for my gold rings. For this my master commanded a negro of his to fetch him a large ox chain. This my master locked on my legs with two padlocks. I continued to wear the chain peaceably for two or three days, when my master asked me with contempuous hard names whether I had not better be freed from my chains and go to work. I answered him, "No." "Well, then," said he, "I will send you to the West Indies, or banish you, for I am resolved not to keep you." I answered him, "I crossed the waters to come here and I am willing to cross them to return."

For a day or two after this not anyone said much to me, until one Hempstead Miner of Stonington asked me if I would live with him. I answered that I would. He then requested me to make myself discontented and to appear as unreconciled to my master as I could before that he bargained with him for me, and that in return he would give me a good chance to gain my freedom when I came to live with him. I did as he requested me. Not long after, Hempstead Miner purchased me of my master for fifty-six pounds lawful. He took the chain and padlocks from off me immediately after.

It may here be remembered that I related a few pages back that I hired out a sum of money to Mr. Robert Stanton, and took his note for it. In the fray between my master Stanton and myself, he broke open my chest containing his brother's note to me and destroyed it. Immediately after my present master bought me, he determined to sell me at Hartford. As soon as I became apprized of it, I bethought myself that I would secure a certain sum of money which lay by me safer than to hire it out to Stanton. Accordingly I buried it in the earth, a little distance from Thomas Stanton's, in the road over which he passed daily. A short time after, my master carried me to Hartford, and first proposed to sell me to one William Hooker of that place. Hooker asked whether I would go to the German Flats with him. I answered, "No." He said I should; if not by fair means, I should by foul. "If you will go by no other measures, I will tie you down in my sleigh." I replied to him, that if he carried me in that manner no person would purchase me, for it would be thought he had a murderer for sale. After this he tried no more, and said he would not have me as a gift.

My master next offered me to Daniel Edwards, Esq., of Hartford, for sale. But he not purchasing me, my master pawned me to him for ten pounds, and returned to Stonington. After some trial of my honesty, Mr. Edwards placed considerable trust and confidence in me. He put me to serve as his cup-bearer and waiter. When there was company at his house, he would send me into his cellar and other parts of his house to fetch wine and other articles occasionally for them. When I had been with him some time, he asked me why my master wished to part with such an honest negro, and why he did not keep me himself. I replied that I could not give him the reason, unless it was to convert me into cash and speculate with me as with other commodities. I hope that he can never justly say it was on account of my ill conduct that he did not keep me himself. Mr. Edwards told me that he should be very willing to keep me himself, and that he would never let me go from him to live, if it was not unreasonable and inconvenient for me to be parted from my wife and children; therefore, he would furnish me with a horse to return to Stonington, if I had a mind for it. As Miner did not appear to redeem me, I went, and called at my old master Stanton's first to see my wife, who was then owned by him. As my old master appeared much ruffled at my being there, I left my wife before I had spent any considerable time with her, and went to Col. O. Smith's. Miner had not as yet wholly settled with Stanton for me, and had before my return from Hartford given Colonel Smith a bill of sale of me. These men once met to determine which of them should hold me, and upon my expressing a desire to be owned by Colonel Smith, and upon my master's settling the remainder of the money which was due to Stanton for me, it was agreed that I should live with Colonel Smith. This was the third time of my being sold, and I was then thirty-one years old.

As I never had an opportunity of redeeming myself whilst I was owned by Miner, though he promised to give me a chance, I was then very ambitious of obtaining it. I asked my master one time if he would consent to have me purchase my freedom. He replied that he would. I was then very happy, knowing that I was at that time able to pay part of the purchase money by means of the money which I some time buried. This I took out of the earth and tendered to my master, having previously engaged a free negro man to take his security for it, as I was the property of my master, and therefore could not safely take his obligation myself. What was wanting in redeeming myself, my master agreed to wait on me for, until I could procure it for him. I still continued to work for Colonel Smith. There was continually some interest accruing on my master's note to my friend, the free negro man above named, which I received, and with some besides, which I got by fishing, I laid out in land adjoining my old master Stanton's. By cultivating this land with the greatest diligence and economy, at times when my master did not require my labor, in two years I laid up ten pounds. This my friend tendered my master for myself, and received his note for it.

Being encouraged by the success which I had met in redeeming myself, I again solicited my master for a further chance of completing it. The chance for which I solicited him was that of going out to work the ensuing winter. He agreed to this on condition that I would give him one-quarter of my earnings. On these terms I worked the following winter, and earned four pounds and sixteen shillings, one quarter of which went to my master for the privilege, and the rest was paid him on my account. I was then about thirty-five years old.

The next summer I again desired he would give me a chance of going to work. But he refused and answered that he must have my labor this summer, as he did not have it the past winter. I replied that I considered it as hard that I could not have a chance to work out when the season became advantageous, and that I must only be permitted to hire myself out in the poorest season of the year. He asked me after this what I would give him for the privilege per month. I replied that I would leave it wholly to his own generosity to determine what I should return him a month. Well then, said he, if so, two pounds a month. I answered him that if that was the least he would take I would be contented.

Accordingly I hired myself out at Fisher's Island, earning twenty pounds; thirteen pounds six shillings of which my master drew for the privilege and the remainder I paid for my freedom. This made fifty-one pounds two shillings which I paid him. In October following I went and wrought six months at Long Island. In that six month's time I cut and corded four hundred cords of wood, besides threshing out seventy-five bushels of grain, and received of my wages down only twenty pounds, which left remaining a larger sum. Whilst I was out that time, I took up on my wages only one pair of shoes. At night I lay on the hearth, with one coverlet over and another under me. I returned to my master and gave him what I received of my six months' labor. This left only thirteen pounds eighteen shillings to make up the full sum of my redemption. My master liberated me, saying that I might pay what was behind if I could ever make it convenient, otherwise it would be well. The amount of the money which I had paid my master towards redeeming my time, was seventy-one pounds two shillings. The reason of my master for asking such an unreasonable price, was, he said, to secure himself in case I should ever come to want. Being thirty-six years old, I left Colonel Smith once more for all. I had already been sold three different times, made considerable money with seemingly nothing to derive it from, had been cheated out of a large sum of money, lost much by misfortunes, and paid an enormous sum for my freedom.

CHAPTER III.

CONTAINING AN ACCOUNT OF HIS LIFE FROM THE TIME OF PURCHASING HIS FREEDOM TO THE PRESENT DAY.

MY wife and children were yet in bondage to Mr. Thomas Stanton. About this time I lost a chest, containing, besides clothing, about thirty-eight pounds in paper money. It was burnt by accident. A short time after I sold all my possessions at Stonington, consisting of a pretty piece of land and one dwelling house thereon, and went to reside at Long Island. For the first four years of my residence there, I spent my time in working for various people on that and at the neighboring islands. In the space of six months I cut and corded upwards of four hundred cords of wood. Many other singular and wonderful labors I performed in cutting wood there, which would not be inferior to the one just recited, but for brevity's sake I must omit them. In the aforementioned four years, what wood I cut at Long Island amounted to several thousand cords, and the money which I earned thereby amounted to two hundred and seven pounds ten shillings. This money I laid up carefully by me. Perhaps some may inquire what maintained me all the time I was laying up my money. I would inform them that I bought nothing which I did not absolutely want. All fine clothes I despised in comparison with my interest, and never kept but just what clothes were comfortable for common days, and perhaps I would have a garment or two which I did not have on at all times, but as for superfluous finery, I never thought it to be compared with a decent homespun dress, a good supply of money and prudence. Expensive gatherings of my mates I commonly shunned, and all kinds of luxuries I was perfectly a stranger to; and during the time I was employed in cutting the aforementioned quantity of wood, I never was at the expense of six pence worth of spirits. Being after this labor forty years of age, I worked at various places, and in particular on Ram Island, where I purchased Solomon and Cuff, two sons of mine, for two hundred dollars each.

It will here be remembered how much money I earned by cutting wood in four years. Besides this, I had considerable money, amounting to all to near three hundred pounds. After this I purchased a negro man, for no other reason than to oblige him, and gave for him sixty pounds. But in a short time after he ran away from me, and I thereby lost all that I gave for him, except twenty pounds which he paid me previous to his absconding. The rest of my money I laid out in land, in addition to a farm which I owned before, and a dwelling house thereon. Forty-four years had then completed their revolution since my entrance into this existence of servitude and misfortune.

Solomon, my eldest son, being then in his seventeenth year, and all my hope and dependence for help, I hired him out to one Charles Church, of Rhode Island, for one year, on consideration of his giving him twelve pounds and an opportunity of acquiring some learning. In the course of the year, Church fitted out a vessel for a whaling voyage, and being in want of hands to man her, he induced my son to go, with the promise of giving him on his return, a pair of silver buckles, besides his wages. As soon as I heard of his going to sea, I immediately set out to go and prevent it if possible. But on my arrival at Church's, to my great grief, I could only see the vessel my son was in, almost out of sight, going to sea. My son died of the scurvy in this voyage, and Church has never yet paid me the least of his wages. In my son, besides the loss of his life, I lost equal to seventy-five pounds.

My other son being but a youth, still lived with me. About this time I chartered a sloop of about thirty tons burthen, and hired men to assist me in navigating her. I employed her mostly in the wood trade to Rhode Island, and made clear of all expenses above one hundred dollars with her in better than one year. I had then become something forehanded, and being in my forty-fourth year, I purchased my wife Meg, and thereby prevented having another child to buy, as she was then pregnant. I gave forty pounds for her.

During my residence at Long Island, I raised one year with another, ten cart loads of watermelons, and lost a great many besides by the thievishness of the sailors. What I made by the watermelons I sold there, amounted to nearly five hundred dollars. Various other methods I pursued in order to enable me to redeem my family. In the night time I fished with setnets and pots for eels and lobsters, and shortly after went a whaling voyage in the service of Col. Smith. After being out seven months, the vessel returned laden with four hundred barrels of oil. About this time I became possessed of another dwelling house, and my temporal affairs were in a pretty prosperous condition. This and my industry was what alone saved me from being expelled that part of the island in which I resided, as an act was passed by the selectmen of the place, that all negroes residing there should be expelled.

Next after my wife, I purchased a negro man for four hundred dollars. But he having an inclination to return to his old master, I therefore let him go. Shortly after, I purchased another negro man for twenty-five pounds, whom I parted with shorty after.

Being about forty-six years old, I bought my oldest child, Hannah, of Ray Mumford, for forty-four pounds, and she still resided with him. I had already redeemed from slavery, myself, my wife and three children, besides three negro men.

About the forty-seventh year of my life I disposed of all my property at Long Island, and came from thence into East Haddam, Conn. I hired myself out first to Timothy Chapman for five weeks, the earnings of which time I put up carefully by me. After this I wrought for Abel Bingham for about six weeks. I then put my money together and purchased of said Bingham ten acres of land lying at Haddam Neck, where I now reside. On this land I labored with great diligence two years, and shortly after purchased six acres more of land contiguous to my other. One year from that time I purchased seventy acres more of the same man, and paid for it mostly with the produce of my other land. Soon after I bought this last lot of land, I set up a comfortable dwelling house on my farm, and built it from the produce thereof. Shortly after I had much trouble and expense with my daughter Hannah, whose name has been before mentioned to this account. She was soon married after I redeemed her, to one Isaac, and shortly after her marriage fell sick of a mortal disease. Her husband, a dissolute and abandoned wretch, paid but little attention to her illness. I therefore thought it best to bring her to my house and nurse her there. I procured her all the aid mortals could afford, but notwithstanding this she fell a prey to her disease, after a lingering and painful endurance of it. The physician's bill for attending her illness amounted to forty pounds.

Having reached my fifty-fourth year, I hired two negro men, one named William Jacklin, and the other, Mingo. Mingo lived with me one year, and having received his wages, run in debt to me eight dollars, for which he gave me his note. Presently after he tried to run away from me without troubling himself to pay up his note. I procured a warrant, took him, and requested him to go to Justice Throop's of his own accord but he refusing, I took him on my shoulders and carried him there, distant about two miles. The justice asking me if I had my prisoner's note with me, and replying that I had not, he told me that I must return with him and get it. Accordingly, I carried Mingo back on my shoulders, but before we arrived at my dwelling, he complained of being hurt, and asked me if this was not a hard way of treating our fellow-creatures. I answered him that it would be hard thus to treat our honest fellow-creatures. He then told me that if I would let him off my shoulders, he had a pair of silver shoe-buckles, one shirt and a pocket handkerchief, which he would turn out to me. I agreed, and let him return home with me on foot; but the very following night he slipped from me, stole my horse and has never paid me even his note. The other negro man, Jacklin, being a comb-maker by trade, he requested me to set him up, and promised to reward me well with his labor. Accordingly I bought him a set of tools for making combs, and procured him stock. He worked at my house about one year, and then ran away from me with all his combs, and owed me for all his board.

Since my residence at Haddam Neck, I have owned of boats, canoes and sail vessels, not less than twenty. These I mostly employed in the fishing and trafficking business, and in these occupations I have been cheated out of considerable money by people whom I traded with taking advantage of my ignorance of numbers.

About twelve years ago, I hired a whale boat and four black men, and proceeded to Long Island after a load of round clams. Having arrived there, I first purchased of James Webb, son of Orange Webb, six hundred and sixty clams, and afterwards with the help of my men, finished loading my boat. The same evening, however, this Webb stole my boat and went in her to Connecticut river and sold her cargo for his own benefit. I thereupon pursued him, and at length recovered the boat, but for the proceed of her cargo I never could obtain any compensation.

Four years after I met with another loss, far superior to this in value, and I think by no less wicked means. Being going to New London with a grandchild, I took passage in an Indian's boat and went there with him. On our return, the Indian took on board two hogsheads of molasses, one of which belonged to Captain Elisha Hart, of Saybrook, to be delivered on his wharf. When we arrived there, and while I was gone, at the request of the Indian, to inform Captain Hart of his arrival and receive the freight for him, one hogshead of the molasses had been lost overboard by the people in attempting to land it on the wharf. Although I was absent at the time and had no concern whatever in the business, as was known to a number of respectable witnesses, I was nevertheless prosecuted by this conscientious gentleman (the Indian not being able to pay for it) and obliged to pay upwards of ten pounds lawful money, with all the costs of court. I applied to several gentlemen for counsel in this affair, and they advised me, as my adversary was rich, and threatened to carry the matter from court to court till it would cost me more than the first damages would be,—to pay the sum and submit to the injury, which I accordingly did, and he has often since insultingly taunted me with my unmerited misfortune. Such a proceeding as this committed on a defenceless stranger, almost worn out in the hard service of the world, without any foundation in reason or justice, whatever it may be called in a Christian land, would in my native country have been branded as a crime equal to highway robbery. But Captain Hart was a *white gentleman,* and I a *poor African,* therefore it was *all right, and good enough for the black dog.*

I am now sixty-nine years old. Though once straight and tall, measuring without shoes six feet, one inch and an half, and every way well proportioned, I am now bowed down with age and hardship. My strength, which was once equal if not superior to any man whom I have ever seen, is now enfeebled so that life is a burden, and it is with fatigue that I can walk a couple of miles, stooping over my staff. Other griefs are still behind, on account of which some aged people, at least, will pity me. My eye-sight has gradually failed, till I am almost blind, and whenever I go abroad one of my grandchildren must direct my way; besides for many years I have been much pained and troubled with an ulcer on one of my legs. But amidst all my griefs and pains, I have many consolations; Meg, the wife of my youth, whom I married for love and bought with my money, is still alive. My freedom is a privilege which nothing else can equal. Notwithstanding all the losses I have suffered by fire, by the injustice of knaves, by the cruelty and oppression of false-hearted friends, and the perfidy of my own countrymen whom I have assisted and redeemed from bondage, I am now possessed of more than one hundred acres of land, and three habitable dwelling houses. It gives me joy to think that I *have* and that I *deserve* so good a character, especially for *truth* and *integrity.* *(While I am now looking to the grave as my home, my joy for this world would be full—If my children, Cuff for whom I paid two hundred dollars when a boy, and Solomon who was born soon after I purchased his mother—if Cuff and Solomon—Oh! that they had walked in the way of their father. But a father's lips are closed in silence and in grief!—Vanity of vanities, all is vanity.)

---

* Note, the closing words in parentheses were omitted in the later editions. It is probable that both improved later, especially so in the case of Solomon, who is well spoken of by elderly men now living, as having maintained a good character.

CERTIFICATE.

STONINGTON, CONN., November 3, 1798.
THESE may certify, that VENTURE is a free negro man, aged about 69 years, and was, as we have ever understood, a native of Africa, and formerly a slave to Mr. James Mumford, of Fisher's Island, in the State of New York, who sold him to Mr. Thomas Stanton, 2d, of Stonington, in the State of Connecticut, and said Stanton sold said VENTURE to Col. Oliver Smith, of the aforesaid place. That said VENTURE hath sustained the character of a faithful servant, and that of a temperate, honest and industrious man, and being ever intent of obtaining his freedom, he was indulged by his master after the ordinary labor on the days of his servitude, to improve the nights in fishing and other employments to his own emolument, in which time he procured so much money as to purchase his freedom from his late master, Colonel Smith; after which he took upon himself the name of VENTURE SMITH, and has since his freedom purchased a negro woman, called Meg, to whom he was previously married, and also his children who were slaves, and said VENTURE has since removed himself and family to the town of East Haddam, in this State, where he hath purchased lands on which he hath built a house, and there taken up his abode.

NATHANIEL MINOR, ESQ.
ELIJAH PALMER, ESQ.
CAPT. AMOS PALMER.
ACORS SHEFFIELD.
EDWARD SMITH.

TRADITIONS
– OF –
VENTURE!
– KNOWN AS –
VENTURE SMITH.*
– COMPILED BY –
H.M. SELDEN.

SEVERAL editions of the Life of Venture have been published successively by his family, and by them circulated throughout the county, but
more in the towns contiguous to his home, where the subject was well
known for his abnormal strength, industry and goodly character, confirma-
tory of the personal narrative. Copies of the remarkable autobiography were
also sent by purchasers to friends abroad. It has long been out of print. To
meet the demand for a new edition and to include traditions gathered by
correspondence, personal intercourse with the aged and supplemented by
some account of his family, is the object of the compiler. Tradition says
Venture's amanuensis was Elisha Niles, of Chatham, who had been a
school-teacher, and also a Revolutionary soldier, like one of the sons of
Venture.

The reader of this new edition will find much in confirmation of the
truthfulness of Venture's statements.

Among the different homes of Venture, the later and favorite one was in
Haddam Neck, near the western shore of Salmon River, on higher ground
and overlooking the cove. His farm was excellent land, fine mellow soil and
very easy to till. In illustration of its fertility an old and current tradition
says: "A black snake was once seen moving on and over the heads of the
standing rye on one of the fields." His house was a one-story unpainted
building, in the upper portion of which he had a room that he called his
office. Here, after his decease, his younger son, Solomon, continued to live
many years. A few rods from where it stood Wells C. Andrews built a large
two-story house now owned by John H. Cone.

---

*Venture assumed the name of Smith in compliment to his latest master, Col. Oliver
Smith, who generously permitted him to secure his freedom by his own earnings.

Venture presented a noble appearance. In mention of himself he says, "Though once straight and tall, measuring, without shoes, six feet one inch and a half, and every way well proportioned," etc. Tradition says he weighed over three hundred pounds and measured six feet around his waist. The tradition of the waist measure was received by the compiler from two sources. The first, from Mr. Orville Percival of Moodus, in 1894, then over 80 years of age, who said Venture measured six feet around his waist, that his feet were very large and twice the width of his (Mr. Percival's) father's feet.

The incident Venture relates of taking upon his knees a tierce of salt has with variation passed into tradition, or the act has been repeated. Mr. Percival gave it as occurring in a store at East Haddam, when Venture burst both of his brogan shoes in carrying the salt across the floor. Mr. Percival added: "A noted wrestler tried his skill in wrestling with Venture, but found he might as well try to remove a tree."

Mr. Alex. M. Clark of Haddam Neck, over 82 years of age, says that Venture worked occasionally for his grandfather, Robert Clark, and with his father, Benajah Clark, at the same time, and that he had often heard them say that Venture measured six feet around his waist, and one or both saw him measured; that Gersham Rowley, a brother of the late Eleazar Dunham Rowley of Young Street, Chatham, was present and assisted in the measurement. Mr. G. Rowley afterward moved to Farmersville, N. Y., where Mr. A. M. Clark visited and heard him relate the occurrence. Mr. A. M. Clark says he heard his father say that Venture weighed over 300 pounds; that his axe weighed nine pounds; that his usual day's work was seven cords of wood, but had cut nine cords in a day; that with his canoe he went often to Long Island, a distance of forty-five miles, to chop, and bring back clams on his return; that by his great strength he made the canoe go very straight and fast. Mr. Clark says that Venture called one day on his grandfather, Robert Clark, for him to stack some wheat, saying in disparagement of himself, "Nigger never know nothing!" Mr. Clark also related the tradition of the salt lifting and mentioned it as occurring in a store in East Haddam. Traditions vary sometimes.

Daniel Cone of Moodus gives the tradition of Venture's axe as weighing six pounds, and that he cut six cords of wood a day. He also repeated the salt-lifting tradition. Another tradition current over forty years ago was that Venture while chopping never raised his axe higher than his head, but forced it into the wood up to the eye at every blow, and further that he said he did not believe in chopping air. This appears to confirm the greater weight of his axe.

Mr. Robert S. Cone of Moodus writes: "About the weight of Venture's axe have no knowledge, but should think six pounds a light weight, for my father used a five and one-half pound weight." Mr. Cone adds: "I have heard father say that he and his brother Horatio cut wood for Venture at thirty-four cents per cord to pay for the use of his scow. When they went to get the scow she was well up on the beach. They thought it impossible to get her off. Venture said, 'Lead me down. True, I am blind, but I can give you a lift.' They led him to the water's edge. Father said the timbers fairly cracked as his great hands touched the scow. She swept into the water like a bird on the wing."

Another tradition, received from various sources, says that when Venture purchased oxen after his sight failed, his method of examining them, besides feeling, was to seize each ox by its hind legs and raise it up to estimate the weight. Again, that Venture while in the house of Ansel Brainerd, Sr., in Haddam Neck—who weighed two hundred or more—stooped down and, placing his hands palm upward on the floor, said to Mr. Brainerd, "You put your feet into my black paws and clasp your hands in my wool and I will raise you up!" This was done and Venture raised him up.

Among the early recollections of the compiler is his visiting an old, unoccupied gambrel-roofed house—the early home of his great-grandfather, Robert Chapman—having narrow outside doors. Tradition said that whenever Venture called, which he often did, he invariably turned sidewise to pass through.

Dea. E. C. Hungerford of Chester, in a letter of April 22, 1895, wrote: "The history of Venture will be interesting, I believe, to a great many. I shall want a copy, perhaps more than one.

"You ask me to rewrite my father's recollections of him. My father (born in 1777) told me that, when he was young, Venture often came to his father's house, and, as he was too heavy a burden to ride on a horse's back, he rode in a sort of two-wheeled cart. Sometimes his horse did not behave well, and then, Venture would put one hand in front of his horse's fore legs and one behind them and jounce the fore parts of the horse up and down a few times and remark, 'There!' The horse would usually behave well after such a jouncing. Father said he used to go behind Venture when he sat in an ordinary chair to look at his broad back and hips, which projected beyond the chair on each side, showing what a large man he must have been."

There is a tradition that the owner of a valuable wood or timber lot, wishing to have some of it cut, had engaged Venture to do it. He arrived later than expected, for which the owner reproved him. Venture, displeased, replied, "You will have cut all you want." At noon the owner came, and to his great surprise and disgust found nearly the whole of his beautiful grove laid low. Robert S. Cone thinks the party whose wood Venture nearly demolished was Capt. Elisha Cone of East Haddam, as his home was

Venture's headquarters when he was on that side of the river, but he must have been aware of Venture's peculiarities. It is easy to suppose similar instances and in a different location.

Dr. A. B. Worthington of Middle Haddam, born in 1819, relates that tradition says Venture had engaged to cradle a field of grain. At noon he returned bearing the cradle, having finished the field, to the great surprise of the owner, who expected it would require more than a day to complete it.

Mrs. Philo Bevin of East Hampton, in her letter of March 12, 1895, which we copy in full, gives a similar occurrence which, perhaps, may have originated the former:

East Hampton, Conn., March 12, 1895.

Mr. H. M. Selden:

Dear Sir—I have been quite interested in the history of Venture, and my mother, who is living with me, at the age of 96 years and 9 months, is possibly the only living person in this vicnity who has personal recollections of him. Mother is the widow of Alfred I. Loomis of Westchester. Her maiden name was Abigail Foote, born in June, 1798, and in her childhood lived in S. W. district, known as Waterhole. Venture used to visit at a neighbor's, Mr. Bigelow, grandfather of D. S. Bigelow, who lives where his grandfather did when she was young. She says Venture froze his feet, and she remembers well that he walked on his knees and could travel quite fast, and for sport used to chase the children. She was afraid of him, and would never allow him to catch her, but Polly Bigelow would let him catch her. She says he was a very powerful man, and Mr. Bigelow one morning set him to cut down trees before breakfast and he hurried to call him away, fearing he would cut down the whole grove of timber. Perhaps you have heard all this, but I don't remember to have seen anything about his going on his knees, and possibly it may have been for only a little while. Mother is very bright and clear in her mind and her memory is better than the average of young folks, so I am sure she cannot be mistaken about this. I have promise of the loan of "Life of Venture" from a lady who lives here.

I don't suppose I have given you any points of interest, except to tell you there is one person living who remembers Venture, and I thought I would venture to write, peradventure it might add to your history.

Very respectfully yours,
MRS. PHILO BEVIN.

It is natural to suppose that the grove cutting on the Bigelow place was later than the one previously mentioned (thought to have been on the Capt.

Elisha Cone farm), from the solicitude of the owner. The incident of the salt lifting related of Venture may have been reënacted by him (as mentioned in the tradition) on being appealed to by curious doubters. It is related of Venture that on the occasion of his marriage he threw a rope over the house of his master, where they were living, and had his wife go to the opposite side of the house and pull on the rope hanging there while he remained and pulled on his end of it. After both had tugged at it awhile in vain, he called her to his side of the house and by their united effort the rope was drawn over to themselves with ease. He then explained the object lesson: "If we pull in life against each other we shall fail, but if we pull together we shall succeed." The success of his later life implies that the lesson was not forgotten by his true and loving wife.

At length, borne down with the weight of years and increasing infirmities, he sickened and died September 19, 1805, in his seventy-seventh year. His heavy body was conveyed in a boat across the Cove and carried thence on a bier, a distance of some three miles, to the cemetery adjoining the First Congregational Church in East Haddam, for burial, by four strong men fittingly chosen. The two in front were white, proving the respect he had won, while two of his own race assisted in the rear. Robert S. Cone writes of the pallbearers: "When Venture was buried, my father was one of the pall-bearers. He was six feet three inches high. Uri Gates was six feet two inches high. Hannawell, a slave of Doctor Moseley, was five feet six inches high, and a slave of Gen. Epaphroditus Champion, about the same height, was his helper. The negroes being behind threw the weight upon themselves, and as they were mounting the long Olmsted hill the darkies complained bitterly. Hannawell exclaimed, 'Durned great nigger! Ought to have quartered him and gone four times. It makes the gravel stones crack under my feet.'"

His grave is marked by a brown-stone slab inscribed:

SACRED TO THE MEMORY OF
VENTURE SMITH,
AFRICAN.
Though the son of a King, he was kidnapped
and sold as a slave, but by his industry
he acquired money to purchase
his freedom.
WHO DIED SEPT. 19, 1805,
IN YE 77TH YEAR OF HIS AGE.

A similar slab at the adjoining grave is inscribed:

SACRED TO THE MEMORY OF
MARGET SMITH,
RELICT OF VENTURE SMITH,
WHO DIED
DEC. THE 17TH, A. D. 1809,
IN THE 79TH YEAR OF HER AGE.

CHILDREN OF VENTURE AND MARGET SMITH.

*Their names with supposed approximate dates of birth are gathered from the autobiography of their father.

1. HANNAH, born about 1752. Her freedom was purchased for £44. She married a free negro named Isaac, and died—. No mention of children.
2. SOLOMON, born about 1756; died about 1773, in his 17th year. His freedom was purchased for $200.
3. CUFF, born about 1758. His freedom was purchased for $200. Was a soldier in the Revolutionary War, credited to town of East Haddam, enlisted January 29, 1781, as a private for three years in Col. Heman Swift's Battalion. He married, but to whom is to the compiler unknown. Had seven children: 1st—Cuff; 2d—George; 3d—Daniel; 4th—Cynthia; 5th and 6th—twins, Jack and Alice; 7th—Venture, Jr., called Young Venture. Most of these were born in East Haddam. R. S. Cone thinks Cuff died in East Haddam. He was a very strong man, over six feet high. While he lived in Haddam Neck he worked some in the quarries and assisted in loading vessels from the quarries with his brother Solomon. While so engaged, they together alone carried aboard some very heavy stone, which on being unloaded in New York those assisting could not believe were carried aboard by two men alone. George, the second son of Cuff Smith, married and had several children, one of whom was Nelson of Haddam, the father of Charles, who was born in Haddam in 1847, and married Ascenath Hurd of East Haddam. They have eight children and reside in Cobalt, worthy decendants of Venture.
4. SOLOMON, 2d, born 1773 or 1774, was a very strong man and over six feet high.

Mr. Robert S. Cone of Moodus, says: "Solomon had seven children. He was married twice. First, to Tamar, a worthy, useful woman. A friend to

---

* Venture in the closing words of his autobiography disparages his sons Cuff and Solomon. The compiler, on inquiry among the elderly people who remembered them well, fails to find sufficient warrant for the language of criticism. Evidently, if any youthful foibles early appeared, they were soon overcome.

everybody, every one her friend. Think she had two children. One, William, lived to grow to manhood, a straight, handsome fellow, well formed and well spoken. Died in Hartford, unmarried.

"I recollect a short episode which occurred in my boyhood days in connection with the above William. We, that is, Tom Summers with others and myself when a lad, were sailing up the Cove in a scow. Summers was tall and very conceited of his strength, thinking himself more than a match for the strong. Solomon's place was noted at that time for its early peaches, delicious apples and fine vegtables, far ahead of his neighbors. As we moved along, when the scow stood opposite Solomon's place, Summers remarked, 'Now for a bag of Sol's apples!'' He jumped ashore, sprang up the hill into the orchard and began to gather. William soon appeared, tall, well dressed and very comely. He very politely asked Mr. Summers to go away. Instead, Mr. Summers showed his two fists in fighting array. William again said, 'Will you go? Will you go?' Summers still showed fight. William, with a cat-like movement, seized him by the nape of the neck and seat of his pants and tossed him down the bank to the Cove with as little effort as we would manage a little child.

"Solomon's second wife was as unlike Tamar as possible. Her name was Peggy. She had six children. Hannah first; then two daughters. Don't recollect their names.* 4th—Henry; 5th—Oliver; then Eliza, for many years head chambermaid on the Hartford and New York line of boats, later on the largest of the Fall River line, the 'Puritan.' Solomon, the father, died in East Haddam at the home of George Palmer, where his daughter Eliza was brought up."

Mrs. L. E. Sexton of Turnerville writes: "I well remember Solomon and his wife Peggy. They came often to the store at Rock Landing kept by John L'Homedieu. One day she came alone and Mr. L'Homedieu kindly inquired after her husband, calling him Sol. (He was often called Sol Venture.) She repeated the name after him in anything but a pleased manner, saying, 'Why, Sol and Solomon are no more alike than Hagar and Phyllis,'' giving him a lecture for speaking of her husband in such a disrespectful manner.

"I remember Solomon as tall, straight and broad-shouldered, but I think she carried her head quite as high as he did. I think only two of their children attended school on Haddam Neck—two boys, one named George Oliver Washington Smith. The other one had a name equally as long, but I only remember one of them, Henry. The winter that Azariah Wheeler taught the school they attended and were his pet class. He had them come and stand by the table. First, he would drill them to get the right kind of bow, then each one had to give his name in full. By that time the whole school

---

* Mary and Harriet.

was interested, but if any smiled too broadly he would try to look severe and rap on the table with his ruler to call the house to order, but I think he enjoyed the fun with them and was quite willing the school should, too. He was a good teacher, and helped to make all the children happy, and that is half the battle whether at school or at home."

The compiler remembers both Solomon and George Oliver W. Smith. The former as being tall and straight, the latter a very bright young man, who married, lived in Middletown and died there several years since, leaving children.

It is related of Solomon that, calling at Capt. Justin Sexton's while he and his boys were engaged in butchering, he quoted the words, "Where the carcass is, there the eagles will be gathered together," and added, "among them comes a black crow and begs a piece of liver." He received some liver. There is a tradition that a large colored family called at Solomon's home early one morning, to remain through the day. They were unwelcomed by Mrs. Peggy, who did not wish a visitation. She placed a small pot inside a larger one and both over the fire. Noon came, long passed, and night succeeded in turn; the pot boiled without ceasing and the hungry visitors at length withdrew. The father remarked later, that for all he knew the "pawt" was still boiling.

Several have claimed, or been claimed by others, as decendants of Venture. Yet the omission of their names from his autobiography casts doubt upon their claims. Among these was Diana, or Dinah Caples, more generally called Dian, and remembered by the elderly people. She often boasted of being a grand-daughter to the king. She made and sold baskets and artificial birds. Of the latter she feared some might learn the manufacture. In person she was of unusual proportions, about five feet in height and nearly as broad.

Robert S. Cone writes: "Tradition says Gideon Quash was Venture's son. He was near the age of Cuff. Both were Revolutionary soldiers. Gid, so said, resembled Venture in form, speech and feature. He was by far the most intelligent negro for miles; accumulated thousands of dollars; married a white wife, whom he told me he obtained her consent to become his, by himself showering into her lap a bag containing ninety-six hard dollars, one year's pay from government. His decendants still live in Colchester, owners of property and respected."

Dr. A. B. Worthington says that Quash called at Isham's store in Colchester and wanted to purchase a "book-tionary and a diction," for his son Jim to learn the meaning of words. Jim later showed his ability by teaching in Colchester.

Alex. M. Clark says, "Sanford, who lived with Solomon, was a son of Solomon's first wife previous to her marriage with Solomon, and that he attended school in Haddam Neck and lived with the family."

MEMOIRS

OF

ELLEANOR ELDRIDGE.

O that estates, degrees, and offices,
Were not derived corruptly! and that clear honor
Were purchased by the merit of the wearer!
How many, then, should cover, that stand bare?
How many be commanded, that command?
How much low peasantry would then be gleaned
From the true seed of honor? and how much honor
Picked from the chaff and ruin of the times,
To be new varnished?—*Merchant of Venice*

PROVIDENCE:
B. T. ALBRO—PRINTER,
1838.

What follows are chapters 2, 3, and 4 of the Memoirs of Elleanor Eldridge. *This biography was first published in 1839. It was written by Eldridge's friend and patron Frances McDougall partly in an effort to help Eldridge recover from financial losses that she had suffered in that year.*

Chapter II.

It should not be considered essential to the interest and value of biography, that its subject be of exalted rank or illustrious name.—There is often a kind of ignis-fatuus light, playing around such names, calculated to dazzle and mislead, by their false lustre; until the eye can no longer receive the pure light of Truth, or the mind appreciate real excellence, or intrinsic worth. On the other hand, it often happens that, by lending our attention to the lowly fortunes of the indigent and obscure, important principles may be established, valuable truths elicited; and pure, and even lofty examples of virtue may be found. Then let no one turn with too much nicety from the simple story of the humble Elleanor, though it may contain few, or none, of the thrilling charms of poetry and passion.

Elleanor Eldridge, on the one hand, is the inheritress of African blood, with all its heirship of woe and shame; and the subject of wrong and banishment, by her Indian maternity on the other. Fully, and sadly, have these titles been redeemed. It seems, indeed, as if the wrongs and persecutions of both races had fallen upon Elleanor.

She was born at Warwick, R. I., March 26, 1785. Her paternal grandfather was a native African. He was induced, with his family, to come on board an American slaver, under pretense of trade. With a large quantity of tobacco, prepared for barter, the simple-hearted African, stepped fearlessly on board the stranger's ship, followed by his wife and little ones.

For some time he continued a friendly exchange of his staple commodity, for flannels and worsted bindings of gay and various colors. Already in imagination, had his wife decorated herself with the purchased finery, and walked forth amid the villages, the envy and admiration of all the belles of Congo; and already had the honest African, himself, rivalled in splendor the princes of his land. Having finished his bargains, Dick, for that was the name of the Congo chieftain, proposed to return;— but his hospitable entertainers would, on no account, allow him to depart without further attentions. Refreshments were handed freely about, with many little presents of small value. Then all the wonders of the ship, with the mysteries of operating its machinery, were to be explained to the intelligent, but uninformed stranger; while appropriate curiosities were displayed before the wondering eyes of his wife and children. By these means the confidence of the simple Africans was completely won.

Gaily the little ones danced along the buoyant deck, hardly restrained
by their watchful and anxious mother; while, ever and anon, they caroled
sweet legends of their own sunny vales, blithe and careless as the sea-
birds, which, even then, were skimming along the surface of the sea,
ruffling the billowy tresses of the deep.— Still the chief was detained; and
still remained unsuspecting; until, to his utter horror, he found that his
detainers, under pretense of illustrating some operation, had carefully
weighed anchor, and were putting out to sea.

Vain were any attempt to depict the horrors of this scene. The African
stood on the deck, with streaming eyes, stretching his arms out towards his
own beautiful Congo; which lay, even then, distinctly visible with the ruby
light of sunset, stealing, like a presence of joy, thro' bower and vale, tinging
the snowy cups of a thousand lilies. There too was his own beloved Zaire,
stealing away from the distant forests of mangrove and bondo,[*] and flowing
on within its lovely borders of tamarind and cedar, until, at last, it rushed
into the arms of the Atlantic, troubling the placid bosom of the ocean with
its tumultuous waters.[†]

Again he caught a gleam of his palm-roofed home, with all its clustering
vines, from the rich forests of Madeira; its beautiful groves of cocoa and
matoba, and its wide fields of masanga,[‡] luno,[§] and maize; all waving richly
beneath the bowing wind, rife with the promise of an abundant and joyful
harvest. Beyond, in holy solitude, stood the tree of his worship, the sacred
mironne,[||] in its garments of eternal green, an apt emblem of the undying
soul. He could almost see the tulip[#] groves where his children played; could
almost see the light garlands of tube rose and hyacinth, their sportive hands
had wreathed; with the rich clusters of nicosso[**] and tamba,[††] they had

---

[*]We cannot conclude this account of the principal vegetable productions of Lower
Guinea, without mentioning that colossus of the earth, the enormous baobab, or Ad-
ansonia digitata, which is here called aliconda bondo and mapou. It abounds throughout
the whole kingdom of Congo; and is so large that the arms of 20 men cannot embrace
it.—*Maltebrun, on the authority of Tuchelli.*

[†]The river Congo, called by the native, Zaire, or Zahire, is three leagues wide at its
mouth; and empties itself into the sea with so much impetuosity, that no depth can there
be taken.

[‡]The masanga is a species of millet, highly pleasant both in taste and smell; the ears
of which are a foot long, and weigh from two to three pounds.

[§] The luno forms a very white and pleasant bread, as good as that made of wheat. It is
the common food of Congo.

[||]The mironne of the same genus, (of the enzanda) is an object of adoration to the negroes.

[#]In every direction there are entire groves of tulips, of the most lively colors, inter-
mixed with the tube-rose and hyacinth.

[**]The nicosso grows in clusters of the form of the pineapple.

[††]The tamba is a species of the bread fruit. *Maltebrun.*

gathered for their evening banquet. He could almost hear the murmurs of the home returning bees, as they lingered in the sweet groves of orange and pomegranate; for despair had quickened the senses: and a thousand objects, with all their thronging associations, came rushing to the mind, in that one agonizing moment, to quicken and aggravate its conceptions of eternal loss.

He stretched out his arms, and, in the agony of desperation, was about to leap into the sea, when his frantic wife, casting aside her screeching children, flung herself upon his bosom, and so restrained him. No sigh, no tear relieved him; but his bosom heaved convulsively; and the muscles and sinews became rigid, as if horror had absolutely taken away the power of thought, or motion. The wife was more violent. With the most fearful cries she flung herself at the captain's feet and embracing his kness, begged for mercy. Then successively she embraced her weeping children; and at last, sank exhausted into the arms of her husband. It was all in vain. They were chained, and ordered below; where the sight of hundreds of wretches, stolen, wronged, wretched as themselves, only showed them that they were lost forever.

No tongue can depict the horrors of that passage. No imagination can form even a faint outline of its sufferings. Physical torture wrought its work. Humanity was crushed within them; and they were presented for sale, more than half brutalized for the brutal market. Few minds ever rise from this state, to anything of their former vigor. The ancestor of Elleanor had one of these few; and though his pride was crushed and his hopes were forever extinguished, still he felt, and acted like a man.

But little more than the foregoing particulars is known to the subject of this narrative, concerning her ancestors, save that his African name was Dick; and that he had four children, one daughter Phillis and three sons; Dick, George, and Robin; of whom the latter was her father.

At the commencement of the American Revolution, Robin Eldridge, with his two brothers, presented themselves as candidates for liberty. They were promised their freedom, with the aditional premium of 200 acres of land in the Mohawk country, apiece.

These slaves fought as bravely, and served as faithfully, under the banner of freedom, as if they had always breathed her atmosphere, and dwelt forever in her temple; as if the collar had never bowed down their free heads, nor the chain oppressed their strong limbs.— What were toils, privations, distresses, dangers? Did they not already see the morning star of FREEDOM, glimmering in the east ? Were they not soon to exhibit one of the most glorious changes in nature? Were they not soon to start up from the rank of goods and chattels, into MEN? Would they not soon burst from the grovelling crysalis; and spreading out the wines of the soul, go abroad in the glad sunshine inhaling the pure air of liberty?

Oh, LIBERTY! what power dwells in the softest whisper of thy syllables, acting like magic upon the human soul! He who first woke thy slumbering echoes, was a magician more potent than ever dwelt in the halls of genii; for he had learned a spell that should rouse a principle of the soul, to whose voice, throughout the wide earth, every human spirit should respond; until its power should be coextensive with the habitations of mind, and coeternal with its existence.

These poor slaves toiled on in their arduous duties: and while they literally left foot-prints of blood, upon the rough flint, and the crusted snow; they carried a fire within their bosoms which no sufferings could extinguish, no cold subdue—the God-enkindled fire of liberty.—They counted their perils and their sufferings joy, for the blessed reward that lay beyond.—Most dearly did they purchase and well they won the gift.

At the close of the war they were pronounced FREE; but their services were paid in the old Continental money, the depreciation, and final ruin of which, left them no wealth but the one priceless gem, LIBERTY. They were free.— Having no funds, they could not go to take possession of their lands on the Mohawk. And, to this day, their children have never been able to recover them; though, by an act of Congress, it was provided, that all soldiers' children who were left incapable of providing for themselves, should "inherit the promises" due to their fathers. The subject of this memoir, attracted by an advertisement to this affect, attempted to recover something for a young brother and sister; but with the success which too often attends upon honest poverty, struggling with adverse circumstances. Her efforts were of no avail.

The spirit of Robin Eldridge was not to be broken down. Before entering the army, he had married Hannah Prophet; and he now settled in Warwick, near the Fulling-Mill; where, by his honest industry, and general good character, he was always held in esteem. He soon became able to purchase land and build a small house; when he reared a large family, all of whom inherit their father's claims to the kindness and respect of those about them. He had, by this marriage, nine children; of whom Elleanor was the last of seven successive daughters. Of these children, only five lived to mature age.

It may now be proper to look back a little, in order to glance at Elleanor's maternal ancestry. Her maternal grandmother, Mary Fuller, was a native Indian, belonging to the small tribe or clan, called the Fuller family; which was probably a portion of the Narragansett tribe. Certain it is, that this tribe or family once held great possessions in large tracts of land; with a portion of which Mary Fuller purchased her husband Thomas Prophet; who, until his marriage, had been a slave. Mary Fuller, having witnessed the departing glories of her tribes, died in extreme old age, at the house of her son, Caleb Prophet; being 102 years old. She was buried at the Thomas Greene burying place in Warwick, in the year 1780. Her daughter Hannah, as we have said before, had been married to Robin Eldridge, the father of Elleanor.

Our heroine had the misfortune to lose her mother at the age of ten years; when she launched out boldly into the eventful life which lay before her, commencing at once, her own self-government, and that course of vigorous, and spirited action, for which she has since been so much distinguished.

During her mother's life, it had often been her practice to follow washing, at the house of Mr. Joseph Baker, of Warwick; a daughter of whom, Miss Elleanor Baker, gave her own name to the little one she often carried with her; and always continued to take great interest in her little colored name-sake. Not long after the death of her mother, this young lady called on Ellenor, and invited her to come and reside with her, at her father's, offering her a home. She asked permission of her father, who consented, but with this remark, that she would not stay a week. The young heroine was not, however, to be so discouraged; but bravely collected herself, and began by making a definite BARGAIN with Miss Baker, before she consented to put herself under her protection, evincing, by this single act, a degree of prudence and wisdom entirely beyond her years.—She fixed her price at 25 cents per week, and agreed to work for one year.

It was Sunday evening, in the changeful month of April, when Elleanor, with her whole wardrobe contained in the little bundle she held, stood with the family group she was about to quit forever. Let not the proud aristocrat smile disdainfully, because the biographer of poor Elleanor lingers a moment here. Home is home, to the lowly as well as the great; and no rank, or color, destroys its sacred character, its power over the mind, and the affections.—The sundering of family ties is always painful; and I have often thought that among the poor it is eminently so. There is nothing which strengthens the bonds of love so much as *mutual suffering*.

> "When joy has bound our hearts for years,
> A sudden storm those hearts may sever ;
> But, Oh, the love that springs in TEARS
> Through time and change, endures forever;"

truly and beautiful says the poet. The ties then, which unite families among the virtuous poor, are wrought from the deepest and strongest and holiest principles of our nature. They have toiled, and struggled, and suffered, together; until bond strengthens bond, and heart is knit with heart, by the

strongest and most endearing ties. The world beyond and above, may perse-
cute, oppress, and wrong them; yet out of these very circumstances springs
a sympathy stronger than the great and the fashionable ever know. In the
little sanctuary of a common home, all may gather themselves together and
cherish this boon as their best treasure. Exterior to home, the poor have no
hope, no pleasure, no ambition, no desires; all the bliss of life is concen-
trated within its charmed circle; and, of necessity, its power is strong.

Our young heroine, having, walked several times through the standing
group, went again to the little nook in the chimney, where neatly ranged on
their little shelves, were her playthings; shells and pebbles from the beach,
little baskets made by her own hand; rag babies, and acorns gathered from
the wood. She loved these things more dearly than the children of the rich
love their gilded toys; for they were full of the pleasant associations of her
early childhood. She looked at them a moment, then turned and looked out
of the window.—There was the little wood where she, with her happy
brothers and sisters, had always played together, and in the bank close by
the window, were her houses and ovens, with their sand pies and mud
puddings, baking in clam and quahaug shells. She turned from the window,
stooped to kiss the baby, that, with waddling steps, was trying to reach her
favorite play-fellow; appearing to have an instinctive perception of something sad in the uncommon silence. The first to speak, for some minutes
was the little brother then only five years old.

He sprung to his sister's arms, and clinging around her neck, cried
"Dont go, Nelly! I play alone. I be tired. I cry!" and, suiting the action to
the word, the poor little fellow burst into tears.

Elleanor swallowed, as well as she was able, the big lump that was
rising in her throat, and comforted him with the promise of coming back
soon.

"How long will be soon?" cried the child, still clinging to his sister,
who was trying to disengage herself from him. "Will it be all night? Say
Nelly?"

She could not answer, but placing her hands silently in those of her two
elder sisters, and pausing a moment before her father, she turned from the
door, wiped the tears away with the corner of her short-gown, and ran along
the road quite fast, to escape the earliest cries of her weeping brother.

The heart of childhood is always buoyant; and that of Elleanor was soon
bounding lightly again; for ambitious projects were, even then, beginning to
germinate in her young bosom.—She paused at a turn in the road, which
gave her a last view of the cottage; and, looking back a moment she wiped
another tear away; and resumed her walk. The distance was two miles; and
Elleanor reached there before sunset. She was kindly received, even by the

old dog and house cat; but she felt somewhat disinclined for society, and she soon begged permission to retire to her little bed; where her slumbers were soft and sweet, as if she bad slept on a bed of down, garnished with the most splendid drapery. Blessed are the slumbers of the innocent! They are kindlier than balm; and they refresh and gladden the spirit of childhood, like ministerings from a better world.

CHAPTER III.

The new relation into which Elleanor had entered, tended to produce mutual satisfaction to the parties sustaining it. Kindness and good feeling, on the part of employers, seldom fail to secure industry and fidelity, in that of the employed. When a mistress, and the several members of her family, manifcst an interest in the welfare of their servants—when they show them that they are considered as human beings, belonging to the same great family of man—that the common rights of humanity are understood and regarded—that those who perform their servile labors are members of the same family, sustaining certain relations, and filling certain places (by no means unimportant ones) in the gradations of society—and are *not the mere instruments of their own selfish gratification*—created to administer to their pleasures; the intcrests of the serving and the served, generally become identified; and the hcart quickens and strengthens the hands in the performance of duty. Those who are governed by these principles know their weight and force; sorrowful it is to think, that the world will not also learn, that kind and judicious masters and mistresses, generally are blcssed with efficient and faithful servants. I, by no means, intend to lay all the follies, vices, and crimcs of servants at the door of thcir employers; but I am persuaded that the comforts, rights, and, more especially, the *moral health* of domestics is shamefully neglected. Instead of being treated as account-able beings—as persons indeed, capable of independent thought, feeling and action—susceptible alike of pleasure and pain, they are considered as the mere appendages of luxury; and being generally left to their own way-ward courses, often sink into depravity and vice, when a little of kindness and good feeling—a little affectionate interest and judicious advice, might restrain and save them. Let them who think lightly of these things, consider the immense value of a single human being! Were this considered and acted upon, a reformation in the department of domostic service, would soon begin; and the blessings which would flow from it, would be greater than a superficial thinker might be made to believe *could* proceed from such a source. But enough of this.

With the early dawn, Elleanor was seen, dashing away the dews with her little bare feet, as she drove the cows to pasture; all the time singing blithely, as the birds themselves. She always had a provident eye on the poultry, and the happiest art of finding their hiding-places. No hen's nest throughout all the varieties of place, stable, hay-loft, wood-pile, thicket, meadow, or out-building, escaped her searching eye. She won the confidence of her feathered friends so entirely, by her zealous attention to their wants, that she could, with all the *sang froid* of her Indian character, cross the path of some sly old turkey, about stealing to her nest, without exciting the least apprehension; and, with apparent listlessness and unconcern, watching all the artful doublings and windings of that wary foul, she would soon creep with a light step, to her chosen sanctum, and so make herself mistress of the poor turkey's secret, *sans ceremonie*. In such cases, when she returned with her coarse apron laden with the mottled treasure, she always met such a warm smile, as was, at once, a reward for the present, and incentive to the future. Not only the family, but every living creature about the house and farm, loved little Elleanor. The dog and cat, the horses, cows, pigs, sheep and poultry, all knew her light step, and in their several ways, manifested their love. And well they might; for when they were well, she fed them; when they were sick, she nursed them; and she always took the kindest care of the young and helpless.

At the expiration of the year, Ellenora received her wages, and commenced a new term of service for two shillings per week.

The marriage, and consequent removal, of her young mistress, to whom she was tenderly attached, was a great trial to her: and for some time she was very melancholy and home-sick; but she recovered, at length, her usual degree of cheerfulness.

With this kind family she remained five years and nine months. During that time she learned all the varieties of house-work, and every kind of spinning; and in the last year she learned plain, double, and ornamental weaving, in which she was considered particularly expert. This shows that our heroine has great mechanical genius; or, to speak phrenologically, that her "constructiveness," "comparison," and "calculation " are well developed. This double weaving, as it is called—i.e. carpets, old fashioned coverlets, damask, and bed-ticking, is said to be a very difficult and complicated process; and I presu me there are few girls of fourteen, capable of mastering such an intricate business; and when we consider that she was entirely uneducated; that her powers had never been disciplined by any course of study, it seems really wonderful that she could enter into this difficult business, at that early age, with so much spirit and success. Yet she was, at the expiration of the year, pronounced a competent and fully accomplished weaver.

In the commencement of her sixteenth year, Elleanor took leave of her kind patrons, and went to live next at Capt. Benjamin Green's, at Warwick Neck, to do their spinning for one year.

At the expiration of the year she was engaged as dairy woman. It appears really wonderful that any person should think of employing a girl, but just entering her seventeenth year, in this nice and delicate business. Yet so it was; and the event proves that their judgment was correct. Elleanor continued in this situation eight years. She took charge of the milk of from twenty-five to thirty cows; and made from four to five thousand weight of cheese annually. Every year our heroine's cheese was distinguished by a *premium.*

We acknowledge to the sentimentalist that these matters are not very poetical; but to the lover of truth, they are important, as giving a distinct idea of the capacity, which early distinguished our subject.

About the period of her nineteenth year, Elleanor became quite a belle; and her light foot in the dance, and her sweet voice in the song, made her an object of great interest among the colored swains. Sad indeed was the havoc which the sweet singing, and the more exciting movements of the dance, wrought among their too susceptible hearts!

Whether Elleanor, herself, ever yielded to the witching influence of the tender passion, remains in the Book of Mysteries to this day. Sometimes, with a low, quick breath—I could almost imagine it a sigh—she would say, "There was a young man—I *had* a cousin—he sent a great many letters—" but further our deponent saith not. Not a syllable more could I ever extract from her. I have asked her for the letters; which, being her veritable biographer, I had a right to do; but she always tells me they are in a great box, with all the accumulated weight of her household stuff resting upon them. Now, dearest reader, if I can ever extract aught further touching this delicate and pleasing subject, I will not fail to make you acquainted with it; or if I can, by any persuasion, get a peep at any letters from this cousin afore-mentioned, I hereby pledge myself that you too shall be advised of their contents.

And now as darkness is closing fast around me, I beg leave to retire from your pleasant company; and so I wish you a very good evening.

CHAPTER IV.

As was remarked in the preceding chapter, Elleanor, at this period, was a belle. During her residence at Capt. Greene's, it seems that her brother, Mr

George Eldridge, had been chosen Governor of the colored election; and was re-elected three successive years. As this title was, in imitation of the whites, invested with considerable dignity, it follows that Elleanor stood among her people, in the very highest niche of the aristoracy. She always accompanied her brother to these festivals, dressed in such style as became the sister of "His Excellency." On some of these occasions she wore a lilac silk; on others a nice worked cambric; then again a rich silk, of a delicate sky blue color; and always with a proper garniture of ribbons, ornaments, laces, &c.—I trust I have acquitted myself, with all honorable exactness, in regard to the dresses; seeing it is important to the world that it should be enlightened on this subject: and no fair reader of marvellous tales, I am confident, would ever forgive me, should I neglect to say in what guise our heroine appeared abroad; for such a course would be entirely without pre-cetndet; and I feel no disposition to introduce a new system. Although I speak of Elleanor in this light, let no one think her story is fictitious; she is none the less a *heroine* because it is *true*.

At the period to which we now refer, Ellenor was light-hearted, and free from shadow as the fairest morning; with the sweet sensations of a happy and benevolent nature quickening within her bosom, like spirits of joy, that tinged all she looked upon with the hues of their own lights and gladness,

> "But all that's bright must fade,
> The fairest still the fleetest,
> All that's sweet, is made
> But to be lost when sweetest."

And so passed away the "dancing days" of Elleanor; bright as the morning rainbow, and like that, too, the presage of darkness and storms.

No doubt, my fair readers are in a state of highly wrought expectancy in regard to the *affaire, du coeur,* of which I barely hinted in the last chapter. Happy am I, to communicate the pleasing intelligence, of new arrivals from that quarter. To descend, at once, from the language of metaphor, to that of plain, sober fact, I rejoice to say that a portion of the correspondence, above alluded to, together with certain facts explanatory thereof, has been laid before me; and, in all confidence, as if the reader were my bosom friend, I hasten to fulfil the promise tendered in the last chapter.

I must beg leave to promise, dear reader, that you shall endeavor to be satisfied with the knowledge of these facts, making no single question concerning them; as I shall, in no wise, feel myself bound to explain any thing in regard to the circumstances by which I became possessed of them.

The manuscripts came to me in much the same order and connection, as

that in which the Editor of *Sartor Resartus,* found those of the lamented
sage and philosopher, Teufelsdroch, when he found out the contents of the
"Bag Capricornus"; when milk bills, love ditties, laundress' bills, poetry,
with torn and yellow scrips of paper, containing all high and unimaginable
thoughts and reflections, came tumbling in a heap together. There may be,
indeed, no further comparison between them: and it may be hinted, even,
that Elleanor's documents want the pith and marrow contained in those of
Teufelsdroch; but of this I am not bound to speak, since my province is not
criticism, but narration.

Let us turn aside, then, for a short time, from the straight-forward path
of history, into the pleasant regions of episode; where, as in a little grotto
apart from the high road, we may indulge in an hour of repose; turning,
mean-while, to the simple story for amusement. Having thus so comfortably
established ourselves, with no evil-minded eaves-dropper to make us afraid;
bend now, dear reader, thy most earnest and delicately adjusted ear; for I
am going to tell thee a *secret.*

Let us come directly to the subject matter in point. Elleanor, when a
buxom lassie of eighteen, by some means or other, became acquainted with
a lad somewhat older than herself, whom we shall designate as Christopher
G—— though whether this was the whole, or any part of his real name,
or one chosen as a screen, behind which to conceal the blushes of the
sensitive Elleanor, is a subject upon which I have no liberty to speak. So
this also may be passed over to the budget of *mysteries.*—Let us, dear
reader, remember the punishment of idle curiosity, as taught in the true and
affecting history, yeclept "Blue Beard;" and, striving to be content with the
facts in the case, seek not to lift the veil, which the sensibility of true love
and feminine delicacy, have alike conspired to draw.

This Christopher, I have found by a course of induction, the process of
which has nothing to do with this story, to be the same true and veritable
person, of whom Elleanor speaks so plaintively, and so pithily, when she
said: "I *had a cousin.*" How much is told in those four little words. They
are, of themselves, a history. They contain all the regular parts of a true
epic; viz: beginning, middle and end; together with outlines, circumstances,
and decorations. We need only shut our eyes; and lo, as if the lamp of
Aladelin were lighted in our presence, all the mysteries stand unveiled
before us, in their true order and connection. But as every one of my readers
may not be gifted, in the highest degree, with the organs of ideality and
"language," I make no doubt they will prefer a translation to the original,
especially as I am enabled to enrich that translation, with numerous notes,
coming from a not-to-be-doubted source.

Certain it is that the youthful cousins, even in the very first interview, began to suspect, (or might have began to suspect, were not love blind, so that frequently he does not know his own image,) *that there are dearer ties than those of consanguinity.*

There was the due proportion of fear, hope, doubt, ecstacy, and moonlight; together with the proper infusion of sighs, tears, &c. "for all such cases made and provided," until at length the important and accustomed tender, was made, listened to—and—accepted. Thus far, all was well. There was the light of hope in the eye of Elleanor, and her footstep had the grace of buoyancy of joy.

Often did the lovers meet, (I feel myself justified in calling them so, since I find all the features of a most undoubted case,) and in the stillness of those beautiful solitudes, which surrounded them, they breathed their vows: unlooked upon, save by the kind moon, and the gentle stars, which, I believe all will agree, are far the best witnesses on such occasions. In the silent grove, and by the solemn sea, they wandered for hours together, creating to themselves a world of fairy-like beauty, which the confidence of loving hearts, warmed and kindled into truth.

> "All lovely things grew lovelier. The flowers
> Bloomed with more vivid brightness, and the grass
> Caught a more pleasant greenness, than, of yore.
> The winds that bowed the forest, or breathed low,
> With a sweet voice of sadness to the flowers,
> Still spoke to their affections; while the moon
> Grew kindlier, and came nearer to the heart,
> Like the familiar presence of a friend.
> The waters and the birds sang, aye, of love;
> Or seemed to chant the story of *their* loves;
> While all the stars had feeling in their light,
> Like the expressive eyes of sympathy,
> Even in the holy silence of the wood.
> When not a wind was breathing, a low voice
> Came with a blessing to their conscious hearts:
> For the sweet presence of undoubting Love,
> Spake to the soul, and these was audible."

And were they poor? No. The had found that which the wealth of kings could not purchase—"the pearl of great price"—the gem of LOVE—and it was safely treasured in the casket of faithful and all-believing hearts.

Then came the first parting, with the mutually reiterated vows of everlasting truth and remembrance; and the succeeding night of wakefulness and tears. But the shadow of absence had scarcely glanced over the fair heaven of Elleanor, when a sunbeam of a letter came: and all was bright again. The letter was as follows.

From Christopher G. to his Cousin.
NEWPORT, March 27, 1805.

My dear Cousin:

I have thought of you, almost with one thought, since I left. How strange it is that wherever I look I see nothing but my dear Ellen. I am well; but my heart is heavy; for I miss the dear eye that always looked on me in kindness; and I don't like to think there may be many weeks before I see you again,— When in Warwick I thought one week was a great while; but now I must learn to bear the pain of absence. I have lately been to the white Election; and I was astonished and disgusted with the behaviour I saw among the whites. I think the white people ought to be very careful what they do, and try to set good examples for us to follow; for whatever they do, whether good or bad, the colored people are sure to imitate them. I am glad that you my dear cousin, do not, like some of your companions, attempt to follow all the extravagant fashions of the white people. If we are ever to rise above our present condition fine clothes will not enable us to do it.

My mind remains the same that it was the last time I talked with you; so this is hoping you are well and happy.

From your affectionate cousin, and true lover.

CHRISTOPHER G——.

LIFE

OF

JAMES MARS,

A SLAVE

BORN AND SOLD IN

CONNECTICUT.

WRITTEN BY HIMSELF.

HARTFORD:

PRESS OF CASE, LOCKWOOD & COMPANY.

1866.

Mars's autobiography, published in 1868, was written in part to remind the New England public that slavery had existed in that region as well as the South. It was also written to help the then elderly Mars earn a little money so as not to be a burden to his children. In addition to telling us about the waning days of slavery in Connecticut, the Mars autobiography also tells us much about the strong sentiment in favor of equal rights among blacks in New England.

TO WHOM IT MAY CONCERN:

These will certify that the bearer, DEA. JAMES MARS, has been known to me and to the citizens of this town for a long period of years, as an honest, upright, truthful man,—a good citizen, an officer in his church, and a man whose life and character have gained the approbation, the esteem, and the good wishes of all who know him. Born a slave, the good providence of God has long since made him free, and, I trust, also taught him that "where the Spirit of the Lord is, there is liberty."

JNO. TODD.

PITTSFIELD, Mass., June, 23, 1868.

INTRODUCTION

WHEN I made up my mind to write this story, it was not to publish it, but it was at the request of my sister that lived in Africa, and has lived there more than thirty years. She had heard our parents tell about our being slaves, but she was not born until a number of years after they were free. When the war in which we have been engaged began, the thought came to her mind that her parents and brothers and sisters were once slaves, and she wrote to me from Africa for the story. I came to Norfolk on a visit at the time the war broke out, and some in Norfolk remember that I was once a slave. They asked me about it; I told them something about it; they seemed to take an interest in it, and as I was in Norfolk now, and having an opportunity to write it, I thought I would write it all through. In telling it to those, there were a great many things that I did not mention that I have written. After I bad written it out, I saw that my brother and my other sister would think that I might give them the same; and my children had often asked me to write it. When I had got it written, as it made more writing than I was willing to undertake to give each of them one, I thought I would have it printed, and perhaps I might sell enough to pay the expenses, as many of the people now on the stage of life do not know that slavery ever lived in Connecticut.

A SLAVE BORN AND SOLD IN CONNECTICUT

THE treatment of slaves was different at the North from the South; at the North they were admitted to be a species of the human family. I was told when a slave boy, that some of the people said that slaves had no souls, and that they would never go to heaven, let them do ever so well.

My father was born in the State of New York, I think in Columbia county. He had, I think, three different masters in that State, one by the name of Vanepps, and he was Gen. Van Rensaeller's slave in the time of the Revolution, and was a soldier in that war; he was then owned by a man whose name was Rutser, and then was owned in Connecticut, in Salisbury, and then by the minister in North Canaan.

My mother was born in old Virginia, in Loudin county; I do not remember the name of the town. The minister of North Canaan, whose name was Thompson, went to Virginia for a wife, or she came to him; in some way they got together, so that they became man and wife. He removed her to Canaan, and she brought her slaves with her, and my mother was one of them. I think there were two of my mother's brothers also. The Rev. Mr. Thompson, as he was then called, bought my father, and he was married to my mother by him. Mr. Thompson ministered to the people of Canaan in holy things; his slaves worked his farm. For a short time things went on very well; but soon the North and the South, as now, fell out; the South must rule, and after a time the North would not be ruled. The minister's wife told my father if she only had him South, where she could have at her call a half dozen men, she would have him stripped and flogged until he was cut in strings, and see if he would do as she bid him. She told him, You mind, boy, I will have you there yet, and you will get your pay for all that you have done. My father was a man of considerable muscular strength, and was not easily frightened into obedience. I have heard my mother say she has often seen her mother tied up and whipped until the blood ran across the floor in the room where she was tied and whipped.

Well, as I said, the South and the North could not agree; the South seceded and left the North; the minister's wife would not live North, and she and her husband picked up and went South, and left my father and mother in Canaan to work the farm, and they lived on the farm until I was eight years old. My mother had one child when she came from the South; I was the first she had after she was married. They had five children born in Canaan,—three died in infancy. I was born March 3d, 1790.

Mr. Thompson used to come up from Virginia and talk about our going South. He would pat me on the head and tell me what a fine boy I was. Once when he was in Canaan, he asked me if I would not like to go with him and drive the carriage for my mistress. He said if I would go he would give me twenty-five cents, or as it was then called, twenty-five coppers. I told him I wanted the money first. He gave me a quarter, and then I would not agree to go, and he put me in the oven; that I did not like, and when I got out I would not give him the money, but his business I did not yet know. He had come to sell his farm and to take us all South. My father said he would not go alive; the minister told him he must go; my father said he never would. Well, the man that had formerly ministered to the people in holy things, sold the farm, and stock, and tools, and effects, with a few exceptions. He kept a pair of horses and harness, a wagon, a bed, and a few such articles. The harness and wagon he kept to take us to the South with. After he sold his place, he took us all to a wealthy friend of his, until he had settled up all his affairs, so as to show to the world that he was an honest and upright man. He would have them think that he feared God and let alone evil; for he was born or raised in the State of New York, and had taught the people of North Canaan the way to do, as you will see, for in former days he spoke to the people from the pulpit morally, and they thought much of the man. He had taught them slavery was right, and that the Great Almighty God had sanctioned the institution, and he would practice it. He now made his arrangements to set out on his journey ; the day was fixed to leave his much-loved people and home for his southern home, where he had obtained a new home and friends and acquaintances.

My father, although a slave without education, was intensely watching the movements of the teacher of the people, but kept all that he saw to himself, yet he was steadily planning his escape. The set day had now within about thirty-six hours come; all went on well with the man from the South. He had had no thought but all was well; those fine chattels were his, and would fetch him in a southern market, at a moderate estimate, two thousand dollars; they would furnish him pocket change for some time, and also his loving wife could have a chance to wreak her vengeance on my father for what she called disobedience.

It was a matter of doubt with my father what course to take,—how he could get away with his family the best and safest; whether to go to Massachusetts, which joined Canaan on the north, or to Norfolk, which joined Canaan on the east. Very fortunately for us, there was at that time an unpleasant feeling existing between the two towns or the inhabitants of

Canaan and Norfolk. He said that the people of Canaan would side with their former pastor, and he found that the people of Norfolk would take sides against Canaan and their pastor; then he thought the best that he could do would be to take his family to Norfolk, where they would be the safest. He concluded to take them to Norfolk, but how was he to get them there with what he wanted to take with them? He came to the conclusion that the horses he had for a long time driven might as well help him now in this hour of distress as not. He got a colored man to help him that was stout and healthy. They hitched up the parson's team, put on board what few things he had and his family, in the still of a dark night, for it was very dark, and started for Norfolk, and on the way we run afoul of a man's wood-pile, for it was so dark he could not see the road; but we got off from the wood-pile without harm, and arrived in Norfolk about one o'clock. I think we stopped at a tavern kept by Mr. G. Pettibone, and in him we found a friend. We unloaded what we had, and father and the man that was with him took the team back to Canaan, so that the parson might set out on his journey and not have to wait for his team, and father returned to where he had left his family. He felt that he had done all for the parson that he well could, for he had taken away his family off from his hands, so that the parson would be relieved from the care that must necessarily occur in such a long journey with a family on his hands to see to, and my father thought that the parson's old Jewel would be relieved from some of her pardoned habits and from a promise she had so often made to him when she got him South. Well, how the parson felt when he had got himself out of bed, and found that he was left to pursue his journey alone, the reader can tell as well as I, for he was a big and bristle man; but I will leave him for a while, and see what is to be done with us.

It was soon known in the morning that we were in Norfolk; the first inquiry was, where will they be safe. The place was soon found. There was a man by the name of Phelps that had a house that was not occupied; it was out of the way and out of sight. After breakfast, we went to the house; it was well located; it needed some cleaning, and that my mother could do as well as the next woman. We all went to work and got it cleaned, and the next day went into it and stopped some time. Father did what work he could get out of the way, where he would not be seen, and it was necessary for him to keep out of sight, for Norfolk was the thoroughfare to Hartford. Days and weeks passed on, and we began to feel quite happy, hoping that the parson had gone South, as we heard nothing from him. At length we heard that he said he would have the two boys at all hazards. It was thought best that the boys should be away. So one dark night we heard that the parson was coming out with his men to find the boys, for have them he

would. A man that lived near to us said he would take the boys where they
would be safe. His name was Cady. It was agreed on, and he went with us
over a mountain, over rocks and logs. It was very rough and steep, and the
night was so dark that we could only see when it lightened. At last we got
through the woods on the top of what is called Burr Mountain. We could
look down in low grounds and see logs that were laid for the road across the
meadow; at every flash they could be seen, but when it did not lighten we
could not see anything; we kept on,—our pilot knew the way. At last we
arrived at the place. The name of the family was Tibbals. The family consisted of an old man, a middle-aged man and his wife and four children, and
a very pleasant family it was. We had not been there long before it was
thought best that my brother should be still more out of the way, as he was
about six years older than I, which made him an object of greater search,
and they were at a loss where to send him as he was then about fourteen
years of age. There was a young man by the name of Butler, from Massachusetts; he was in Norfolk at the time, studying law; he said he would take
him home with him, and he did so, as I supposed, and I saw him no more
for more than two years.

I stopped with the family a few days, and then went home, or what I
called home. It was where my parents and sister were. I found them very
lonely. I had not been home many days before our quiet was disturbed, for
the parson had his hunters out to find our whereabouts. He somehow found
where we were. My sister and myself were at play out at the door; we saw
two men in the woods, a little from the house, coming very fast, and they
came into the house. My father was not far from the house; mother was in
the house. The men were Captain Phelps, the man who owned the house,
and Mr. Butler, the law-student. They told us that we must now say whether
we would go with the parson or not, and we must decide quick, for the
parson was coming, and he would soon be on the spot, and there was no
time to lose. Mother had said she was not unwilling to go herself, if it was
not for father and the children, and the parson had made her such promises
that she was somewhat inclined to go. The parson talked so fair to her, he
beguiled her, I suppose, somewhat as our first mother was beguiled in the
garden. The beguilers were both, I do not say preachers, but they were both
deceivers, and he talked so smooth to mother that he beguiled her. He told
her if she would go to Canaan and see to his things and pack them up for
him, then if she did not want to go, she need not. Mother talked with father;
he did not incline to go, but finally he consented. The parson ordered a
wagon, and it was soon on the spot; but where was Joseph?—he is not here.
"I want him to go with us, that we may be all together," said the parson.
Father saw what the parson's plan was: he told him the boy was on the

way,—he could get him when we got to Canaan. I should have said that those two men that came to tell us that the parson was coming, hid in the barn before the parson arrived, and were not seen by him. They had a few words with my father while the parson went for his team. We set off for Canaan, and in the land of Canaan we arrived that day. Where is Joseph? Father said he would go for him the next day in the morning, or in the day. Father went, as the parson supposed, for Joseph. The parson was loading; mother was packing; all was now going on well. Night came, and when all was still, for father had told some one it would be late before he got back, he came and took the parson's horses, and took mother and the two children on horseback, and instead of going South, went to Norfolk, and got there about two o'clock in the morning. We stopped at a tavern kept by Captain Lawrence. The horses were sent back for the parson, for he said he should start the next day; but it seemed that he did not start for old Virginia, for we often heard of him after that day.

We stopped with Capt. Lawrence a few days. It was thought best by our friends that we should not all be together, for it was found that the parson was still in the land, and on the lookout for us. I was sent to a woman in the neighborhood, by the name of Darby—a poor woman. I stopped with her a few days, with instructions to keep still. The old lady had but one room in her house. You may wonder why I was sent to such a place; most likely it was thought she had so little room that she would not be suspected of harboring a fugitive.

A man by the name of Walter lived near by; he was in the habit of coming in to see how his boy did, as he called me. Ho told me when any one came there I must get under the bed. I used to sit in the corner of the room, so that I should not be seen from the window. I stayed there a number of days,—I do not now remember how many. One day I ventured to take a peep through the key-hole; the door was locked. Some one came to the door; I made a bound, and then a roll, and I was out of sight. The door was opened, and it was my friend Mr. Walter. He was quite amused to hear the performance; he said he would take me with him the next day, he was going to work in a back lot where it would be out of sight. So the next day I went with him; it was quite a treat. At noon we ate our dinner in the field; that was new to me. After dinner Mr. Walter lay down on the ground; he told me he should go to sleep, and I must keep a look-out to see if any one came in sight. If I saw any one, I must wake him. I kept watch, but there was none came to disturb him in his repose. The day passed away, and we returned home at night—all well, as I supposed; but it seemed that the parson had his pickets out, and had got an idea that I was somewhere in the street. That night I had to leave my place at Mrs. Darby's, and went about a mile to a man's house by the name of Upson; he lived on a back street. I thought him to be a friend; I do not know but he was,—but as I find that men now act in relation to slavery, I am inclined to think otherwise. The next morning the man went to his work; he was painting for the minister in Norfolk. Mrs. Upson sent me to the brook, a little way from the house, to fetch a pail of water. I did not like going into the street very much, but being taught by my parents to obey, I went without any words. As I got to the brook, a man rode into the brook with a cocked hat on. I did not much like his looks. I did not know who he was. Said he,—"My boy, where is your father and mother?" I said, "I don't know, sir." "Where is your brother?" "I don't know, sir." "Where do you live?" "I don't know, sir." "Whom do you stay with?" "I don't know, sir." I did not then know the name of the man. He rode off, or rather I left him asking questions. He looked after me till I got to the house, and rode up. I asked Mrs. Upson who it was that came to the brook when I was there. She said it was Mr. Robbins, the minister. I thought nothing of it, for I thought all the people in Norfolk were our friends. In a few hours, the woman sent me to the neighbor's to get some water from the well. It was a widow woman where I went to get the water, and there I found my father. He said that Capt. Lawrence had been there and told him that Mr. Robbins had sent his son to Canaan to tell parson Thompson that he had seen one of his boys, and we must go in the woods, for he thought the parson would come out to look for me. Father took the water and went with it to the house that I brought the pail from. The family where I went for the water, I shall always remember with the kindest feelings. We have ever, from that day to the present, been on the best terms, and I believe three of them are living now. Two of them live in that same house that they then lived in, and the transactions of this narrative took place sixty five years ago. Their name is Curtiss.

When father came back, we set off for the woods pointed out by our friends; we went across the lots and came to a road, and crossed that into another open field. The woods were in the backside of the field. As we went on, we ascended a ridge of land, and we could see the road that led from Canaan to Norfolk. The road then went past the burying-ground, and we could see it from where we were. We saw fourteen men on horseback; they were men we knew; the parson was one of them. We hid behind a log that was near us until they got out of sight; we then went into the woods, and there we found my mother and sister; they had been sent there by the man that had told us of the parson's information of where I was. We all remained there. This I should think was about two or three o'clock in the afternoon. Very soon the thought of night came to mind; how we were to spend the night, and what we should do for something to eat; but between sundown and dark a man passed along by the edge of the woods, whistling as he went. After he had passed on, father went up where the man went along, and came back with a pail or basket, and in it was our supper. We sat down and ate. The man we saw no more that night, but how were we to spend the night I could not tell; it was starlight, yet it was out in the woods, but father and mother were there, and that was a comfort to us children, but we soon fell asleep and forgot all our troubles, and in the morning we awoke and were still in the woods. In due time the man that passed along the night before, came again with more food for us, and then went his way; his name was Walter. We spent several days in the woods,—how many I do not remember. I think it was the fore part of the week when we went into the woods; we were there over the Sabbath, for I well remember a man by the name of Bishop had a shop where he fulled and dressed cloth not very far from where we were, and he came to the back door of his shop and stood and looked out a while, and went in and shut the door. I felt afraid he would see us. We kept very still, but I think he did not know that we were there; if he did, it did us no hurt. We were fed by kind friends all the time we were in the woods.

One afternoon, or towards night, it was thought it would be safe to go to a barn and sleep. After it was dark we went to a barn belonging to a Mr. Munger and slept, but left it while the stars were shining, and so for a few nights, and then it was thought we might sleep in the house. The next night after dark, we went in the house of Mr. Munger for the night. My sister and myself were put up in a back chamber, behind barrels and boxes, closely put together, out of sight for safe-keeping. We had not been there long before mother came and told us we must get up, for Captain Lawrence, our friend, had sent word that the parson said he would have the boys at any rate, whether he got the parents or not. His pickets were going to search every house within a mile of the meeting-house that night, or search until he found them. But we went into the woods again; we were there awhile again; when it rained, we went sometimes into a barn when we dared. After a time it was rather still, and we were at one house and sometimes at another. We had pickets out as well as the parson. It was thought best that I should not be with the rest of the family, for the hunt seemed to be for the boys. My brother, I have said, was out of the State. I was sent to one family, and then to another, not in one place long at a time. The parson began to think the task harder than he had an idea; it rather grew worse and more perplexing; he did not know what to do. He was outwitted in all his attempts; every effort or trial he had made, had failed. He now thought of giving my father and mother and sister their freedom if they would let him have the boys to take with him; this they would not do.

After some time was spent, the parson or his pickets had an idea that we were all at Capt. Lawrence's house, shut up there ; how to find out if we were there or not, was the puzzle. They contrived various plans, but did not succeed. Finally there was one thing yet. They knew that Mr. Lawrence loved money; they thought they would tempt him with that; so they came to his house and made trial. They met together one day and wanted to search his house; he would not consent for a time; they urged and he refused. He finally told them on certain conditions they might go into every room but one. They went into all the rooms but one. They then wanted to go into the room that they had not been into; they offered him money to let them go into the room,—how much he did not tell, as I know of. He finally consented. The much-desired room was a chamber over the kitchen. Mr. Lawrence opened the door at the foot of the stairs, and called and said, "Jupiter! (for that was my father's first name,) you must look out for yourself now, for I can not hide you any longer." He then told the parson's pickets they must take care, for Jupiter says he will kill the first man that lays hands on him. They hesitated some; they then went up stairs still, and stopped a short time, and then with a rush against the door, it gave way, and they all went in. They found the landlady sitting there as composed as summer, with her knittingwork, unconscious of an arrest to go south as a slave! but they found us not, although the room they last went into was the one we had occupied all the time we were in that house, sometimes one night, sometimes a week, and then in the woods or elsewhere, as was thought best to keep out of the way.

The pickets returned to the land of Canaan to see what was to be the next move. The parson then proposed to give my father and mother and sister their freedom, if they would let him have the boys. That they would not do; but the boys he said he must have. As my brother was away, it was thought best that I should be away. I was sent to Mr. Pease, well-nigh Canaan, and kept rather dark. I was there for a time, and I went to stay with a man by the name of Camp, and was with him a time, and then I went to stay with a man by the name of Akins, and stayed with him a few days, and went to a man by the name of Foot, and was with him a few days. I went to another man by the name of Akins, and was there some time. The parson was not gone south yet, for he could not well give up his prey. He then proposed to sell the boys until they were twenty-five, to somebody here that my parents would select, for that was as long as the law of Connecticut could hold slaves, and he would give the other members of the family their freedom. It was finally thought best to do that if the purchasers that were acceptable could be found. Some friends were on the lookout. Finally a man by the name of Bingham was found; it was a man that my father was once a slave to; he would take my brother, then a man by the name of Munger would buy me if they could agree. Mr. Bingham lived in Salisbury, Mr. Munger lived in Norfolk; the two men lived about fifteen miles apart, both in Connecticut.

The trade was made, and we two boys were sold for one hundred pounds a head, lawful money,—yes, sold by a man, a minister of the gospel in Connecticut, the land of steady habits. It would seem that the parson was a worshiper with the Athenians, as Paul said unto them when he stood on Mars Hill, he saw an inscription on one of their altars; and it would seem that the parson forgot or passed over the instruction of the apostle that God made of one blood all nations of men for to dwell on all the face of the earth.

The parson was a tall man, standing six feet in his boots, and had no legitimate children to be heirs to his ill-gotten gains. The bargain was made on the 12th of September, 1798. Then I was informed that I was sold to Mr. Munger, and must go and live with him. The man I did not know, but the thought of being sold, not knowing whether I was ever to see my parents, or brother, or sister again, was more than I could endure; the thought that I was sold, as I did not then know for how long, it was hard to think of; and where were my parents I knew not: It was a sad thought, but go I must. The next morning (I was to go the morning of the 13th) was a sad morning to me. The morning was clear, without a cloud. I was told where the man lived, and I must go, for he had bought me. I thought of my parents; should I, oh! should I never see them again? As I was taught to obey my superiors, I set out; it was a little over a mile. The way was long. I was alone. Tears ran down my cheeks. I then felt for the first time that I was alone in the world, no home, no friends, and none to care for me. Tears ran, but it did no good; I must go, and on I went. And now sixty-five years have passed away since that time; those feelings are fresh in my memory. But on my way to my new home I saw my father; I will not attempt to describe my feelings when he told me he had taken rooms in the same neighborhood, and should be near me. That made the rough way smooth. I went on then cheerful and happy. I arrived at the place. I found a man with a small family; it consisted of himself and wife and three daughters. The oldest was near my age. The family appeared pleasant. I ate a bowl of bread and milk, and was told to mount a horse that was at the door with a bag of rye on his back, and ride to the field; that was about a mile off. The man went with me, and on the way we passed the house of Mrs. Curtiss, where I mentioned in the former part of this narrative of going for well-water for Mrs. Upson. We went to the field and worked that day; went home at night. The family appeared very pleasant, and I felt pleased to think that the parson had gone, for I was told that he went the same day that I went to my new home. In a short time my father and mother and sister came into the neighborhood to live. I was allowed to go and see them one evening in two weeks. They lived about sixty rods from where I lived. Things went on well. I was very contented, and felt glad that the fear of being carried south was at an end. The parson was out of town and out of mind. I soon became acquainted with Mrs. Curtiss' boys, for I passed the house where they lived every day, as Mr. Munger's farm was beyond where they lived. I soon was feeling contented and happy. There was one thing that was unfortunate for me; Mr. Munger was not a stout, strong man, and not very healthy, and had no other help but me, and of course I had many things to do beyond my strength. I do not complain of many things, yet there are two things more I will mention. One of them I feel to this day, and that I feel the most is that I did not have an opportunity to go to school as much as I should, for all the books I ever had in school were a spelling-book, a primer, a Testament, a reading-book called Third Part, and after that a Columbian Orator. My schooling was broken and unsteady after the first and second winters, as Mr. Munger had no help, and had to go something like two miles for his wood. He would take me with him to the woods, and he would take a load and go home, and leave me to chop while he was gone. The wood was taken off from a fallow where he had sowed rye. It was in piles. Some had to be cut once, and some twice, and some three times. I went to school the most of the first winter; after that my schooling was slim. The other thing was, he was fond of using the lash. I thought so then, and made up my mind if I ever was the strongest I would pay back some of it. However, things went on, and I thought a good deal of Mr. Munger; yet I wonder sometimes why I was not more contented than I was, and then I wonder why I was as contented as I was. The summers that I was thirteen and fourteen, I was sick; they began to think I had the consumption. They sometimes would say to me, "If you should die we should lose a hundred pounds." I do not know as Mr. Munger ever said that, but it was said to me. But I will pass on with my story.

I soon found out that I was to live or stay with the man until I was twenty-five. I found that white boys who were bound out, were bound until they were twenty-one. I thought that rather strange, for those boys told me they were to have one hundred dollars when their time was out. They would say to me sometimes, "You have to work four years longer than we do, and get nothing when you have done, and we get one hundred dollars, a Bible, and two suits of clothes." This I thought of.

Some of the family or friends of the family would tell me what a good boy I should be, because Mr. Munger saved me from slavery. They said I must call him Master; but Mr. Munger never told me to, so I never did. If he had told me to, I should have done so, for I stood greatly in fear of him, and dreaded his displeasure, for I did not like the lash. I had made up my mind that I would not stay with him after I was twenty-one, unless my brother did with the man he lived with. My brother had been home to see us, and we went once to see him. I asked my brother how long he was going to stay with Mr. Bingham. He said Mr. Bingham said he should have his time when he was twenty-one. Well then, I would have my time, I said to myself. Things went on, and I found Mr. Munger to be a very good sort of a man. I had now got to be fifteen years of age. I had got my health, and had grown to be a big boy, and was called pretty stout, as the word is, yet I was afraid of Mr. Munger. I actually stood in fear of him.

I had now got to be in my sixteenth year, when a little affair happened, which, though trivial in itself, yet was of consequence to me. It was in the season of haying, and we were going to the hayfield after a load of hay. Mr. Munger and I were in the cart, he sitting on one side and I on the other. He took the fork in both of his hands, and said to me very pleasantly, "Don't you wish you were stout enough to pull this away from me?" I looked at him, and said, "I guess I can;" but I did not think so. He held it toward me with both his hands hold of the stale. I looked at him and then at the fork, hardly daring to take hold of it, and wondering what he meant, for this was altogether new. He said, "Just now see if you can do it." I took hold of it rather reluctantly, but I shut my hand tight. I did as Samson did in the temple; I bowed with all my might, and he came to me very suddenly. The first thought that was in my mind was, my back is safe now. All went on well for two months or more; all was pleasant, when one day he—or Mr. Munger, I should have said—was going from home, and he told me, as was usual, what to do. I went to my work, and did it just as he told me. At night, when he came home, he asked me what I had been doing. I told him, but he did not seem satisfied. I told him I had done just what he told me. He said I had not done what I ought to have done. I told him I had done what he told me. That was more than I had ever said before. He was angry and got his horsewhip, and said he would learn me. He raised his hand and stood ready to strike. I said, "You had better not!" I then went out at the door. I felt grieved to see him in such a rage when I had done just as he told me, and I could not account for it. If he had been a drinking man, I should not have wondered; but he was not, he was a sober man. I could not get over my feeling for some time, but all was pleasant the next day. I said to his daughters that I would not stay there a day after I was twenty-one, for I did not know what their father meant. I did just as he told me, and thought I was doing what he would be satisfied with. They told me not to mind it. Things went on from that time as well as I could wish. From that time until I was twenty-one, I do not remember that he ever gave me an unpleasant word or look. While I lived with him, after that time, I felt that I had now got as good a place as any of the boys that were living out. I often went with his team to Hartford and to Hudson, which the other boys did not that lived in the neighborhood. I now felt that I could do anything for the family; I was contented and happy.

The year that I was eighteen, Mr. Munger was concerned in an iron establishment, manufacturing iron. He had a sister living in Oneida county, and he learned that iron was high or brought a good price there. He told me be thought he would send a load out there and get a load of wheat, and asked me if I would go out with a load. I told him I would if he wished me to; he said he did. He got every thing ready, and I set out the 17th day of October, and thought it would take me about two weeks or thereabouts. On I went, and when I got there I could exchange my iron for wheat readily, but none had their wheat out, and their barn-floors were so full that they could not thrash. I had to wait a week. As soon as I got my load, I set out for home. I was gone a day or two over three weeks. After I got to Norfolk, I passed the house where my parents lived. They told me that it was very current with the people that I had sold the horses and wagon, and was seen by some one that knew me, and was on my way to Canada. They said that Mr. Munger said he did not believe it,—he said he should not trouble himself. Yet I went on home. He was glad to see me; asked if I had any bad luck. I told how it was, and he was satisfied, and said when he saw the team that they were in better condition than they were when I left home. "Now they may talk as much as they please; you and the team, wagon and load are here." And when I told him what I had done, he said he was perfectly satisfied, I had done well; he had no fault to find. Every thing went on first-rate. I did my best to please him, and it seemed to me that the family did the same. I now took the hardest end of the work. I was willing to do what I could. I was willing to work, and thought much of the family, and they thought something of me. Mr. Munger was receiving his share of offices of the town, and was from home a portion of his time. I felt ambitious to have our work even with others. He said his work went on as well as if he was there.

When I was in my twentieth year, a nephew of Mr. Munger came to board with him; he was studying law. Mr. Munger and I were accustomed to talk about my term of service with him. I told him I did not mean to stay with him until I was twenty- five. He said he thought I would if I meant to do what was fair and just. I told him that my brother had his time when he was twenty-one, and I wanted my time. He finally had some talk with his nephew, who said that he could hold me. But finally Mr. Munger made me an offer of what he would give me if I would stay. I thought the offer was tolerably fair. I had now become attached to the family. I told him that I would stay, as he had often said he thought I ought to stay after I was twenty-one. I thought I would divide the time with him in part, as the offer he made would not cover the whole time. All was fixed, and I worked on. Nothing more was said for a long time about it; then the thing was spoken about, and the same mind was in us both, and I felt satisfied. The fall previous to my being twenty-one came; all was right, as I thought. The winter came and nothing was said. The last of February came. I heard it hinted that Mr. Munger had said that he should not make any bargain with me, but if I left him he would follow me. The thing was understood by us, and I paid no attention to it. March came, and nothing was said. The third of March was my birthday. All was quiet, and I kept on as before until the first of April. It was told me that Mr. Munger said that his nephew had examined the law and found that he could hold me, and what he gave me would be his unless he was bound by a written agreement. As there were no writings given, I began to think it was time to know how it was. There was another thing now came to mind.

When I was thirteen years old, Mr. Munger bought a calf of my father, and gave it to me, and said he would keep it until it was two years old, and then I might sell it and have what it brought. He kept it. were two. He had a mate for it, and when the steers were two years old he sold them for twenty-four dollars. He then told me that he would give me a heifer of the age the steer was, and when she had a calf he would take her to double in four years. When I was seventeen he gave me a heifer, and she had a calf that spring, and the first of April he said he would take her, and at the end of four years from that time he would give me two cows and two calves. That was agreed on. The next year, in March or April, one of his oxen hooked my cow; it hurt her so that the cow died. Well, now, what was to be done? He said at the time agreed on I should have my cows. I was content with that and worked on, feeling that all would be made right. I thought I should have two cows with those calves when I was twenty-one, and that would be a beginning. Afterward I agreed to stay with him until I was twenty-five; I could let them until that time. I will now go on with my story. I asked him for my cows and calves. He said he should not let me have any. He said if I stayed and did well perhaps he would give me a cow. I asked him if that was all that I was to have if I stayed until I was twenty-five. He said he would see. I asked when he would see. He said when the time came. I then told him I had been told that Warren (that was the name of his nephew) had told him not to give me what he had agreed to, and I wanted to know if he would do as he had agreed to or not. He said I belonged to him,

and I could not help myself. I told him I would stay with him as I had said if
he would give me a writing obligating himself to give me the sum we had
agreed upon. After hesitating a short time, he said he would not give a
writing; he would not be bound. I told him I had got that impression, "and if
you say you will not give me what you said you would, I will not work
another day." He then said if I left him he would put me in jail and keep me
there a year at any rate. This was on Saturday. The next day I picked up
what few duds I had, and at evening, as it was the Sabbath, I told him I had
done all the work for him that I should do. I then bade him good night and
left his house, and went to my father's. The next day in the afternoon, Mr.
Munger and nephew came to my father's with a sheriff. I was not in the
house. He told my father that he would pay my board in jail for one year,
and I could not help myself. They took what few clothes I had, and went
away before I got home. It was well it was so. I told my father that I would
stay in jail as long as Mr. Munger would find money. I sent the word to Mr.
Munger. He sent me word that I should have an opportunity to. My people
wanted to have me go away for a time. I thought at first I would. Then I saw
that I had nothing to go with, and had no clothes for a change. I would not
leave. I told them I would go to jail. I thought perhaps I could get the liberty
of the yard, and then I could earn something to get some clothes, and then I
would leave for Canada or some other parts.

A few days after, I heard that Mr. Munger said he would leave it to men
how it should be settled, and he sent me such word. I sent word to him, no, I
was going to jail, if he would keep his word. He finally said as I had always
been faithful, he would not or had rather not put me in jail. My parents said
so much, they did not want to have me go to jail, that I finally said I would
leave it to three men if they were men that I liked: if they were not, I would
not. He said I might name the men; their judgment was to be final. The men
were selected, the time and place specified. The day came, the parties met,
and the men were on hand. Mr. Munger had his nephew for counsel; I plead
my case myself. A number of the neighbors were present. Mr. Munger's
counsel began by saying that his uncle had bought me, and had paid for me
until I was twenty-five, and that he had a right to me. I then told his nephew
that I would have a right to him some day, for he was the cause of all the
difficulty. He said no more. The arbitrators asked Mr. Munger if he had
anything against me. He said he had not. They asked him, in case they gave
him anything, if he wished me to work it out with him; he said he did. They
went out a few moments, and returned and said that I must pay Mr. Munger
$90. He then asked me to go home with him, and he would hire me. I told
him I would go and get my clothes, for that was in the decision. He said I
could have them. His nephew did not want me to live with his uncle, if he

boarded with him. I told Mr. Munger that I would not work for him. I hired to another man, and went to work in the same neighborhood. This nephew kept an eye on me for a long time, and always gave me the road whenever he saw me coming. Mr. Munger and family always treated me with attention whenever I met them; they made me welcome to their house and to their table. If that nephew had not interfered, there would have been no trouble.

Things all went on pleasantly. In about four years I went there again to work, and in a short time Mr. Munger and his two daughters joined the church of which his wife was a member. I joined the same church, and was often at his house. Mr. Munger was unfortunate and lost his property, not as people lose their property now. He was poor and not very healthy, and his wife and the daughter that was not married, not being healthy, and he being a man advanced in life, it wore upon him and his family, and his daughter went into a decline. I went west, and was gone about three months, and on my return went to see the family, and found the daughter very much out of health and wasting away. I called again the next day but one. As I had been accustomed to take care of the sick, she asked me to stop with her that night. I did so, and went to my work in the morning. The second day after, I called again to see her, and she made the same request. I staid and watched with her that night. She asked what I thought of her; I told her I feared she would never be any better. She then asked me to stay with her if she did not get any better, while she lived. I told her I would. A cousin of hers, a young lady, was there, and we took the care of her for four weeks. I mention this because it was a time to be remembered and cherished by me while I live. We were in the daily habit of speaking of her prospects and how she felt. She would speak of death with as much apparent composure as of any other subject. She said very little to her friends about her feelings. The day that she died was the evening of the Sabbath. About six o'clock in the afternoon, or rather all that day, she did not appear to be as well; but at the time just mentioned she sunk away and seemed to be gone for a short time, when she revived as one out of sleep, suddenly, and seemed surprised, and said, "There is nothing that I want to stay here for; let me go." She then bade her friends farewell, and told them not to weep for her, for she was going. Her countenance seemed as if lit up with heavenly love, and for a short time she seemed to be away from the world, and then was still and said but little. About eleven o'clock she wanted to be moved. She was moved. She then wanted to drink. I gave her, or put the glass to her lips. She did not swallow any. I saw there was a change, and before her friends could get into the room her spirit had fled.

That was a scene that I love to think of. It makes me almost forget that I ever was a slave to her father; but so it was. I staid until she was buried, and then I went West again. Her parents were broken-hearted indeed. I returned from the West, and spent a part of the summer with Mr. Munger.

I afterwards worked where I chose for a few years. I was frequently at Mr. Munger's house. He seemed depressed, his health rather declined, and he finally sank down and was sick. He sent for me; I went to him, and he said he wished to have me stay with him. I told him I would, and I staid with him until he died, and closed the eyes of his daughter when she died, and his also. And now to look back on the whole transaction, it all seems like a dream. It is all past, never to be re-acted. That family have all gone, with one exception.

APPENDIX.

This Appendix is by request of those that have read what is before it:—

After the death of Mr. Munger, I married a wife and lived in Norfolk a few years; we had two children. We went to Hartford after a while; I worked for the then known firm of E. & R. Terry. There was a man came to Hartford from Savannah, with his family; he came to school his daughter. He brought a slave girl with him to care for the smaller children. My wife washed for the family. All went on well for about two years. The Southern man's name was Bullock, and the slave's name was Nancy. One day when I was at work in the store, a gentleman came where I was; he asked if this was deacon Mars. I said "Yes, sir." He said Mr. Bullock was about to send Nancy to Savannah, "and we want to make a strike for her liberty, and we want some man to sign a petition for a writ of habeas corpus to bring Mr. Bullock before Judge Williams; they tell me that you are the man to sign the petition." I asked him who was to draw the writ; he said Mr. Wm. W. Ellsworth. I went to Mr. Ellsworth's office with the man. I signed the petition. I then went to my work. I told Mr. Ellsworth that it would cause an excitement; if he wanted me at any time, I would be on hand. The writ was served on Mr. Bullock, and he was brought before Judge Williams, but Nancy could not be found. The court adjourned till eight o'clock the next morning. At night Nancy came to the house where they were boarding; she had been out as she was accustomed to go with the children. Mrs. Bullock told Nancy to go to bed. She somehow had an idea that all was not right; she opened the door, and gave it a swing to shut, but it did not shut, as she said afterwards. She thought she would see what they were talking about. She said Mrs. B. told Mr. Bullock to start in the morning at 4 o'clock with Nancy for New York; "never mind the bond, and send Nancy South." I omitted to mention that the court put Mr. Bullock under a bond of $400 to appear the next morning at 8 o'clock. The plan to send Nancy South was fixed on. Nancy said to herself, "When you come where I be, I wont be there." She went out of the house, and went to the house of a colored man and stopped for the night. The next morning the court sat; master and slave were both there. The court said it was the first case of the kind ever tried in the State of Connecticut, and the Supreme Court of Errors was to meet in ten days, and was composed of five judges; he would adjourn the trial until the session of that court.

During those ten days I had a fair opportunity to see how strong a hold slavery had on the feelings of the people in Hartford. I was frowned upon; I was blamed; I was told that I had done wrong; the house where I lived would be pulled down; I should be mobbed; and all kinds of scarecrows were talked about, and this by men of wealth and standing. I kept on about my work, not much alarmed. The ten days passed away; the Supreme Court of Errors sat; Judge Williams was chief judge. The case was argued on both sides. When the plea was ended, then came the decision:—two of the court would send Nancy back to slavery; two were for her release; we shall hear from Williams to-morrow at eight o'clock.

At the time appointed all were in attendance to hear from Judge Williams. The Judge said that slavery was tolerated in some of the States, but it was not now in this State; we all liked to be free. This girl would like to be free; he said she should be free,—the law of the State made her free, when brought here by her master. This made a change in the feelings of the people. I could pass along the streets in quiet. Nancy said when she went into the court-house on the last day she had two large pills of opium; had she been sentenced to go back, she should have swallowed both of them before she left the court-house.

Now to my family. I have said I had two children born in Norfolk, and six in Hartford. One died in infancy. I lived in Hartford about sixteen years. I took a very prominent part in the organization of the Talcott Street Church. I moved from Hartford to Pittsfield, Mass. When I had been there three years and a half, my wife died in November; the May following I lost a son sixteen years of age. My oldest son enlisted in the U.S. Navy when he was eighteen, and has followed the sea ever since. I had another that went to sea, that I have not heard from for eight years. My oldest daughter went to Africa, to Cape Palmas; she went out a teacher, and has been there five years. I have one son who, when the war broke out, when the first gun was fired on Sumter, wanted to enlist, and did enlist in the navy, and went out on the brig Bainbridge, and served until she was stopped for repairs. He then went on the Newbern and served his time, and has an honorable discharge. Another, and the last one, enlisted in the artillery and went to New Orleans, but never, no, never came back, nor will he ever come again. I have a daughter in Massachusetts, of a frail constitution. She has a family to care for. I have none to care for me that has anything to spare, yet my children are willing to help as far as they are able. As they are not able I feel willing to do all that I can to help to get my living. The question is sometimes asked me if I have not any means of support. The fact is, I have nothing but what I have saved within the last three years. I have spent a portion of that time with my book about the country. I am now in my eightieth year of age, I cannot labor but little, and finding the public have a desire to know something of what slavery was in the State of Connecticut, in its time, and how long since it was at an end, in what year it was done

away, and believing that I have stated the facts, many are willing to purchase the book to satisfy themselves as to slavery in Conecticut. Some told
me that they did not know that slavery was ever allowed in Connecticut,
and some affirm that it never did exist in the State. What I have written of
my own history, seems to satisfy the minds of those that read it, that the so
called, favored state, the land of good morals and steady habits, was ever a
slave state, and that slaves were driven through the streets tied or fastened
together for market. This seems to surprise some that I meet, but it was true.
I have it from reliable authority. Yes, this was done in Connecticut.

August 22d, 1866, I had a fall and uncapped my knee, that laid me by ten
months, so that I was unable to travel or do anything to help myself, but by
the help of Him that does all things well, I have got so as to be able to walk
with a staff. During the time that I was confined with my knee, I met with
kind treatment, although I was away from home. I was in the state of New
York at the time of my misfortune, away from any of my relations, still I
was under the watchful care of a Friend that sticketh closer than a brother.
He has thus far provided for me, and I feel assured that He will if I trust
Him, with all my heart and soul and strength, and serve Him faithfully,
which is my duty, the few years or days that are allotted to me, and it is my
prayer that I may have grace to keep me, that I may not dishonor the cause
of Christ, but that I may do that which will be acceptable in the sight of my
Heavenly Father, so that I may do good to my fellow-men.

One thing in my history I have not mentioned, which I think of importance. Although born and raised in Connecticut, yes, and lived in Connecticut more than three-fourths of my life, it has been my privilege to vote at
five Presidential elections. Twice it was my privilege and pleasure to help
elect the lamented and murdered Lincoln. I am often asked when slavery
was abolished in Connecticut; my answer is, the Legislature in 1788, passed
an act that freed all that were born after 1792, those born before that time
that were able to take care of themselves, must serve until they were
twenty-five; my time of slavery expired in 1815. Connecticut I love thy
name, but not thy restrictions. I think the time is not far distant when the
colored man will have his rights in Connecticut.

THE LIFE

OF

WILLIAM J. BROWN,

OF PROVIDENCE, R. I.

WITH PERSONAL RECOLLECTIONS OF
INCIDENTS IN RHODE ISLAND.

PROVIDENCE:
ANGELL, 1883.

William J. Brown's autobiography, first published in 1883, is an incredible bit of historical serendipity. Although Brown spent the bulk of his working years in a fairly ordinary occupation—that of a shoemaker—he was nonetheless an incredibly astute observer of human affairs and a participant in many of the major events that shaped the Providence black community in the nineteenth century. More than that, as the narrative shows, Brown, despite limited education, was an able chronicler of the events that he witnessed. Perhaps equally important, Brown was able to preserve the oral traditions of his parents and grandparents, providing us with a unique window on the world of eighteenth century New England slavery.

PREFACE.

In presenting this work to the public, the object of the author may be looked upon in a two-fold sense, viz., that he is totally blind, afflicted with paralysis, and without means to meet his obligations and support himself; and as a necessary resort to accomplish his object, he herein presents to the public a review of his past life, believing that it will commend itself to the favorable notice of his many friends, and to the public generally.

Secondly, it is evident that a great change has taken place in our community in the past sixty years, the survivors of that period have nearly all passed away, aud if the events of those times are not soon recorded, there will be no one to present them to the public; and the rising generation will have but faint conception of the discouragements and disadvantages with which their parents had to contend, which greatly impeded their progress in moral and religious culture. And should the question arise in the minds of the present or future generation, why the people of the free States have made so little progress in wealth and literary acquirements, a reference to this work will satisfy every one seeking for information, as to the real cause, and also convince every candid mind that under the varied circumstances which then existed, the success of their efforts could by no means be excelled, and the men of the present day must make large and heavy strides on the road of improvement to compare favorably with their fathers, or fall in the rear.

The author has given particular attention to every detail in this work, that a faithful and true record may be presented of himself and his ancestors, the success of their efforts under the trials, disadvantages and discouragements with which they had to contend, and their unflinching perseverance to the end. And believing that he has the sympathies of many friends who wish him success, he now presents this book to an appreciative public.

WILLIAM J. BROWN.

CHAPTER I.

I was born in the town of Providence, State of Rhode Island, November 10, 1814. The house in which I was born was situated on a street running from Power to William street, the house standing on the southwest corner of a lot belonging to Dr. Pardon Bowen, his mansion being located on the northeast corner of the lot, facing the south side of Power street. My father's name was Noah Brown; his father was Cudge Brown and his mother Phillis Brown. Grandfather Brown was born in Africa, and belonged to a firm (named Brown Brothers) consisting of four, named respectively, Joseph, John, Nicholas and Moses Brown. They held slaves together, each brother selecting out such as they wished for house service; the rest of the slaves to perform out-door labor. I am not positive, but believe my grandfather was brought from Africa in the firm's vessel. He had two or three brothers. One was named Thomas, and the other Sharp or Sharper Brown, and they worked for Moses Brown. My grandfather was occupied as a teamster, doing the team work for two farms, the one on which Mr. Brown lived, and the other to the northward towards Swan Point Road. My father married Alice Greene; her maiden name was Alice Prophet. She was a widow, having lost her husband, Uriah Greene, several years previous to her second marriage. They were married in Cranston, R.I., the 25th of December, 1805, and commenced keeping house in that town, but being engaged in a seafaring life, he removed to Providence, and rented a house of Dr. Pardon Bowen, situated on Wells street. During his residence in Cranston, he had a son born, July 10th, 1810, and named him Joseph George Washington Brown. My sister, Mary Alice, was born Sept. 1811, in this city. My brother George was born Sept. 23d, 1817. After residing in Dr. Pardon Bowen's house five years, we were obliged to move, as Mr. Bowen wished to make a strawberry bed in the garden where the house was located. My father hired a house called the Red Lion, near the junction of South Main and Power streets, on the north side, the place where the Amateur Dramatic Hall now stands. My brother Henry was born there in 1820.

Worthy mention may be made of Mr. Moses Brown, one of the owners of my father. He belonged to the Society of Friends, and was highly esteemed by every one, and considered himself a Christian man, and would not allow his people to live in adultery if he could help it. My grandfather was married to Phillis, Nov 20th, 1768, and they went to keeping house, living in one towards the north end of Olney street, owned by Mr. Brown, where he kept his teams.

Newport, his oldest son, was born April 22d, 1769. Rhoda, his oldest daughter, was born Sept. 27th, 1776, and Noah, my father, was born September 20th, 1781. James was born November 17th, 1788. My mother, as I stated, was a widow when she was married to my father. I never had any knowledge respecting her first husband's relations. My mother's relations were the Prophets, who belonged to the Narragansett tribe, and resided in Cranston. My grandmother's father was a man of note and one of the chiefs, and called, Grandfather Jeffery. Whether he was a prophet by name or by title I know not. He had two daughters, but whether he had any sons I know not, but think he had none. One of grandfather Jeffery's daughters married a white man, preferring civilized to savage life. The other daughter, my grandmother, purchased a colored man and married him, by whom she had five children, one son and four daughters, John, Phebe, Mary, Alice, and Eunice. Her father being very much displeased with her management, gave his effects to the first, who married the white man, and the fourth generation are living in the city at present, and moving in upper circles. After some years his anger abated towards his daughter's husband and he rendered some aid to the family. My grandmother said her father had a place where he dug money. It belonged to the tribe, and was called Old Blood's mine. No one except the tribe knew where it was located, and could get none of the money. By the request of my grandmother, her father took grandfather, who was then living about nine miles from Providence, with him to the mine. When the time arrived, which was in the evening, grandfather accompanied him, both being mounted and with saddle bags to bring their money in. Grandfather said the road was filled with Indians all the way. After riding some four hours, they arrived at a huge rock, and without saying a word, dismounted, and walked around the side of the rock until they came to an opening sufficient to admit a single person. Jeffrey entered, and grandfather followed. As they advanced the place grew larger. Jeffrey came to a halt, took a tinder box and struck a light.

They found themselves in a large place under the rocks, and everything around them glittered with brightness. There were picks and shovels in the place, and other tools to work with, and Jeffrey commenced digging, and continued till he filled his bag, but grandfather, being frightened, did nothing. He said he saw a large Indian with his head cut and the blood streaming from his wounds, and the ground seemed to shake under him. When Jeffrey had filled his bag they returned by the way they came. When grandfather came home it was daybreak, and he said he would never go again for all the silver there was in the world, and he kept his word. Jeffrey said he neither saw or beard anything. The reason grandfather saw it was because he did not belong to the tribe. He gave a part of the silver to grandmother. She said the white people knew there was a mine, and had searched for it but could never find it. At one time they got him intoxicated, then hired him to show them where it was. He carried them within a few rods of the place, and said, "It was somewhere around here; it is enchanted ground, and you cannot get it if you try." That was all they could get out of him; but be continued to pay his visits to the mine and bring his silver in to sell. This is the statement grandmother and uncle frequently made respecting the silver mine belonging to their tribe.

In the year 1842 I went to my grandmother, Chloe Prophet's, funeral. She was buried from a meeting house in Cranston, situated four miles from her residence and five miles from the city of Providence There were twenty-six carryalls and wagons filled with her grand-children, each one containing four persons, making a total of 104 grand-children. And that was but a portion of her relations. This was the first country funeral I ever attended. The services were performed by a white minister. He represented her as one of the sisters of the church, spoke highly of her character and exhorted the people to take pattern thereby, and told how the Lord had blessed her with long life, to see the age of ninety-six years. After the services the remains were placed in a nice, clean lead-colored farm wagon, partly filled with straw, and started from the meeting house about half-past eleven o'clock, for the old Indian burying ground. The procession moved in line, on a trot. After riding for the space of half an hour we came to the turn of the road, where, at the corner, we found a house and shop. The procession stopped, and many got out to get something to drink. My sister remarked that she supposed that was the fashion they practiced at the Indian funerals. I answered, I presumed it was an ancient practice. A great many were unused to this, and remained in their carriages. After regaling themselves we continued our journey, and by fast driving arrived at the ground at half-past one o'clock. When we started from the meeting house the manager, a tall Indian man, started on foot. When we arrived at the ground he was there. We found the grave all ready, and without further ceremony, she was lowered into it. After she was buried and the grave filled up, the manager placed a large stone at the head, and said to the assembly, "You all know where Granny is buried by this large stone at the head; now we will take our carriages and go home." The burying ground was the most wild and lonesome place I ever saw. I should think by appearances that thousands of Indians had been buried there. On our return home the stopping place at the shop was not forgotten. When the procession stopped I turned out of the line and continued homeward.

My grandmother was born in the year 1744, and my mother in the year 1771, making grandmother 27 years old when mother was born. I have never been able to ascertain the date of grandmother Jeffrey's marriage, but learned that she purchased her husband from the white people, in order to change her mode of living. It was customary for the woman to do all the drudgery and hard work in-doors and out. The Indian men thought it a disgrace for them to work; they thought they did their part by hunting and procuring game. The Indian women observing the colored men working for their wives, and living after the manner of white people, in comfortable homes, felt anxious to change their position in life; not being able to carry out their designs in any other way, resorted to making purchases. This created a very bitter feeling among the Indian men against the blacks. The treatment the Indian women received from the husbands they had purchased was so satisfactory that others were encouraged to follow their example, notwithstanding every effort was made to prevent such union. My grandmother Phillis, on father's side, I know but little about; I do not recollect of ever seeing her or grandfather. I do not know whether she was raised on a farm or came from Africa on one of the vessels which brought slaves here. My grandfather being a teamster she remained home to prepare his meals. It was his duty to fill the demands of both farms. He was allowed to send his children to school in the winter season while young. In this way they learned to read and write, but as soon as they were large enough they found work for them on the farm, where there was plenty to do. My father during his youth worked on the farm belonging to Moses Brown, and at one time had occasion to find fault with his food, which displeased Mrs. Brown very much. She was accustomed to save all their turkey carcasses until they were musty, and then make soup for the men. So every morning they were treated to some musty soup for breakfast. Week after week this was continued, and no one dared say anything for fear of offending some one. One morning after the horn had been blown for breakfast, father came in advance of the men, and looking on the table beheld the soup and exclaimed, "Musty soup again—damn the musty soup." Then to his surprise he saw Mr. Brown partly behind the door wiping his hands. "What did thee say, my boy?" said Mr. Brown. "I said musty soup," said father. "Is that soup musty?" said Mr. Brown. "Yes, sir," said father. Mr. Brown ordered a spoon, and tasted of the soup, which he ordered to be put into the swill. By this time the field hands had come in. Mr. Brown asked them how long they had been eating musty soup. They replied, "Several weeks in succession." Mr. Brown sent for his wife to come into the kitchen, and said to her in the presence of the men: "Is not my house able to give my help good victuals? Here you have been feeding them week after week on musty soup. I have tasted it; it is fit for nothing but for hogs. I don't wish you to give them any more such stuff; they work hard and should have good victuals, and I am able to give it to them." Then to the men he said: "Why did you not speak to me about your victuals? You have been going on week after week and said not a word, until this boy had to speak for you. Hereafter, if everything is not right, come to me." After Mr. Brown's departure his wife called my father a black devil, and said he should not sleep with the men any longer, but should have his lodgings in the attic room. This was quite a severe punishment to my father, as he was compelled to retire soon after eight o'clock. Mr. Brown was very particular that his men should not be over-worked, and allowed no punishment on his farm. He was always willing to grant his men leave of absence whenever they desired. This made them the more willing to work, and in seed time they were never late in getting their crops in, so that when election time came the planting was all done, and the last Saturday in June was set apart by the laborers as a holiday or election day. This was an ancient custom got up by the farmers in order to get their crops in the ground in season; and the workmen would work extra hours to get the planting all done. They also made preparations before the day came to celebrate it, procuring some suitable place near a country tavern, making a contract with the tavern-keeper to entertain them, and to give the company a free treat at his own expense. After that they had to purchase their own liquor. The landlord agreed to get up a dinner for them, each one to pay for his own, and at night to procure a hall for them to dance in. The order of exercises during the day was as follows: At 11 o'clock to form in proces-sion for a march. This would take place immediately after they had elected officers. These officers were a governor and lieutenant-governor and trea-surer; then accompanied by music they would march up and down the road, after which they would retire to the tavern and refresh themselves, then take up a collection and dismiss until dinner; after dinner they would amuse themselves any way they choose until the time for dancing. It was custom-ary at this election, if any one had any animosity against another, male or female, to pay of their old debts by fighting. During Sunday they would get sober, so they could return to work on Monday.

These elections were kept up annually, and the colored people came from every quarter, anxious to have a good time. Those who were pious did not care about attending them. In the year 1832 the people had lost their interest in having them. The first check that the election had was through their treasurer, who inquired of the governor what he should do with the money. He was informed it was to be given to the poor.

The money was locked up in a box and the key was given to the lieutenant-governor. The treasurer at the close of the day took his wife and went home. That night he laid awake thinking who the poor were, and thought no one poorer than himself. So he took part of the money and then nailed up the box. The next night being again troubled about the poor, he came to the conclusion that his wife was as poor as any one, and took the rest of the money out and nailed up the box. At the next election he made his appearance with the box, and when it was unlocked to their surprise there was nothing in it; and when asked what disposition he had made of the funds he honestly told them what he had done, and the company wisely concluded not to take up any more collections; so that was stopped. The next and final check was in 1841. The people had appointed their election in Warwick, or thereabouts. The day was beautiful and the people had repaired there in good numbers, anticipating a nice time. The landlord had given his free treat, the officers had been elected and they had made their parade, when a very dark man, mounted on a horse, adorned with a belt and sword at his side, introduced himself as General Amey. After riding around for half an hour, he ordered the hostler to put up his horse. He then walked up to the bar and regaled himself; then walked around among the assembled crowd, like some officer in authority, but finding no one willing to acknowledge him as bearing rule over them, again went out and ordered the hostler to get his horse, which was done according to orders. After riding up and down the road another half hour, be returned and again ordered his horse put up. His orders were obeyed but not as pleasantly as at first, for he either forgot to remuncrate the hostler or was ignorant of the customs of the times. On again demanding his horse the hostler kindly reminded him that hostlers generally get pay for waiting upon gentlemen. Gen. Amey replied, "Do as I bid you, and bring my horse." The hostler obeyed, and he rode away. In an hour's time he again made his appearance, giving the same orders as before. The hostler agreed to put it up, but told the General that he should not again bring him out without pay. The General reported him to the landlord, who told the hostler not to put him up unless he was paid for doing so. Shortly the General came and ordered the horse brought out. The landlord being present, informed the General that according to custom, the hostler must be remunerated. The General declared he would pay nothing. Some cross words passed between them, when the landlord threw a half brick, hitting him on the head. The General fell backward to the ground like one dead, and the cry soon went forth that General Amey was killed by the landlord. Much excitement was created. The General's brother, Hardin, was in the garden playing cards, when, hearing the report, went like a madman after the man who killed his brother. By the time he reached the stable the General came to, and the enraged brothers started for the landlord, who seeing them, fled into the house for refuge. They followed rapidly, and as the landlord fastened the door they broke it down. He fled to a second room. They broke that door in. The landlord then made his escape through a window, and was joined on the outside by twenty men, who armed themselves with sticks of wood. The two Ameys proceeded towards the landlord and his men, who dropped their sticks and fled towards the Pawtuxet. Everything was in commotion. The table being ready the people helped themselves, eating up the victuals and drinking up the landlord's liquor. After they had finished regaling themselves, they advised the women to go home. They went after their apparel, but the landlady refused to give it up, and called on her help to assist her to keep the things, but they were overpowered by the women, who took their apparel and started for Providence. The men learning that the landlord had gone after the Pawtuxet company of soldiers, armed themselves with sticks of wood and formed themselves in a line, and awaited the arrival of the company. In a short time they heard the fife and drum. The company came up and formed a line in front of the men. The captain ordered them to surrender themselves prisoners, but they refused either to surrender or lay down their sticks. The captain threatened to fire on them if they did not surrender. They told him coolly to fire if he pleased, but it would be the last firing he would ever live to do. The commander withdrew his men and marched for Pawtuxet. The people stayed around the tavern for some time, then returned to their homes. For a week nothing more was heard of the affair, or the landlord. Harden, brother of the wounded man, after getting over the fight, thought best to go and settle with the landlord. He informed Mr. Halsey (for he was foreman on his farm) what he had done, and thought it best to go and see the landlord and make amends. Mr. Halsey advised him to stay away, but Harden's convictions were such that he went the following Sunday to see him. He informed him of his errand, and was applauded for his noble act. The landlord told him to be seated, as it would take some little time to make up his account. Mr. Amey consented to wait as he had no pressing business. The landlord immediately dispatched a messenger on horseback to Pawtuxet, and a large nnmber of men sooh arrived, and locked Amey up in jail. And before he could be released, Mr. Halsey was obliged to go to Pawtuxet and pay five hundred dollars to settle the case. That was a death blow to the election. They tried several times to revive it, but failed in the attempt.

CHAPTER II.

In the first chapter, I gave a short sketch of my ancestors; the place of their birth, the times in which they lived, and some pleasing accounts of slavery days in Rhode Island. Mr. Brown, my grandfather's master, seemed well satisfied with his help and thought that although they were his property, yet they had amply paid for themselves by their labor, and hence wrong for him (being a Christian man) to confine them any longer in servitude. Also Mr. Knight Dexter had slaves, but entertaining the same opinion concerning the system of holding property in human beings, they both emancipated them. This was some time before the general emancipation in the State. My grandfather then drew wages for his labor. He saved his earnings and purchased a lot of Mr. Brown situated on Olney street. They sold land at that time by the running foot. He bought over one hundred feet in width of Mr. Brown, and thirty feet of Mr. Carlisle, adjoining the lot he purchased of Mr. Brown, and over two hundred feet in depth. He dug a cellar and raised a frame of a house, but before he had time to cover it there came a storm and blew the frame down. Soon after, he was taken sick, and the frame remained down. About this time father left Mr. Brown and hired himself out to Mr. Thomas P. Ives, living on South Main street, in the house where the old Providence Bank is. After living there some time, he took a notion to follow the sea, and being 24 years old, obtained protection from the Custom House, June 7th, 1806, and shipped on a vessel, as seaman, bound for Liverpool, there he went ashore. While walking on the street, be observed several sailors running and dodging around the corner of a street. He passed on not taking any particular notice of them, but had not proceeded far, when he was met by a squad of soldiers, who commandered him to halt. They asked him what was the reason he could not go and serve the King. He answered that be was an American seamen, belonging to an American vessel lying alongside the dock, and as for the King he didn't know anything about him. They replied, "You don't? then we will make you know. Fall in the ranks." He accordingly obeyed, and they marched him to the guard-house. There he remained until Monday forenoon without seeing any one, and receiving no drink or food. On Monday the drum

and fife was heard and the guards appeared, unlocked the prison, and ordering him to fall in the ranks, they marched him down to the English privateer, and there he remained until the ship put to sea. They cruised about four
or five months, and fell in with no prize. One morning the captain came up,
dressed in full uniform, and told the crew that this day was his birthday and
he was going to celebrate it, and they should have all the rum they wanted;
and he ordered it by the bucket full, and they all drank as much, and as
often as they wanted, serving it also to the helmsman. The weather was fine,
the wind was light, and they were all enjoying themselves, but the enjoyment was stopped, by the man on top crying out, ship "ahoy." The second
officer was pacing the deck, and hearing the cry from the top, caught up the
glass and sprang up the rigging; after recononitering the sail he came down
and exclaimed with an oath, "we are taken." The captain hearing that
announcement from the second officer, drew his sword and asked how he
dared make that assertion; "repeat it," said he, "and will run you through."
The officer exclaimed, handing him the glass, "there is a Spanish launch
bearing down upon us." The captain took the glass and surveying the
launch, prepared to meet the enemy, calling all hands to duty. Meanwhile a
shot from the enemy crossed the bow of our ship as a signal for them to
heave to, which they immediately obeyed, and returned the shot. Both ships
being in readiness, they prepared for action. The engagement lasted but a
short time, as their ship was mounted with 18 pounders and carried but two
miles, while the Spanish ship mounted 32 pounders and carried three miles.
Soon as the launch ascertained the power of their guns, they withdrew to the
distance of three miles, being out of reach of the English ship's guns, and
continued cannonading in perfect safety. The Englishmen not liking their
position, got under way, endeavoring to make their escape. The Spaniards
observing this joined in the chase. The English ship made every possible
exertion, and set every sail that she was capable of carrying. The launch
continued the chase, and being larger, having more sail, and a good light
breeze, she sailed a third faster than the English ship, keeping up the firing
at the same time, until a shot struck the English ship below water line,
which compelled her to heave to and strike. The ship began to sink, and the
officers thought it best to leave the ship and take to the small boats. They
were soon made ready, and all jumped into them except four, two white and
two colored men, who could not get in, there being no room for them. They
remained on the ship's deck, the Englishmen promising to return for them
as soon as they arrived at the launch. The ship settled so fast they became
impatient, and father told them that if they remained much longer they
would go to the bottom in the ship. They found they had no time to waste;
they must either leave the ship or be lost. Father's shipmate said he could

not swim, and they must save him or he must go down with the ship. Father said he could not, as he didn't know as he could save himself, as the launch was three miles away and the small boat has not yet returned and they would probably have to swim all the way to the launch; at any rate, they would risk their fate, and they jumped overboard. As soon as they reached the water the cook grabbed father by the ankle, crying "Save me Noah, save me." Father cried out, "let me go, I can't save myself." He kept crying, "save me," until a huge shark swam along and cut him in two; he made one screech, his grasp was broken and he sank to rise no more. In the midst of the excitement, father gave one spring and found himself clear. He soon came up and passed the other men, and speeded his way towards the launch, and when he began to get near the launch, the small boat came up, and passing by father to pick up those who were behind, he cried out for them to save him. The men on board told him to continue on, be was doing well enough; they were going to pick up the other two which were behind, then would return and rescue him, which they did, and took them all safe to the Spanish launch. After they were all on board, seeing the captain with his uniform on, they stripped it off and threw him into the sea. He swam around the ship, got hold of a rope and was climbing up to get in again, but as he reached the railing, an officer, who was pacing the deck, picked up a hatchet and cut his hands off. The captain fell into the sea and was seen no more. The English crew were alarmed, expecting to meet a similar fate,but the Spaniards treated them kindly. After arriving on the Spanish Main, they were taken to a place called Dartmouth prison. It was a one story building, a quarter of a mile or more long, having attached to it a large yard, where the prisoners could exercise. Every man was allowed a seven foot plank for a bed, and a stone for a pillow, and was compelled to work at his trade, if he had any, and if he had none to learn one, for they all had to do something towards their support. Father having no trade, was permitted to have a choice in one to learn. He chose to learn to braid palm leaf hats. They learned him how to braid, sew and cover them. After learning, he, with others, was given a daily task, which if they accomplished, they were paid for all over-work. Among other very unpleasant things in prison life was vermin, which troubled them very much, so much that they were obliged to brush them off each other every morning. A great many prisoners were confined there, and when their task was finished they were allowed to exercise in the yard, which was very large, and occasionally they were allowed to walk down to the sea shore, but when the gun was fired at sunset from the fort, every prisoner must return to the prison, and the gates were closed. When any news was received that an English vessel had taken a Spanish vessel, the officers of the prison were cross, and would not allow the prisoners to go outside of the gates. They were also very harsh, and the prisoners had to be very careful when they were so to attend closely to work and keep out of the officers' way as much as possible.

Father and the shipmates who were saved with him kept together and away from the other seamen. One day, after completing their task, they went out to enjoy themselves in the yard. Several officers were seated, smoking cigars. Seeing his shipmate, who was very limber, displaying his dexterity by walking on his hands with his feet in the air, then rolling himself in a heap and tumbling over, at the same time calling father to see him, one of the officers arose, walked up to the man who was tumbling, and without saying a word drew his sword, cut off his head and took his seat again as if nothing had happened. This conduct greatly alarmed grandfather and his comrade, so that they were more afraid of the officers after that than ever, and they at once began to watch for a chance to make their escape. Consequently, they did all the over-work they could, and saved their money to bribe some one who would aid them in their plan to escape. Shortly after this, having finished their task, they started to take a walk. Father being ahead reached the gate first. Just then a man came running past him and disappeared. He raised his hand to open the gate when a man on the outside with a knife stabbed him in the wrist, and was about to give him another cut when father cried out. He drew back and said,"You are not the man. I meant to kill the man I was chasing." That was all the apology he made for his rash act, and went his way. The officer at the prison took father to the hospital, attended to his wound, took off his clothes, washed and dressed him in a clean white suit, and told him to remain there until the doctor said he was well. He said he was very sorry, when the time came for him to leave the hospital and return to the prison, for he had a good bed and plenty to eat, very much better than his prison fare, and was free from those vermin called lice, which were so abundant in the prison.

They continued their work until they had saved up a good sum of money by over-work. They would often go out and watch for a chance to make their escape. One day while walking on the sea shore they fell in with a ferryman, and in conversation with him asked if there were ever any American vessels in the harbor. He replied, "Yes, occasionally, as Spain and America are on good terms with each other." They told him they had saved the money they made by over-work, and each had a small bag full, and asked if he would row them across the river when the next American vessel came in. He said he would, providing they would come down and get in the boat just before the gun fired, lay down in the bottom of the boat and cover themselves up with a piece of canvas he would have for that purpose, and he would be on the shore some distance from the boat, pretending not to know anything about it. After the gun fired he would come and get in the boat and row over as fast as he could. He said he would keep a sharp look out, and when one did arrive, he would board her and ask the captain if he would take the two men to America, telling him they were prisoners of war and Americans by birth, captured from an English man-of-war, and would find out when they would sail so as to have them on board the night before. In the meantime he wanted them not to speak to him or take any notice of his boat, lest they should be seen by some one, and suspicion would rest on him when they were missing, but to walk along the shore frequently, and when they saw a stick sticking up in front of the boat, that would be the signal for them to get in. This being agreed upon they departed. Each day one of them would walk on the shore, it being near the prison, covered by a hill. Many weeks passed before the signal was given, when one day to their great joy, they saw the boat and signal, and sallying forth with their money went to the shore, and walked around until it was nearly time for the gun to be fired, then went in the boat and covered themselves up with the canvas. Only a few minutes passed when the gun was fired. The boat man soon came leisurely along, got into his boat, took his oars and rowed away. By the time he had crossed the river it began to grow quite dark. They went aboard the ship, and learned that she belonged to Providence, and was commanded by Capt. Olney, who, after inquiring their names, said to father, "I am well acquainted with your father. He told me when I sailed if I came across you to bring you home." He told us to go below and keep out of sight until he had passed the fort. His shipmate, Major by name, was an Englishman, father to James Major, now residing at No. 487 North Main street, with whom I had a very pleasant conversation a short time since concerning his father being a prisoner of war with my father, both of whom are now dead. They had a pleasant passage, arriving safe in Providence, after losing a number of years in English servitude. The English thought they had a right to press any American seaman into their service. After father's return he followed coasting, running from Providence to New York on a vessel commanded by Capt. Comstock. At that time England and America were at war. Privateers were cruising around New York, picking up any vessels coming in their way as prizes, and it was very hazardous for vessels to sail, as they might be picked up. Consequently, vessels carrying two six-pounders each would go in company for each others' protection. At one time five vessels left New York in company for Providence, and Capt. Comstock was the second packet out. Father always went prepared, having a big jug of rum and a bottle of laudanum, so that in case they should be captured to charge the rum with laudanum, and treat the English seamen to a bountiful supply, knowing them to be dear lovers of the article, and would have it if any was found on board. And drinking of it freely they would soon be unable to do anything. They could then re-capture the ship, for he had no notion of going back again into English servitude. He had lost too much time by them already. It was a pleasant day and a stiff breeze was carrying the vessels along rapidly to their destined port when a privateer hove in sight and saluted our commanders very abruptly, saying, "Drop your main-sails, you damned rebels, and come under my lee." The first sloop obeyed the summons, but Captain Comstock answered the salutation by saying, "Yes, sir, when I have nothing else to do," and continued his course. They fired but did not hit him, and not caring to follow him and lose the other sloops, gave up the chase, and captured the other three vessels. Captain Comstock arrived safe in port. He was a fine man. He was a neighbor and schoolmate of father's, and seemed much interested in him.

Grandfather was now getting very feeble, unable to do anything. He went on board to see father, and the captain asked him, if his property was all paid for and clear of all incumbrances. Grandfather said it was. Captain then asked him if the deed was recorded. He said he never had any deed; that Mr. Brown had often promised, but had never given it to him. But Mr. Carlyle had given him the deed for the lot he sold him. The Captain told him to go and get the deed of Mr. Brown, and have them both recorded. Grandfather said he would. Time passed, and the Captain frequently asked father about the deed. He also told grandfather again, but he was in poor health; was always going to get it, but never went. Finally when the vessel was ready to sail for New York, the Captain came on board about ten o'clock in the morning, and said to father, "Noah, has your father got the deed yet?" Father said, "No." He said, "Your father is feeble—is liable to drop off any time; then it will be too late to get those deeds recorded. Now stop your work at once; get your father and go to Mr. Brown's house and see that Mr. Brown gives him his deed. You must do no more work until you get that deed and get them both recorded. Father stopped work, washed, changed his clothes, and went and took grandfather to Mr. Brown's house. When entering the driveway a carriage drove in ahead of them. They went to the house, ent ered the kitchen, sat down and rested awhile, then sent word for Mr. Brown to come out ; they wished to see him. Soon Mr: Brown came into the room, and father told him what he came for, and Capt. Comstock's anxiety about having the matter attended to at once, so much so that he made him stop his work; get his father and come and get the deed. Mr Brown replied I have company from New Bedford and cannot attend to it now; you must come some other time, and I will draw up the deed. It will take some time to make one. Father told him he was about to sail, and when he returned would come again. Mr. Brown said it should be ready. Father went back to the vessel and told the Captain about the interview. He told him when they returned he must attend to it. The next day they sailed for New York and did not return for some four weeks. During that time, grandfather died. When the vessel returned, father learned of his death and burial Captain Comstock said he feared it would be so, and "probably you will have trouble in getting the deed." Father made no further attempts, but continued with Captain Comstock until Fall; then left the Captain and went a voyage at sea. During his absence grandmother sickened and died, her daughter Rhoda took care of her. Soon after her mother died, she was taken sick and was cared for by her two daughters, Ann and Lucy, but both being out of employ they were without means, to get the things that were really wanted, and as her condition required good care and proper food she opened an account with Mr. Angell where her mother had an unsettled account at her death Her health failed so rapidly, that Mr Angell thought it best to look after his debt. After making out his bill, he sent his son Robert, accompanied by Mr. Peck, a butcher, to see Aunt Rhoda, presented his bill and wished her to secure him on the land. They could find no deed of the property purchased of Mr. Brown, so she secured him on the lot deeded to her parents by Mr Carlisle. Soon after this was done Aunt Rhoda died. When father returned, he learned of the death of his mother and sister. Mr. Angell told him what had happened, and said he would buy father's share or sell his own. Father told him he would think of it and the subject dropped. Father married and settled down, intending not to take any more long voyages, but labor along shore or go coasting. He ploughed his land, and began to cultivate it; and for several years raised vegetables enough to supply his family. Mr Angell kept quite uneasy; wanting to sell or buy. About this time Uncle James, who had been absent for a long time, returned home, and went with father to see Mr Brown about the deed, as Mr. Angell said he had bought the land (he, father, was occupying) of Mr. Brown. He said that Mr. Angell wanted the lot, and he let him have it. Father said to Mr. Brown, his father had paid for the land but had received no deed, he came with his father one time for the deed at Captain Comstock's earnest request, just before grandfather died. A carriage drove in, with company from New Bedford to see you, you told us to come again, you could not attend to it then. Mr. Brown replied, "I recollect it but did not think about it when I sold the lot; now as your father lived in my house for a good many years, I guess we are about square; but there is a strip, ten feet wide, I will give that to you." And that was all my father received. He then took Mr. Cato Green with him and called on Mr. Angell, saying, "you want to sell your strip of land or buy mine. He said, "yes." "What will you give for my land," said father. He said, "twenty five dollars, and no more; what will

you take for yours?'' He said, ''twenty-five dollars.'' ''When will you give
the deed?'' said father. ''As soon as you pay the money,'' he said. Father
drew his wallet, and in Mr. Green's presence counted out twenty-five dollars, and asked for the deed immediately. Mr. Angell was surprised, not
thinking father had the money. He drew up the deed, had it duly executed
Father took it and gave him the money. Uncle James found so small a strip
coming to him, he gave it to his niece, Ann Macklin, and she sold it to
father. He then had possession of the thirty feet which grandfather bought
of Mr. Carlisle, and the ten feet which Mr. Brown gave him by deed,
making his lot forty feet wide and two hundred and twenty feet deep. This
was the land which my grandfather once owned, somewhere about 150 feet
in width, when he attempted to build his house, now narrowed down to
forty feet in width and is that now occupied by brother George and myself.

CHAPTER III.

I have remarked that father moved into a house called the Red Lion. This name was given to the house because of its former occupants, which did not bear a very good character. Providence being a commercial place, always having a large amount of shipping in port, consequently there was a large supply of sailors, who could be seen at all times in the day. In this locality there were a large number of sailor boarding houses to accommodate them; and for their convenience there were very many grog-shops to refresh themselves in; and their numerous attractions enticeing many lewd females. The house which my father rented being located in the south part of the town, near the water was a very desirable location for such characters, hence it received the name of Red Lion. It was a gambrel roofed house, covered with planed boards like clapboards, and painted red. The front of the house was towards Power street with windows fronting the same. Seats were placed on each side of the door, long enough to seat three persons each, with a back of wooden railing. A pretty flower garden each side of the door made a very tasteful appearance in the summer season. A brass knob was also put on the door, adding somewhat to the grandeur of the Lion. On the west side was a door and two windows, one over the other, and two doors on the north side, one leading into the cellar, the other into the back yard, with two windows the same as in front. The inside of the house was arranged as follows: two rooms on the first floor, the largest used for a kitchen, the other for a sitting room or bed room. Adjoining us on the east was a sailor boarding house kept by Mr. James Axum. From our east window could be seen a fine garden filled with various kind of vegetables belonging to Mr. Axum. There were two rooms upstairs arranged the same as below, having access by a stair-way in a small entry three feet by six, on the north side of the west room. When we first moved in we occupied the upper rooms, until the family below could vacate their rooms, which was some six months after we moved in. Two rooms was considered quite a genteel tenement in these days for a family of six, especially if they were colored, the prevailing opinion being that they had no business with a larger house then one or two rooms. The family occupying the lower floor of our

house were considered the upper crust of the colored population, Mr.
Thomas Reed by name, by trade a barber, and kept a fashionable shaving
saloon. They occupied the whole house, using the rooms upstairs as a
genteel boarding house. He did not accommodate sailors, and thus regained
the reputation of the house, which had previously been occupied and pa-
tronized by the lower classes. I well remember what a change was wrought
upon my mind when we first moved into the house, having lived in a short,
narrow street, in the rear of South Main and back streets, now called Benefit
street. Wagons and carriages seldom passed through, and very few persons,
except those living on the street. But from our house we had a view of
Power and South Main streets, the last named, a general thoroughfare for
carriages and teams, and easy of access from either the north or south side.
We there had a fine view of the sailors in their varied condition, the working men coming and going from labor, and the men of note. We also had a
fine view of the beautiful waters of the Narragansett Bay, fairly alive with
its ships, brigs, schooners, crafts, and small boats, sailing to and fro, thus
displaying a grandeur unequalled in any city of its size. And in addition to
these attractions, there were two brass foundries, one located on the northwest corner of Power and South Main streets, owned and occupied by
James Wheaton, the other on the southeast corner of the same streets, occupied by Josiah Keene. The work commenced at sunrise and continued until
sunset,. with the exception of one hour for dinner. The continued sound of
the hammer was very pleasing to me, as children like music and noise, and
though but six years old, I felt that in comparison with the place formerly
occupied, it was livlier My ears were gratified with the sound, and my eyes
with the sight. I was astonished to hear older people say to mother when
they called to see her, especially her sisters in the church, "Why, sister
Brown, what a horrid situation you live in? why, it is next in kin to Baby-
lon; why you can't hear, yourself think, let alone speak." When you spoke
to any one, you had to raise your voice above the sound of the hammer, or
you could not be understood. In the Fall Mr Reed's family moved out and
father's family moved down stairs, taking the whole house. He was responsible for the rent to Mr. Tillinghast and other heirs, to whom it belonged. It
was forty dollars per year. There being more room then be needed or could
afford to pay for, he rented the upper part for fifteen dollars per year; which
reduced his rent to twenty-five dollars. The landlords received their rents
quarterly. Every one knew, in those days that a man having a family of six
could not pay the rent of four rooms, unless he robbed or went on the
highway to get a living. If he intended to live by robbing, he had only to
keep a sailor boarding house; for the poor fellows when they came from a
voyage, as it was proverbally spoken of them, were full of money as a dog

is full of fleas, generally fell a prey to the land lords and their accomplices. It was frequently the case when they shipped for another voyage they would go aboard in debt to the landlord. This practice was generally kept up, not only with sailors, but with any one wishing to go to sea.

Many years ago there was one of those boarding houses and shipping offices at a house corner of South Main and Transit streets, known as Simmons' boarding house. The landlord's name was Ambrose Simmons. He had a large run of boarders; and any one that wanted to go on a voyage, went to his place of business. At one time, it was said a man from the country took an odd notion to follow the sea, and was directed to Simmons's shipping office, but just at that time there did not happen to be any ships ready for sea, so he took up his abode with Simmons, doing odd jobs as he thought for his board, filling the office of, what is it called on shipboard, lob-lobby-boy. Whilst being there, hearing the tales of the sailors numerating the various hardships they had to pass through, his ardor dampened, and he came to the conclusion that he would not attempt to follow the sea. He then told Mr. Simmons of his convictions, who in order to catch him, coincided with him. Notwithstanding his labor during the time he had been there, Mr. Simmons calculated to have pay for the time. Soon after, a pennant was seen floating from the top of a ship as a signal that hands were wanted. Mr. Simmons soon appeared on board, and completed the agreement to furnish the amount. The day arrived for the ship to sail, and Mr. Simmons addressed his greenhorn, saying, there is a ship going to drop down the river today. I want you to go on board and help to get her down; and when the pilot leaves her, you can get aboard of his boat and return; the fellow readily complied, went aboard, got underway and stood down the river. Having a good breeze, she was ready to discharge the pilot, who took leave of his crew and went over the side to his boat. The fellow cried out, to the pilot, "hold on; I am going up with you." The captain answered, "Going up where?" The man replied, "To town." The captain said, "You are not going until the voyage is up." The man said, " I am not going any voyage!" "You aint going," said the captain, "what did you ship for ?" " I have not shipped, I only came to help get the ship down. Mr. Simmons told me when the pilot came to get on board and come up with him." The captain asked, "Have you ever been to sea?" He answered, "No; I came from the country with that intention, but having heard so much about its hardships, I gave it up, and was going to return home." The captain said, "Mr. Simmons has shipped you as an able seaman at $17 per month, and taken your first month's advance; now I can't go back after another man, and I don't want to go to sea with one man short. Now I will put you in the cabin as a steward and allow you $10 per month, as you have never been to sea, and will put the steward before the mast. And as you have no clothes for that purpose, I will furnish you out of the slop chest." And the man willingly agreed to it, and went on the voyage and was gone some fourteen months. When on their return home, the captain said to the steward, "As you do not intend to follow the sea, but are going into the country to settle, I want you to play a trick on Simmons." The man replied, "I shall never trouble the sea again as long as I can stay on land." The captain said, "Well, as soon as you arrive in port, go to the counting room and I will see the owners and settle with you and I will tell the owners what a trick Simmons played upon you, and as soon as you receive your pay, go to Simmons's office, tell him you have just arrived home, and made out first rate; had a good voyage, and you want a suit of clothes from top to toe, and five or ten dollars for pocket change, and to-morrow he can go up and settle your voyage and take out his pay that you owe him for board that you had before you went to sea, and your suit of clothes." He told him he would do it. So when the ship arrived in port, the captain went to the Custom House to enter his ship. The steward went ashore and to the counting room. The captain soon arrived, and after stating the case of the steward and Simmons, the merchant immediately settled with the steward, and he made his way to Simmons's shipping office. On entering, he saw Mr. Simmons, and saluted him, saying, "How are you, Mr. Simmons; I am safe home again." Simmons looked somewhat surprised, when the steward said, "Don't you know me? I am the chap from the country that came to your office to get a voyage, and as there was no ships ready for sea at that time, I stopped at your house and did odd jobs for some weeks, and you sent me on board of a ship to help haul her down the stream, and said I could come up with the pilot, but I went the whole voyage, had a first rate time, and have come home safe." Simmons grabbed him by the hand, gave him a hearty shake, saying, "I recollect all about it; you see I have made a man of you; I am glad to see you: you are going to stop here ain't you?" The steward replied, "Certaily, I am. Come, Mr. Simmons, let us have something to drink; come, boys, take hold." After they had had a drink all round, those that were in the shop at the time, the steward remarked, "Mr. Simmons, I want a new set of sail; I must go and see the ladies; can't you rig me out?" "Certainly, certainly; what do you want?" The steward said, "I want a pair of blue pantaloons, a vest, and jacket, also a light pair of shoes and stockings, and a couple of handker-chiefs." He supplied himself with the whole. After dressing himself up, Simmons said, " You are a nice looking fellow." Then said he, "I would like a decent looking hat." That was readily furnished. He then called for something to drink, and two cigars, and then said to Mr. Simmons, "Loan me ten dollars, I can't put to sea with a swept hold." Mr. Simmons supplied his wants, and bidding him good-night, he said as he was going out the door, "Now remember, see to my voyage tomorrow." Simmons replied, "All right; I will attend to it." The steward then started for his home in the country, and that was the last seen of him. Simmons waited till the afternoon of the next day for the steward to appear, but he did not come; and he thought he would go himself to see about it. He went to the counting room, and said to the merchant, I have come to settle the voyage of a steward that went in your ship." The merchant asked where he was. Simmons said, "I don't know; he went off last night and promised to come to my office to-day. I suppose he went with the girls, and became intoxicated and has not got sober yet. When he left my office, he requested me to settle the voyage, and I have come for that purpose." The merchants asked the steward's name. Mr. Simmons readily informed them, and they said "he settled his own voyage yesterday afternoon, soon after the ship arrived; we have paid him every cent we owed him; you can step here and see his signature to the receipt on the books." Mr. Simmons was struck with astonishment. He informed the owners how he had obtained an out-fit from him, also borrowed the sum of ten dollars. The merchants said they were sorry, but could not help it. Many a poor sailor was taxed after that to make up that amount. I relate this circumstance to show one of the various ways that landlords practiced on sailors to relieve them of their money, which was downright robbery.

The house which was next to our's on Power street was a sailor boarding house. There were two more in the neighborhood. The ships were continually arriving and clearing, and made business very lively. It was common to see boys with pitchers and decanters going for liquors; and this practice continued throughout my youth. After we had taken the lower tenement of the house, mother said to me one day, that it was my birthday; "that I was born on the 10th of November, and was seven years old, and it was commonly stated that the boy at seven years is old enough to earn his own living, but, I think seven years is too young, but I want you to remember when your birthday comes." And from that day forth I have never forgotten it. In the spring, some ladies called at our house, and speaking about Sabbath School, asked mother if she could send her children. She said she had three that could attend, if there was any one going who could see to them. Miss Wescott, the lady living up stairs, and a member of the First Baptist Church, with my mother, offered to take us to school, which was to be kept in the town house at the corner of Benefit and College streets, and was to commence at one o'clock and close at half past two, as the church commenced at three. The Sabbath School was something new, and the people had many conjectures about it. At the proper time we left home, and we arrived at school. I remember being much pleased with my nice clothes, and still more so, as I saw so many boys and girls of all sizes at the school, all dressed so nice and clean, also some beautiful ladies and gentlemen. I thought it one of the most charming sights I ever beheld. Soon the school commenced, classes were made up, and whilst I was training to see everybody and hear everything that was said, some one tapped me on the shoulder, and turning round, a beautiful lady spoke a very pleasantly, asking my name. Miss Wescott, who went with me told her. She wanted to know if I was coming steadily. The lady said I was, and said these children are sister Brown's. I came to show them the way, and look out for them. She said she was glad to have us here. Then she got some cards and heard me say the alphabet. As I had learned a good part of them from my brothers and sisters, I was a good hand in repeating the alphabet. The lady came soon after, and brought some beautiful cards, which pleased me much, and asked me to come next Sunday. I told her I would. After the school closed, I went to the first Baptist church in company with Miss Wescott, climbing up three or four pair of stairs to where the colored people sat. There I was carried away with astonishment at being up so high, as I thought, and seeing the people in the gallery and down stairs, and the minister in the pulpit. I looked until I fell asleep. I slept until Miss Wescott woke me to go home. On arriving home I did not know how to commence telling what I had seen and heard and what I had passed through. My mind was employed the whole week in thinking of that day, and anxious for Sunday to come again. I continued going to the Sabbath School and was delighted, more so than at the church, as the school was more lively, children and people were talking and whispering, and they distributed pretty cards and books to the children; but at the church no one was talking or whispering but the minister, and I soon got tired of hearing him. After singing was over there was no enjoyment for me, and I went to sleep. In the Fall I waited anxiously for my birthday to come. I kept run of the months and days until the time came, and had the pleasure of telling mother that that was my birthday. I was eight years old. That was the time mother said a boy was capable of earning his own living, in her opinion. I tried to make myself useful by running errands and doing work around the house that mother wanted done. I frequently went out with brother Joseph, who was four years older than myself. He was a stout, thick-set boy, and often get into trouble with other boys. At one time he got into a fight with a colored boy belonging to Mrs. Ayers, from the south. He was taller than brother, but not so stout built. What the fight commenced about I could not tell. There were a dozen or more boys, mostly white, encouraging them to fight. The boy from the south was dressed very nicely; the rest of the crowd were very roughly dressed; I think the colored boy's dress must have excited them to jealousy. After exchanging many angry and wicked words, to the great joy of the crowd, for they all seemed to be delighted, they soon commenced to fight. My brother was too stout and heavy for the other boy, who did not understand the science of fighting, consequently got the worst of it, and becoming more and more angry he said, "I will beat your brains out;" and running back made a half halt, and bending over suddenly, came forward and struck such a blow with his head that he knocked my brother over. Seeing his success, he made another attempt, and came up full force, but brother holding up his heels, his head came in contact with them. This nearly stunned him, and raised a shout from the boys. Mother hearing the noise, came out to see what it meant, and learning that brother was one of the combatants, she made him go into the house. The boy coming to himself, was nearly crazy with anger. It was impossible for the people to calm him; he kept crying out, "I want that Joe Brown, the northern skunk." He tried to force the door open to get into the house. Just at that time, Mr. Ayers, his master, came along, and perceiving the noise coming from his boy, hailed him, and ordered him home. The boy calmed down at once, and went home. Mother had a task to keep brother in his place, as he was twelve years old, and father was away to sea. Soon Mr. Eaton, a gentleman from Framingham, a relative of Judge Staples's wife, wanted a boy, and hearing of brother Joseph, came to see mother about him. He made an agreement to take him a year on trial, for his victuals, clothes, and schooling, and he went home with Mr. Eaton on trial for a year. After he left home my services were required doing chores around the house, cutting wood, etc. This was before hard coal was brought in use in Providence, and every one burned wood, which cost four or five dollars a cord. The small sticks were given to me to cut. About this time some ladies opened a free school for colored youth. One of the teachers in this enterprise was Miss Eliza B. Gano, daughter of Dr. Gano, a Baptist minister, afterwards Mrs Joseph Rogers. She interested very much in the colored people, in order to secure the attention of the children, which she succeeded in doing, and the school opened early in spring. It was located on Middle street, on the west side of the town, and was taught on the Lancasterian plan. I was large enough to go into the lowest class. A semi-circle was painted in front of the teacher's desk. When the class was called each scholar had to toe the circle. It extended across the room and would accommodate some twelve children, who stood front of the teacher to read and spell, the teacher remaining at her desk. My class read from a large alphabet card; then there was prepared for us a long desk with seats, on top was a place one foot wide and one inch deep, filled with sand. A piece of board was used to stroke the sand smooth, then a copy of A B C was made for the scholars to learn to write, using wooden pens flattened out like a spoon-handle. Each scholar had his own space to write on, 18 inches long and 12 inches wide. When the space was filled each one had to sit up straight, as a sign that we had filled up the spaces, and the teacher would call a monitor to level the sand and set another copy.

Thus the time during the interval was occupied. As regards the other classes I knew but little. This school continued six months. Near the close of the term Miss Latham, the teacher, wishing to show the ladies who employed her, and the parents of the scholars, the progress she had made, proposed to have an examination. She selected pieces for the scholars to read and speak on the occasion; every class had a piece, and I was selected from my class to recite a piece, and as I could not read, she taught me how to speak it, and I have never forgotten it. It was as follows:

> "Who could expect one of my age
> To speak in public on the stage,
> And if I chance to fall below
> Demosthenes or Cicero,
> Don't view me with a critic's eye,
> But pass my imperfections by.
> Large streams from little fountains flow,
> Tall oaks from little acorns grow.
> Although I am but small and young,
> Of judgment weak, and feeble tongue,
> Yet all great learned men, like me,
> First learned to read their A, B, C.
> Let Rhode Island boast as great
> As any other sister state.
> But where the boy that three feet high,
> Has made improvements more than I?
> These thoughts inspire my youthful mind,
> To be the greatest of mankind.
> Great, not like Ceasar, stained with blood,
> But only great as I am good."

After speaking my piece and making a low bow, I descended from the stand, as I had been instructed to do by Miss Latham. I spoke it to her satisfaction, and the praise and admiration of all present, who declared that I was to be a great man, and if the necessary measures were taken, there was no doubt but that I would be of great use to my people; but that was the winding up of this school. Preparations were being made to open a school in the vestry of our new meeting house, which was just finished. This building was commenced in 1819, but for the want of funds it was not finished until 1821, two years after its commencement. Prior to this time, the people had no place of worship of their own, and were obliged to attend the white people's churches. Some attended the Congregational church, Rev. James Wilson, pastor; some attended the Methodist church; some attended the Episcopal church, Dr. Crocker, pastor; a few attended the Unitarian church, Rev. Mr. Cady, pastor; and a large number attended the First Baptist church, Dr. Gano, pastor. Some were members of each of the above named churches; the largest number, however, were Baptists, and belonged to the First Baptist church, but many attended no church at all, because they said they were opposed to going to churches and sitting in pigeon holes, as all the churches at that time had some obscure place for the colored people to sit in. Finally they came to the conclusion to build them a house of worship large enough to have the vestry for a school room. This was eleven years after the Emancipation of the State of Rhode Island, which took place in 1808. The General Assembly passed a law to the effect "that all who wanted to be free, could secure their papers of freedom, but those who remained in slavery, if they ever came to want, or needed assistance, they should be maintained out of there owner's property, if they were worth anything, before they could receive assistance from the town." Most all the colored people took their freedom, and secured their papers, except a few old ones, who declared their masters had been eating their flesh and now they were going to stick to them and suck their bodies. The colored people called a meeting in 1819 to take measures, to build a meetinghouse, with a basement for a school room. After appointing their Committee to carry out their wishes, they sent a special committee to Mr. Moses Brown, to inform him of their intentions and see what he would do towards aiding them, knowing he belonged to the Society of Friends and was a very benevolent man, besides some of the members of the committee had been in his service. Mr. Brown, after hearing their statements, highly commended their movement, and said, "I always had it in my heart to help the colored people, whenever I saw they were ready to receive. Now go and select you out a lot, suitable for your purpose, and I will pay for it." This so pleased the committee, that they went to work in good faith. They notified the different pastors of the several churches, and called a meeting in the vestry of the First Baptist church. When they were assembled their object was laid before the people by Henry Jackson, a young Christian gentleman, belonging to the First Baptist church, and of high standing in the community. There were present that time several ministers of the Gospel, namely: Dr. Stephen Gano, Dr. Crocker, Rev. Jas. Wilson, Rev. Mr. Snow, and the pastor of the

Methodist church. The statement of Mr. Brown was made by the committee, and was received by them, and steps were taken to carry out the project,
under the directions of the other committee. The lot was selected, and Mr.
Brown purchased it as he agreed, and then conveyed the lot to the colored
people of Providence, and appointed three feofees in trust, to carry out the
object, namely: his son, Obadiah Brown, Henry Jackson, and George Benson. The house was finished in 1821. The committee lost some time in
trying to find a teacher, to instruct the school under the Lancasterian plan.
After searching in vain they procured a white gentleman by the name of Mr.
Ormsbee, to teach them. The school was opened in the vestry, but not a free
school, the price of tuition being $1.50 per quarter. The colored people sent
their children and they soon had the number of 125 scholars. I attended the
school at the opening, being the second school I ever attended. The scholars
behaved pretty well, and he read over to them, at the opening of the school,
his rules of order. On the east side of the vestry there was a part which had
never been dug out and made level with the rest. It was petitioned off,
leaving a dark hole 20 feet long and 10 feet wide, having a door that opened
in the vestry, and this door had a hole in the top, 15 inches wide and 18
inches long. Whenever any of the scholars misbehaved they were put in this
hole. The children were very much afraid to be shut up in this place, for
when they were digging the cellar they dug up a coffin and a man in it. No
one could tell how the coffin came there. It was nearly consumed, but they
supposed it must have been some Indian that was buried there. Mr. Ormsbee was a very severe teacher; he used the cowhide very freely. After
keeping the school for one year his labors came to a close, and for a year
and a half the school was suspended, not being able to procure a teacher.
Colored teachers were very rarely to be found, and it was difficult to procure a white teacher, as it was considered a disgraceful employment to be a
teacher of colored children and still more disgraceful to have colored children in white schools. But there was one gentleman who would take a few
colored scholars. His name was John Lawton, belonging to the Society of
Friends. He was a highly educated man, and his school consisted of white
and colored scholars. His price was high, and very few of the colored
people could afford to send their children.

He did not keep school to accommodate colored people, but for the sake
of the money, and those who attended his school, if they could be taught
anything, were always learned. My father, when a boy, attended his school.
He was celebrated for teaching the Mariner's art. His scholars had given
him the name of "old Toney Latin," and he was known by that name more
than by his own. After waiting a long time the Lord sent us a teacher, and a
preacher, Mr. Asa C. Goldberry. He was an octoroon, and many people

took him to be white. He filled the pulpit on the Sabbath, and on week days taught the school. He was here some two years, when he got married and went to Hayti. After his departure we succeeded in getting a white teacher, and he remained six months and left. The next teacher was the Rev. Jacob Perry, a colored man. He preached in the meeting-house, and taught the school, having the same salary that the former teacher had. The school was well attended by small and great. Among the large boys was Jim Brown, well known among colored people as the bully. He was about 17 or 18 years old. Stephen Gibbs, Edward Green Jerry Benson, and half dozen more, were of the same grade. These large boys frequently did pretty much as they pleased. They held conversation with the teacher and seemed more like his equals than scholars. In the fall of the year, the boys were allowed an intermission in the forenoon for a few minutes. The large boys paid a visit to Mr. Dorr's orchard, and came to school with their pockets filled with fruit, and would present some to the teacher, and then commence eating it. The small scholars would ask for some, and they would tell them to go and get some for themselves, and when asked where they got it, replied, in Dorr's orchard. They continued going to the orchard during the recess, for weeks, each time treating the teacher to some stolen fruit, who said on receiving it, "you will get caught bye and bye." The smaller boys followed the larger ones to the orchard and I joined them. In going there we got over the fence at the southeast corner. The large boys had nearly stripped the trees in the upper end of the lot, so we had to go down towards the middle of the lot to get any. I had filled my hat nearly two thirds full, went back to the school, and gave my teacher a share, which he took and put into his desk, to eat at leisure. When I went home at night, I carried some home to my mother. She asked where I got them, they were so nice. I told her "in Dorr's orchard." She asked if Mr. Dorr gave them to me. I said "No." She wanted to know how I came by them; did I steal them. I said "No." She knew I had no money to buy them, and if Mr. Dorr did not give them, how I came by them. I said "all the boys get them, and no one says anything, or troubles us." She said, "the boys were stealing them, and would get in jail, and I to, if I kept on going there." She told me not to go again. I promised that I would not. The other boys continued to go, and when I asked for some, they would say, "You know where they are, go and get them." So on Friday afternoon I thought I would go once more, notwithstanding I had promised my mother only the Tuesday before that I would never go again. I went during the recess, found most of the trees stripped, and I had to go quite a ways down to get any. One of the boys discovered a man coming and gave the alarm. I ran to the southeast corner and climbed the fence, and there saw the man crouched down ready to receive me. I jumped back and ran to the northeast corner; the man not knowing which way I was going, stayed there for some moments. I had scaled the fence, and was making my way towards the school-house, when a colored man by the name of Marquis, who lived with Mr. Dorr, sprang for me, but I dodged him and made my way for Prospect street. He followed on, and when I reached Prospect street I turned towards Olney street, and was leaving him far behind, and would have got clear, but two men made their appearance, one of them, a cousin of mine, coming up Prospect street, from Olney street, and Marquis exclaimed, "Stop that boy," which they proceeded to do, having canes, and I was compelled to give up. Then I wished I had minded my mother and kept away, but it was too late. I had stolen and the man had caught me. When he came up he asked me my name, how old I was, where I lived, if I went to the school, how many boys there were that stole, and what their names were; and I told him the truth, and how I came to go there. He let me go and I returned to school. The schoolmaster said he expected I would get found out. That was all the consolation he gave me. When I returned home, I told mother the whole story, and she told me that was the result of bad actions of wicked people. It always led them to get found out and caught. I was in a terrible state of mind. I knew I had disobeyed my mother, done a wrong act, and now I feared an officer would come and carry me to jail, and all the next day, which was Saturday, I was weeping, and if any one came to the house I thought an officer was after me. But no officer came that day. I solemnly promised that I would never be again caught in such a wicked act.

It was a serious time with me on the day following, (Sunday.) I thought of my crimes, and how wrong it was to take that which belonged to others; so I formed new resolutions, and have kept them. Monday morning I went to school, and everything went on well until ten o'clock, when to our surprise two constables came in, took out a paper, and called the names of the several boys, requesting them to answer to their names. The call was responded to, with the exception of about six boys, who were absent, and those were the large boys. The constables marched us by twos down to Squire William Aplin's office. The large boys, getting wind of what was up, kept out of the way, and could not be found. We were all arranged in a row at the squire's office. Mr. Dorr being sent for, soon made his appearance, and after viewing us, asked our names, our parents' names and residences, then addressed us as follows: "Boys, you have stripped most all my trees of their fruit; you commenced as soon as the fruit began to ripen, at the upper part of my orchard, and you have cleaned up the trees. Now I could put you all in jail, you are in my power. Do you want to go there?" We all answered, "No sir." He said, "If you continue stealing it will bring you all to

the gallows. One crime will lead to another until you commit some desper-
ate act. Now if I let you go, will you promise to be good boys, never to steal
again, and attend to your school?" We all answered, "Yes, sir." Then he
said, "I will forgive you; never steal again." Mr. Aplin spoke, saying, "I
want you to recollect that your names are all on the town book, and should
you ever get caught stealing again you will all have to go to prison. Mr.
Dorr is a gentleman, and has forgiven you for what you have done. If he
was like some men, you would be marched from here to prison. Now you
may go; but remember, never be caught doing such acts again." I don't
think any of the boys have practiced stealing since. It had great effect on
me, and I have had no desire to steal since. Soon after this happened Mr.
Perry, our teacher, got married and moved away, and we could not procure,
a teacher for some time. I was then about twelve years old, had learned to
write a good hand. The colored people, under the leadership of Minor Hall,
a Methodist man, formed a society, each member paying into the treasury
25 cents a month. This money was given to a committee of three to buy
lottery tickets, and as none of them could write they took me into the
society, promising that if I would do their writing they would not charge me
any fees, and I should have a share of whatever they drew. I promised to do
so. This practice was followed up, buying tickets as fast as they could get
the funds, but drawing nothing, until they got weary of paying out and
getting nothing in, and gave it up. Afterwards, I suggested to my comrade
boys, to organize a society and have a bank, each member to pay in six
cents per month until money enough was raised to purchase instruments to
learn to play on. This suggestion met their approval, and twelve of the best
boys we could find were selected for the purpose. There names were
Charles Cozzens, George C. Willis, Charles B. Burrill, Isaac B. Bowen, Jr.,
Samuel Brown, Daniel Wiley, William J. Brown, Wm. K. Howland, Isaac
Robinson, George W. Gardiner, Cæsar H. Gardner, and Henry Banister.
Afterwards, two more were received to our number, James Gumes and
Gilbert D. Gardiner; after which we concluded to have a treasurer, and I
was chosen. We held meetings every Tuesday night, in, front of Rev. Mr.
Edes's church, and appointed a committee to find a place where we could
hold our meetings when the weather became cold. A vote was then passed
that the boys who joined our company should use no bad language and keep
no bad company, also, to keep ourselves from the company of boys whose
characters were not good, and if any of our members were in trouble to do
what we possible could to get them out; if any were sick and had no parents,
to see that they were cared for in some good family; if any got sick, whose
parents did not reside in the city, safely to convey them to their parents, and
if any got arrested and locked up, as soon as it became known, to draw

some money and pay for their release; as they had a law to arrest any one they caught in a row at night and put them in the watch-house, and if no one appeared before nine in the morning, and paid a dollar for their release, they were carried to the work-house for two weeks to pick oakum. And for a second offence, and if no one came and paid their fines they were sent to the work-house for four weeks, and received two dozen lashes on their nude back, at the whipping post. Soon after we were orginized, we learned that a military company from Philadelphia were going to pay a visit to our city, and were to be accompanied by a colored band, led by Henry Johnson. We were very glad to learn this, as we had never seen or heard a full band play, and did not know what instruments to purchase. By seeing them we would learn what kind we should need. We had, what was called in those days, a band playing field music, consisting of a bugle, played by a man named Hamilton, two claronets, two trombones, one French horn, two fifes, one bass drum, and two kettle drums—eleven pieces in all. This was the only band we ever heard or knew of. The day arrived, and the company made their appearance, bringing with them Frank Johnson's band, consisting of twenty-six pieces. The company was received by the Rhode Island Infantry, at the steamboat wharf, on the west side of Carrington's block, foot of Transit street. The Philadelphia company was brought up at the foot of Transit street and formed, the Infantry taking the right of the line. They marched up South Main street, led by Hamilton's band of eleven pieces. The leader, a tall Irishman, possessed of more pride than wisdom. When near Market Square, Johnson's band opened with music such as never before, in my recollection, graced the city of Providence. Reaching the City Hotel they dismissed and went in to refresh themselves. Some of the gentlemen told Hamilton that he could not begin to play with the colored band's leader. He replied that Johnson's bugle was much better than his. The gentlemen wished them to change with each other, which they did. Johnson took his bugle and beat him. This made him so angry that he struck Johnson, and with an oath threw his bugle on the floor. Johnson being the shorter and stouter man of the two, immediately knocked him down. The people were obliged to put a stop to the affray, condemning Hamilton for his conduct towards the former, and commending Johnson for knocking him down, because he deserved it. The company finished their visit, enjoying themselves very much, and accompanied by their band were escorted down to the wharf and sailed for Philadelphia. Our band learned what instruments were needed, and made arrangements to purchase them, but the weather began to be so cold it became necessary to have a place to hold our meetings in. So we took our funds, and built a small room 10 by 12 feet on Benevolent street, where Brook street came through, on the south side. We bought a stove and put it in to warm the room. We were now well situated, and held our meetings once a week, although we had no instructor. I had an inclination to visit New York, and obtained father's and mother's permission from Capt. George Childs, commander of the sloop Venus, to work my passage on and back, promising when I returned to go errands for him whenever he wished. I went on board the day before she sailed. John Smith, the cook, a friend of father, showed me how to perform the duty of a steward. He took me in the cabin and showed me how to make up beds, (there being thirty two berths,) clean the cabin, etc., set the tables, which I did to their satisfaction, and put things in good order, then went on deck and helped to get in readiness to sail. We got under way and cleared for New York, where we arrived after a seven days' sail, being heavy ladened, with a light wind nearly all the way. We laid there three weeks, then shipped a cargo and returned. While I was away the committee found a white man willing to teach school and hired him. Captain Childs took a great liking to me, and wanted me to live with him. Father said he was willing, providing he would give me my victuals and clothing, and schooling one half each day, which he consented to do, but I was to sleep at home. I went and liked very well. The captain and his wife were very fine people. He was tall, straight, good looking, and well dressed. She was handsome and very kind. They had two children, a boy and a girl, Frances and George by name, three and four year old. My work was very light, such as going, on errands, etc. They had just moved into the upper part of a house corner of John and Hope streets. We took our meals all at the same time. I learned that Mrs. Childs formerly belonged to a Methodist church, but being young and, gay had neglected her religious duties, until she began to think she never was a Christian. She soon changed her mind and became favorable to the Universalist religion. The captain was fond of amusing himself, and as I was a dry kind of a boy, he asked me "what I thought of the Universalist religion?" I told him I did not know much about them but some said that everybody would be saved, let them be ever so bad. The Bible says no man can serve God and man; if he clings to the one, be will hate the other. Now if you believe all will be saved, I don't. You certainly can't; you swear too much. This pleased him, and he began to tell the merits of the Universalists, and asked, "if I thought such a good being as God would burn up people after he had made them." I answered, "The Bible says the wicked shall be turned into hell, with all the nations that forget God. I am satisfied to believe what the Bible says." He could get no more out of me; so he left me. Mrs. Childs wanted a cook, so she hired one from Newport to come and live with her, by the name of Abby Young. Abby thought because I was a colored boy that I was obliged to wait on her and mind her. She soon commenced ordering me about. I obeyed for a time to see what she was trying to do. at last I told her I didn't come to wait on her, I was working for Mrs. Childs. She threatened to report me. I told her I didn't care what she did. So she then asked Mrs. Childs if Bill could do what she wanted done. Mrs. Childs said "yes, if you can get him to." I was listening, and heard the conversation. She came out and said, "Mrs. Childs says you must do what I tell you." "Yes,"I said, "if you can get me to do it." She perceived that I had heard the conversation, and stopped troubling me.

When I was sent on an errand I generally took my own time. When Mrs. Childs wanted an errand done quick she would send me just before meal time. I noticed mornings, when I returned, Abby would have my coffee poured out and prepared for me, saying, "Bill, your coffee is all warm and ready for you." I thought it very curious that she should be paying so much attention to me, all at once, for I knew she set no great store by me; so one morning when sent on an errand, I made good speed back, and as the kitchen door was ajar, I peeped in, saw Miss Abby take the children's coffee slops, after they had been playing with their fingers in it, pour it in a bowl, drop a little fresh milk in it, and set it down by the fire. When she got all through, I went in in great haste, and she said, "Come Bill, get your breakfast, I want to finish cleaning the table off." "Oh, yes," I said, and walked to the pantry, and took a cup and saucer. When she asked what I was going to do with that cup and saucer. I said, "I am going to get some coffee." "Here is your coffee," said she, "I have kept it warm at the fire for you." I told her "I was not going to drink that coffee. I was going to help myself out of the coffee pot." Mrs. Child's hearing the noise, came out to see what was the trouble. She told Mrs. Childs what she had done, and I had refused to drink the coffee. Mrs. Childs asked the reason why I would not drink it. I told her that Abby had been in the habit of pouring out my coffee, and I suspected it was not done with any good intent; so I hastened home, and caught her pouring the children's coffee slops into a bowl, then putting a little fresh milk in it, and set it by the fire to keep warm for me to drink. Now if I can't have clean coffee to drink I will go home. She tried to deny it, but I was looking in at the time and saw her. Mrs. Childs told her not to trouble Bill's coffee anymore, and let him help himself to anything he wants. At twelve o'clock Capt. Child's came to his dinner. His custom was to remain home until three, but he told his wife he must go back as soon as he had finished his dinner. Mrs. Childs said, "why must you go immediately back; what is your hurry?" "I have $700 of the owner's money in my pocket, which I intended to leave at the office, but came in a hurry and forgot to leave it." "If that is all," she said, "let Bill take it down." He said, "I dare not trust it with him, for fear he will lose it, or some boy take it away from him." Mrs. Childs said, "I'll risk Bill; he won't lose it and no one can take it away from him." So the Captain called me to come and get my dinner right away, and get ready to go to the office. She said "No; let him go before dinner. If you give him his dinner now, he won't return until the middle of the afternoon." "If that is the case," said the Captain, "then start right away now, Bill." Taking the package from his breast pocket, be handed it to me, saying, "Now, Bill, there are $700 in this package; don't you open it, or stop to talk with any of the boys, but carry it right to Potter & Eddy's store, and tell either of the firm that may be there, that there is $700 in the package, freight money, which I intended to leave at the store, but came off to my dinner and forgot it. Now go down just as quick as you can go." I answered, "Yes, sir," and put the package in my pocket, starting off on the run. In a short time I arrived at the store, saw Mr. Eddy in the office, and gave it to him, also delivered my message. He opened and examined the package and exclaimed, "all right." I immediately started for home. On my way back I commenced thinking of the Captain's words, "go as quick as you can," but said to myself he never said a word about coming back quick; now I am not going to hurry myself; I am going to take my time, and I will break up this foolishness. Pretty soon it will get so every time they want me to go an errand they will send me off before I can eat, so as to make me go and come back quick. The fact is, the old woman is half right, its no mistake, for I don't hurry myself when I get away from the house, but that's neither here nor there. I don't want to be sent off every time before dinner or breakfast is ready, and I will not hurry myself back. If they say anything to me when I return, I will say to them you told me to hurry down there, and I did, but you said not a word about coming back quick; it is a very hot day and I ran so fast that I took my time coming back. I thought this would be a good excuse, so I walked along leisurely till I arrived at William street, looking for a good place to rest. Having crossed Thayer street, I stretched myself full length on the grass face downward, playing with the spears of grass, until I fell asleep. How long I slept I cannot tell, but not coming back as soon as the Captain expected, he began to be uneasy, and went to the window several times to see if he could see me coming, but as I had not come in sight he said to his wife, "Surely, something has happened to the boy." She, too, began to be alarmed, on account of my long absence, and said to him, "You had better go and see what has become of him." He put on his hat and coat and started to look for me. Coming up William street, he discovered me lying prostrate on the grass, and putting his foot on my back shook me, saying, "Bill." I awoke, and at first could not tell what was shaking me. He again shook me saying "Bill, Bill." I knew his voice, and with a low, grumbling sound, said, "Be still, be still." "Are you asleep," he said. "No sir, be still." He said, "What are you doing?" "Listening, listening." Listening for what," he said. I answered, "To see what plants are coming up here next year." Not understanding what I said, I raised up my head and said, "To see what plants are coming up here next year." He burst into a laugh, and said, "What have you done with the money." "Oh, I carried that long ago, and he said it was all right." The Captain said, "If that is so, listen on, then," and left me to go to the vessel. I jumped up and went home. Mrs. Childs asked me where I had been so long, and if I saw the captain." I said "I had, the money was all right, and I stopped to listen." She asked what I stopped to listen for? I said, "Oh, nothing more than I wanted to see what plants were coming up next year among the grass." She said, "Bill you are a curious genius, go eat your dinner." I did without a second bidding. Shey took care never to send me again before dinner. During my stay there, Mrs. Childs had a son, and they called his name Edwin Forrest. The captain's mother, who resided in Warren, came and stayed three months, during Mrs. Childs's illness. She was getting ready to go home, and was to leave the following Monday morning. The Sunday before she was to leave we were all sitting at the breakfast table, with an addition of two extra ones—Captain Childs's brother Nathan and Mrs. Childs's sister Jane. The Captain was telling about a new play they had in New York, with which the people were much pleased, describing it, to give them an idea of the play. It had been played two or three weeks in succession. The Captain's mother was an elderly lady, and listening to the description the Captain had given, exclaimed, "I would like to see that play." Mrs. Childs said, "Why, Bill knows a song about Cold Black Rose." The Captain said, "Do you know that song, Bill?" I replied ,"yes sir." The Captain said, "well sing it for us." I told him I could not sing it, that the day was Sunday. He replied, "what of that; there is no harm in singing it. I answered,"I do not sing songs on Sunday for anybody." The Captain's mother said, "Now you will sing it for me, Billy." I told her, yes ; I would sing it for her on the morrow. She said "I am going away to-morrow morning early, and I want to hear it to-day." Then I answered, "you will not hear me sing it, for I am not going to sing songs on Sunday for any one, whether they are pleased or displeased." Captain Nathan offered me half a dollar to sing it. I told them they needn't ask me any more, for I would not break the Sabbath to please any one. They could neither coax or hire me, so they ceased troubling me.The baby was now six or seven months old. Mrs. Childs said to me one day, "I have business for you this summer." I asked what it was. "To take care of my baby and rock it in the cradle." "Very well," I replied, thinking all the time that I was not going to rock anybody's baby. Abby had gone on a visit to Newport, so the duties of

washing the dishes and cleaning fell to me. The next morning after breakfast and I had done up all the work, Mrs. Childs came in and said, "I am
going to get the baby to sleep, and lay it in the cradle, and I want you to sit
by it, and if he wakes up, rock him; I have got you a book to read, Bill,
while you sit by the baby." I said, "yes ma'am." She knew I was fond of
reading, and brought the book to interest me. Her son George was a mis-
chievous boy and did pretty much as he had a mind ; no one could do
anything with him but myself, and I expected the baby would be much the
same in regard to behavior, and if I had anything to do with him I would
break him of those bad tricks. While Mrs. Childs was getting him to sleep, I
slipped down the back stairs, cut me a stick about fifteen inches long, and
shaved down all the knots, so as to make it perfectly smooth, repeating the
words which my father used when preparing sticks to whip me and my
brothers with, for not obeying him, "I will smoothe these knots down for I
am not going to tear your hide but tingle it." After preparing my stick, I ran
it up my sleeve, and went into take charge of the baby. She placed a small
rocking chair by the side of the cradle, and I took the book and watched
Mrs. Childs to see what she was going to do. She fixed her hair before the
glass, and said, "I am going down stairs to see Mrs. Burr, the lady living on
the first floor. After she went out, I commenced reading and continued
reading for an hour and a half, while the baby slept and came to a very
interesting part of the story, when the baby awoke. I rocked him and tried to
get him to sleep again; the more I tried to soothe him the worse he acted. I
said to myself, he has got to be broken of this, and I might as well begin, or
he will be like the other children, and wouldn't mind any one; so I began
scolding him. That made him still worse. I turned down the covering, took
my stick, and put it on to him. He kicked and hollored. I heard Mrs.
Childs's step on the stairs, and I ran my stick up my sleeve and began to
coax him. She came in and asked me what the matter was with the baby? I
replied, "the dear little creature is afraid of me, I think." She said, "I guess
not." I said, "Oh, I guess he must be, for Iam black you know, and he ain't
used to me." She said, "Well, he has got to get used to you"; and taking him
out of the cradle said, "you may go out now, Bill." The next day I was
called again to the cradle. The babe after sleeping awhile, began again to
kick up and holler. I didn't coax him much; but gave him a little dressing
down, and after awhile he got easy. Soon after Mrs. Childs came and
relieved me of my charge, saying, "he didn't act so bad to-day as he did
yesterday." I replied, "no ma'am; I guess we will bring him to." The third
day I was called on duty again. When he awoke I shook my stick and spoke
to him. He began to snuffle, so I gave him two or three cuts on the quilt, he
opened his eyes, looked at me, as much as to say, do you mean it? and

soon became calm. When Mrs. Childs got ready, she came up stairs, and looking in the cradle, beheld the baby wide awake, playing with his fingers. She exclaimed, "Why Bill, you have got this baby so that he likes to lay in the cradle. I guess he loves you." "Oh, yes" I said; "I have not the least doubt but that he loves me." I had no occasion to use the stick any more, and Mrs. Childs had no occasion to get him to sleep. I would say to her, "Lay him in the cradle, I will take care of him." She did so, and if he began to make a noise, I would shake my finger at him and that would be sufficient. When she had him in her lap, and he made any noise, she would call me and I had only to take him, or speak to him, and it was all over, he would be silent. She often told her company, when they called, how attached the baby was to me. He turned out to be the best child she had. When he was 18 months old, she took a notion to go to New York with her husband. I heard them talk about going, and say, "we must have Bill go by all means." I did not care to go. They asked me if I would like to go to New York. I said I would not. I asked if Abby was going. They said she was, but they wanted me to go because I could manage the baby better than any one else. I told her I had no clothes suitable to wear. When the Captain came to dinner, she told him what I had said. The Captain called me and wanted to know the reason I could not go. I said, the first was, I didn't want to, and the second I had no suitable clothes to wear. He was very crafty and knew just how to take hold of me. He said "Bill, when you wanted to go to New York, I let you go to accommodate you, and treated you well, did I not?" "Yes, sir," I replied. Now Mrs. Childs wants you to go to accommodate her, because the baby loves you, and you can get along first rate, and I want you to go because Mrs. Childs wants to be accommodated; one good turn deserves another, does it not?" I said "Yes, sir." "Won't you go with us to New York." I said, "yes, sir, providing you furnish me with some nice clothes, to go with; I don't want to disgrace myself." He said, "go down to Joseph Mason's shop and tell him to take your measure for a pair of calf skin square-toed shoes, what else do you want?" "I want two or three pair of white socks, and two pair of pantloons, two vests and two jackets, and a new hat, and a fife." The Captain said, "Anything else?" I told him "no sir." He said, "get yourself ready, for we shall go in ten days; and I will have your things for you." I went that same afternoon, and got measured for a pair of shoes. They got all my things for me except a hat and fife ; he said he would get them in New York, and asked if that would satisfy me. I said it would. When the time arrived we went on board, about ten o'clock in the morning. When we were well under way, I said, in the presence of Abby, "I expect to be sick." She said, "don't you go to being sick; Mrs. Childs and myself are going to be sick, and you have got to take care of the baby." I wanted to find out what they intended to do, and that was just what I wanted to learn. The day was beautiful, and I walked about enjoying myself until about five in the afternoon. I then went down and got into one of the lower berths, and laid with my shoes sticking out of the berth. The Captain came into the cabin, and noticing my feet, said to the steward, "whose feet are those sticking out?" He said, "your Bill." The Captain said, "what is the matter, Bill?" I told him I was sea-sick. He said, "take your shoes and put them under the berth, if that is the case." I obeyed, for that was what I wanted. I had no trouble with the baby during the passage. When we arrived in New York, I did not forget to speak to the captain about my hat and fife. The next day the captain went up into the city and bought a white fur hat, which he paid four dollars and a half for. I told him I did not want a white hat. What a curious taste you have said he. He told Jack, the cook, to go with me, take the hat back, and let me select one for myself. The next day Jack and myself went to the store, and I selected a hat to suit my taste; the price was $1.87. On my return the captain asked if I was suited. I said, "yes, sir." He laughed when I told him the price. The next was my fife, which I spoke of to him. He asked the price. I said one that would cost $1.50 would answer. He asked if I was willing to take round a paper and get it by subscription. I told him I had no objections. He drew one up, which read as follows: "The bearer has came to the conclusion that he is blessed with a musical talent, and desiring to obtain an instrument suitable to his taste, and not having the means to obtain one, is obliged to call on the public to accomplish his object, and if ever he should be caught in the war, he will endeavor to console and comfort the wounded by his melodious notes." He then signed twenty-five cents, and gave me the paper. I handed it to Captain George Brown first. He asked me if Captain Childs drew up the paper. I said, "yes, sir." He laughed and signed his name and gave twenty-five cents. I passed it around to several of the captains. They all gave me something. I ended with Captain Nathan Childs, who after reading the paper, said, "come into my cabin about eight o'clock to-night and bring your paper. I am going to have company there this evening. We will see what we can do for you." I told him I would. In the evening I went to his cabin. There was a large company of gentlemen and ladies present. They read my paper, passed it around, and then laid it on the table. They wanted me to sing a song. I noticed a storm coming up, when I went on board. I sung a song, and it commenced to rain hard, I felt anxious to go, but they asked me to sing another, and another. When I was in the middle of a song, there came a heavy clap of thunder, and it lightened very sharp, which so terrified me that I stopped singing. They wanted me to continue singing. I told them I could not sing anymore. They tried to persuade me, but I said no, and was about to go back to my shop, without stopping for money or anything else. They saw how scared I was, and made up the amount of four or five dollars for me. I went to our shop, and was enabled to purchase my fife for $1.25. We started for home in a few days, where we arrived in safety. Abby went home to stay awhile, and a portion of her work was assigned to me, such as setting the table, washing up dishes, etc. Whilst doing that, I thought I would examine the closet, and see what I could find by way of good things. I could not discover anything but a little loaf sugar and a demijohn. I found it nearly full. I poured some out and found it was liquor. I helped myself to some and put it back again. After finishing my work I took another taste of it. I undertook to get my wood for the night. I began to feel very happy, and began to sing. I brought an armful up, but part of it fell down stairs. The noise it made brought Mrs. Burr to see what the matter was. I apologized for the noise, saying I accidentally dropped some wood. The next armful I dropped some wood again. This brought Mrs. Childs to the head of the stairs. She discovered that something was the matter with me, and asked me if I had been drinking any liquor. I told her I had been tasting a little. She told me I had better go home. I remembered hearing people say that when a person was intoxicated, if they ran fast, people would not notice it. I came out the rear door, and started on the run for William street; got home as soon as possible and went to bed ; was sick all night. In the morning I got up and went to my work, feeling bad enough and ashamed, for I knew they must have seen me when I was going home. I determined never to be caught so again.

When I reached the house in the morning, Mrs. Childs told me to go down in the kitchen and make a fire, as the woman was coming to wash. I was busy in making my fire, when Mr. Burr, the gentleman that lived in the lower tenement, put his head in the door and said, "Take care, Billy, don't let the fire get down your throat, and don't get too near, for your breath may take fire." Then I knew that they had all seen me, so I braced myself up and prepared for the worst. At the breakfast table Capt. Childs took me to do, saying, "Bill, I have heard some very bad news about you, and am very sorry to hear it. I thought you was very pious awhile ago; we tried to coax and hire you to sing 'Cold Black Rose' to my mother; you would not because it was Sunday. Mother was going away Monday morning, and she wanted to hear it very much, and you would not gratify her nor Mrs. Childs nor me, and my brother Nathan tried to hire you, and you wouldn't, because you was so religious. And you are running down Universalist people, thinking you are better than they are. Now, I understand, last night you was so drunk you could not walk straight. I don't think, your religion is as good as Universalist religion, and I am ashamed of you; ain't you?"

I said, "Yes, sir, I am so devilish ashamed I don't want to hear any more about it, and I ain't going to do so again." This set them all to laughing, and they didn't trouble me any more about being drunk. That act had a good influence upon me, for I then saw the folly of becoming a slave to liquor.

Our school was again broke up, the teacher moving from the city. My father said he wanted me to get through my studies, my progress was too slow, going only half a day. He wanted me to go all the time, of course I had to leave my place for that purpose.

CHAPTER IV.

By the request of my father I left Captain Childs and made preparations to go to school regularly, until I should complete my studies. The following week I entered Mr. John Lawton's school, kept in the brick school-house on Meeting street. He occupied the lower room in the building, and kept a private school. He had kept there for many years, and was called an excellent teacher, but his health was so feeble that he was unable to continue his school more than two quarters after I entered. He then broke up and went to live with his son in Newport.

The next man that took the school was Mr. John G. L. Haskins, a white preacher in the Methodist Church. In his school I began to cipher, using Daboll's Arithmetic. It was a hard study and required a strong mind and a clear head to master it. Father told me that if I paid for my own schooling, and wished to stop a day or two, I could do so; but if he paid it, I must go every day so as to finish my studies and go to work. I preferred to pay for my own schooling, which was three dollars a quarter. I also joined the evening class, paying one dollar and fifty cents a quarter, and twenty-five cents for ink and pens, which the teacher supplied us with. When the money for the quarter became due, I had no money to meet it, and told the teacher that, having no money, I thought I had better stop. He said I was improving very fast and had better keep on with my studies, as I was in the first class, and used an English reader and Walker's dictionary, which I was to purchase as soon as I could get the means, as I had to borrow. My friend James Gumes, a lad much younger than myself, also owed for a quarter's schooling. Mr. Haskins was anxious to have us continue in the school, and he gave us a job of sawing wood to encourage us. We got our saws sharpened by James's uncle for nothing, for he wanted to help us. The wood was walnut, and hard to saw. It was cold winter weather and the wood was covered with snow, and James got very sick of his job, and declared he would never saw wood for anybody any more. I had to saw a greater part of the wood in order to finish it. But it was no difficult task for me as I had been accustomed to saw wood ever since I was eight years old.

The second quarter became due, and I had not paid my first quarter.

James was also in arrears. We made up our minds to leave, but Mr. Haskins coaxed us to stay, and still continued to dun us, saying: "Can't you bring me a little this afternoon?" I would tell him I had no possible prospect of getting anything, and had better stop coming. But James was very tender-hearted, and would say: "I don't know, I will try;" and that kept him always dunning us. My bill had run up to two quarters day schooling, and three quarters night, and money also for ink and pens, in amount eleven dollars and twenty-five cents. I had no means of paying this, and I wanted books and a pair of shoes. I made up my mind to stop.

The next Monday I expected he would tease me again for the money, and I asked mother to lend me some. She told me to go to father, for she had no money. I was ashamed to do this, because I had undertaken to pay my own way. My bill got so large that cousin Lydia, who was staying at my house, asked mother if she had twenty-five cents; if so, give it to William, and she gave me twenty-five cents more, saying, "Go and buy a ticket as you go to school." I stopped at Mr. Baker's lottery office and purchased a ticket. Everybody bought tickets at that time, as it was very fashionable. The teacher again asked for money, but I hadn't any. I continued going to school until Thursday morning, when he talked so pitiful, I told him I would try and get some in the afternoon. At noon I made my teacher's wants known to mother, and she said, "You ought not to have undertaken to pay for your schooling; you must go to your father." Not being able to raise any, I started off toward the school-house. I hardly knew whether it was best to go or not, or what I should tell him. I passed Mr. Baker's lottery office and cast my eyes in. Thinking I had better go in; perhaps I might have drawn a little something, I went, and asked Mr. Baker what my ticket which I had purchased Monday had drawn? He said, "What was the class, and what the numbers?" I told him, and, looking over his books, said, "You little skunk, you have drawn seventy dollars, where is your ticket?" I told him it was at home, and I would get it, which I quickly did. I gave it to him, and he gave me the money, taking out the draw-back. I then went over to Mr. Wilcox's store and purchased an English Reader, a Walker's Dictionary, a quill, a nice pen-knife, a plated-top ink stand, a sand box, a quire each of blue, pink, yellow and white paper, and a box of wafers. Having them all done up, I went to the school-house. I opened my packages, took out the things I had bought and put them in my box.

Mr. Haskins came up to my desk, saying, "Well, Billy, you have made a raise." I replied, "yes, sir." He said, "Have you brought me some change; can't you spare me a little." I answered, "Yes, sir; make out your bill in full." Mr. Haskins immediately did so. He then asked, "How much shall I credit you with?" I said, "Receipt the bill in full," at the same time taking

out my pocket-book I had purchased. He stood amazed, and looked at me a
few moments, and exclaimed, "Where did you get so much money; I hope
you have not got it wrongfully. I would rather give you your schooling than
have you take a cent wrongfully." Every head was raised, an every eye in
school was on me, waiting to hear my reply. I very coolly and deliberately
answered, "Oh, no, sir, I think myself above that." "But," said the teacher,
"where did you get it?" After hesitating a few moments, I explained how I
came by the money, which relieve him very much. I then made up my mind
that for the future I would try to keep out of debt, and to search around to
find some jobs to do between school hours and on Saturdays, to enable me
to finish my studies, and learn some kind of a trade. The next day I had a
call to saw and split two cords of wood for Capt. Harding, commander of a
Philadelphia packet. It was at his house on Bridge street, in the lower part of
the town. I agreed to do the work, and commenced the next morning, as he
wanted the work done before he sailed. I thought I would give my friend
James Gumes a chance to earn a little money, so that he could pay his
school bill. I called on him and told him the job I had got, and asked him to
help me, and he should receive half of the money. His mother was very glad
that I called on him, and said, "You are not like some boys, that wish to get
everything themselves, and don't care about their neighbors. You have got a
good principle in you, and I hope it will always continue; for in helping
yourself, you always like to help others." Gumes agreed to help me. I told
him to be ready at five o'clock in the morning, and I would call for him, and
at seven o'clock we would go home to our breakfast. I told him it would be
a very warm day, and we must do as much as we could in the morning. It
was then in the latter part of June. I called the next morning little before five
o'clock. Gumes was not up. I knocked at the door, and aroused him up. He
was inclined to wait until after breakfast before he went. I was opposed to
that, and told him he must save time as much as possible, for the man
wanted his work done as soon as possible, and if we didn't do it he would
get some one else, and losing half an hour or so would put us back; so we
commenced on our work. About half-past six Gumes got hungry, and said
he couldn't work without having something in him to work on, and it was
with great difficulty that I could get him to work until the clock struck
seven. Then we stopped work and went to breakfast, agreeing to return at a
quarter before eight, taking three quarters of an hour for breakfast. I had
twice the distance to go that he had to reach home. I ate my breakfast and
returned to Gumes's house; he had not had his breakfast, and I was delayed
again, and it was half-past eight before we got at our work again. We
worked on until the clock struck ten, when Guines had to stop and get some
water. After an absence of a quarter of an hour he returned. At half-past ten

he went again. When he returned he worked for a quarter of an hour or so, and commenced complaining of the heat, and said he was never going to saw wood in the summer time again for any one.

I said to him, "Last winter you said you was not going to saw wood for any one in the winter, and now you find fault with the summer. I see that you are not used to sawing wood. Now as soon as the clock strikes eleven, you had better knock off and go to splitting the wood—I will finish sawing it," for I had come to the conclusion that I would have nearly all the sawing to do. He commenced splitting. I finished up the sawing at about two o'clock. We were getting along so fast we thought we would not go to dinner, but finish the job. Our work was complete by five o'clock. We went into the house to receive our pay. I said to Gumes, "I don't want you to say anything at all, I am going, to do the talking," and he agreed not to interfere. I said "You commenced to work at eleven and quit at five o'clock, which is six hours. We had ten cents an hour for splitting and fifty cents a cord for sawing wood; your work comes to sixty cents for splitting." Gumes said that was correct. When we had got into the house, I said to the lady, "We have done your work, and put it in the cellar as agreed." She asked me what the price was? I replied, $1.90. Gumes said, "It ain't so much as that." I told him it was. Gumes said, "Oh, well, no need in cheating the woman." Those remarks made my very angry, and I told him to please mind his business, I knew what I was doing. The lady said, "Come, don't go to quarreling here; you had better go to the Captain and let him pay you." After we got out of the house, I said, "Gumes, what under the sun do you mean ? Did you want to make that lady believe I was cheatiing her? I didn't want you to say anything, for I knew you would make just such a blunder." He replied, "Well, you were cheating her." I said, " What do we have for sawing wood, and what did this come to?" He said, "The sawing was one dollar." I said, "What did your splitting come to for six hours?" He said, "Sixty cents, and that was what the bill was." I asked him what time I left off sawing? He said, "Two o'clock." "What did my splitting come to for three hours? Don't that make the bill $1.90? He said he forgot my splitting. I said to him, "You are a clever fellow, an honest fellow; but you have a curious way of showing it. You look at but one side of the thing, and by so doing, you make trouble for other folks and yourself, too." Gumes was a very peaceable and honest man, and he carried that trait of character with him during his entire life.

The next day we went aboard the Captain's vessel, to settle. I made off the Captain's bill and presented it. After reading it he asked me how much my bill was. I said "That is my bill, $1.90." He said "But what is your part alone?" I said, "We work together, in partnership, and have fifty cents a cord for sawing wood, and ten cents an hour for splitting it. We sawed two cords, which was one dollar, and split nine hours which is ninety cents." The Captain said the sawing is one dollar. I replied, "Yes, sir," "And how long did you split?" "Three hours, and Gumes six hours." Then he said "Your splitting and sawing amounts to $1.30." Then counting it out, handed it to me, saying, "This pays you." Then to Gumes he said, "I am not going to give you ten cents an hour; you ain't worth it. My wife said she sat at the window during the time you was working, and she said you was a lazy lubber. Brown did nearly all the sawing, and in three hours split as much as you did in the six; besides, every little while you would run off somewhere, so I shall pay you but six cents an hour, which is thirty-six cents. You ought to be ashamed of yourself, to let that little fellow do twice as much work as you, when you ought, by good rights, to do twice as much as he." Gumes said, "He is older than I am." The Captain said, "I know better." Gumes said, "He is, sir; ain't you, Brown?" I replied, "Yes, I am." "How much older," said the Captain. "Four years." The Captain said, "No wonder you couldn't do any work; you are all legs; you grow too fast. Go home and tell your mother to put a big flat stone on your head to stop your growing so fast.

We left the Captain, and I divided my money with him. He then said, "You need not come after me to saw any more wood, for I am not able to saw wood and I ain't going to for anybody." I soon had another call to saw, split and pile up six cord of wood. The sawing was three dollars, and the splitting two. I finished it in four days. I soon found that I need not again be caught in such circumstances as I had been, for the people gave me a great many jobs at that time, and I was known as the "little wood sawyer."

Our society continued holding meetings, and we decided to abandon the idea of having a band, for we learned that we could not get such instruments as we wanted for less than $150, and we could put our money to a better use. We then increased our number of members, and used our funds to assist each other in case of sickness, according as they should be in need. So we called a meeting on the 17th of June, 1828, and organized under a constitution, having a preamble, setting forth our intentions and our constitution for government, making provision for the appointment of officers for the government of the society. I was appointed president, Charles Cozzens treasurer, and Samuel Brown secretary. The constitution made provision for a committee of seven, five of whom were a quorum, for the transaction of all business. The name of the society was the "Young Men's Union Funds Society."

Our numbers increased, and we held our meetings every Tuesday. We passed resolutions that if any male citizens died to attend their funerals, out of respect, as well as attending the funerals of our own members; and if any female society wished our attendance, we would escort them. Our uniform was dark dress coat, white pantaloons and white gloves, with a gilded star with blue ribbon attached to it on the left breast; and a blue roll fifteen inches long, with a gilt edge three inches long. As we admitted no spectators to our room, we kept our business to ourselves. The people became very suspicious of us. This made us the more anxious to keep our business a secret.

We soon became the gossip of the city. Some said it could be for no good object that we met every week. Finally, William Scott, one of our members, died. The society sent a committee to Mrs. Scott to ascertain if it would be agreeable to her for us to attend in society order, as he was a member. She consented to our request. Accordingly at the appointed hour the society under command of our Marshall, James A. Gumes, attended the funeral in a body and formed in line in front of the house. When the procession was ready to move the society took up their line of march in front, and when the procession returned we opened to the right and left, with raised hats, until the procession passed through, then passed on. This was our first appearance in public, and it attracted great attention. The applications for membership among the young men of our town were numerous. There was one other society among the colored people, the Mutual Relief Society, and consisted of elderly and settled persons, and had been formed two years previous. Their object was to assist each other in case of sickness and distress—a very worthy object.

In reference to our meeting house and school room: It was commenced in 1819 and finished in 1821, and was dedicated to the worship of Almighty God in 1822. It had been finished and in use six years prior to the time of our society's turnout. It had a nice audience room capable of accommodating five hundred persons, so that the first Baptist with all other churches which had separate seats to accommodate colored people, were forsaken except by a few, who, still holding their membership with those churches, felt it their duty to attend. The school room was also well filled up, and would accommodate from 150 to 200 scholars. At the time of the church dedication the colored people made great preparations to celebrate the day. A committee met at the house of Hodge Congdon, on Benefit street, to make arrangements for a suitable acknowledgement of their gratification.

The young colored men formed a military company (called the African Greys) to escort the African societies to their new house of worship. The procession in line of march was to pass Meeting street by the Friend's meeting house. There the Friends were to join the society and the procession move up to Meeting street church, where the service of dedication was to be performed. The Friends were not aware they were to have a company escort them. When the procession arrived in front of where the Freinds were to join them, seeing they had a band of music and a military company to escort them, they refused to join in with them, preferring to go by themselves.

The African societies wore their regalias. The president of the societies, who was their commander, was dressed to represent an African chief, having on a red pointed cap, and carried an elephant's tusk in his hand; each end was tipped with gilt. The other officers carrying emblems, decked with lemons and oranges, representing the fruits of Africa, and other emblems. The military company wore black belts and carried muskets, and the officers with their side arms. When they reached the meeting house they were informed that Mr. Brown was opposed to having arms carried into the house; so they were stacked outside, while the company marched in. After the services were closed the company paraded the streets, commanded by Col. Geo. Barrett, a man well posted in military tactics, and had attended some military officer, from whom he acquired his knowledge; and it was said that General Carrington procured his services when he was ordered to take a post off Fox Point, which the colored people had voluntarily thrown up to receive a British frigate, which threatened to come up the river. Finding there was a fort erected and commanded by Black Cloud in readiness to give them a warm reception, they declined the visit.

This same Col. Barrett, when marching with the African Greys, arrived at Market Square, and in making a wheel—the streets being covered with ice—slipped and fell down. This was quite amusing to the spectators who were looking on. Just after that accident one of the officers was tapped on the shoulder, and a bill was presented to him by an officer, charging him five dollars for a pair of boots. This was concocted by some men to make sport. The company immediately came to a halt, and after ascertaining the difficulty, Corporal Cato G. Northrup drew out his pocket-book, took out a five dollar bill, and passed it to the officer, and by order of Col. Barret the company resumed their march as if nothing had happened. The trick which they thought would create such beautiful fun, passed off unnoticed.

Now I will speak of the management of our school. Our people continued their school in the meeting house; having organized themselves into a society, hired their own teachers, charging each scholar one dollar and fifty cents a quarter, and agreeing with the teacher that if he could not collect fifty dollars a quarter from the scholars they would make up what was short of the amount. It was frequently the case that at the end of the quarter they would have to collect some money to make up the deficiency. A great many were unable to pay.

The town officers, learning that the colored people were turning their attention to getting houses to live in, concluded that, as they were accumulating property, they should be taxed. So they levied a tax on them. This made a great commotion among them, and they called a meeting in the vestry of our church to consider the propriety or impropriety of paying the tax. The meeting was called to order, and Geo. C. Willis appointed chairman, and Alfred Niger secretary. Several colored gentlemen addressed the meeting, among whom were Messrs. Geo. McCarty, Edward Barnes, Ichabod Northup, James Harris and others. The amount of taxes levied was forty dollars, or near that amount, annually. But very few colored people had any real estate at that time.

After the feeling was understood by those who had spoken, they appointed a committee to meet the next general assembly, and inform them of their disapproval to meet the tax, for they believed taxation and representation went together; and they were unwilling to be taxed and not allowed to be represented. Some of the members of the house said it was perfectly right; if the colored people were to be taxed they should be represented. But the members of the house from Newport were bitterly opposed to colored people being represented, saying: "Shall a Nigger be allowed to go to the polls and tie my vote? No, Mr. Speaker, it can't be. The taxes don't amount to more than forty or fifty dollars; let them be taken off." So the taxes were taken off.

At that time the colored people had little or no protection. It was thought a disgrace to plead a colored man's cause, or aid in getting his rights as a citizen, or to teach their children in schools. The teachers themselves were ashamed to have it known that they taught colored schools.

It was the custom for children on seeing their parish teacher or minister to raise their hats and speak to them, and the girls to make a courtesy. The instruction was taught to them by their parents when small. It was often stated by elderly people that children must be seen and not heard. When company were in the house they were not to make much noise, and when they came into their own house they must take off their hats and sit down. If they did not know enough to take of their hats they would soon teach them that their heads must be uncovered while in the house. They would also teach them, as a general thing, that they must not come to the table to eat their victuals until they were called. They did not allow their children to be the first at the table; and when called they did not suffer them to help themselves, but to wait until they were helped; when they wanted anything always to ask for it, and when they had finished eating to rise from the table and thank their parents. My parents were so strict that they did not allow us to come to the table until they had finished eating; then they would put victuals on our plates and call us. When we came to the table we had to stand up to eat, not to sit down in chairs. We had to eat just what they put on our plate, and to have our plates cleared before we could have them replenished. When in the street to be respectful to every one, and be very careful not to run against any elderly person. If we did we were liable to feel the weight of their cane; also, to be particular when sent on an errand to a person's house, to knock at the door, and when we enter take off our hats and make a low bow, holding our hats in hand until we went out.

We learned this from our spelling books. If we neglected any of these marks of politeness we would be put in mind of our duty by any elderly person who might be passing, first saying to the boy, "Whose boy are you? Where do you live? What are your parent's name?" They would then say to us, "Go home and tell your parents to teach you some manners." When they had said this, the boy or girl had better leave as soon as possible, and show no wry faces or impudent looks, for if you did there would be forthcoming a box on the ear, or a stroke of a cane; and if you went and told your parents, all the satisfaction they would give would be "they served you right; you deserved it." But it was considered such a disgrace for white men to teach colored schools that they would be greatly offended if the colored children bowed or spoke to them on the street. Mr. Anthony, who was at one time teaching the colored school, became very angry because Zebedee Howland met him on the street, spoke to him, raised his hat and bowed. He took no notice of his dark complexioned scholar, but the next Monday morning took poor Zebedee and the whole school to task, saying, "When you meet me on the street, don't look towards me, or speak to me; if you do, I will flog you the first chance I get."

The feeling against the colored people was very bitter. The colored people themselves were ignorant of the cause, unless it could be attributed to our condition, not having the means to raise themselves in the scale of wealth and affluence, consequently those who were evil disposed would offer abuse whenever they saw fit, and there was no chance for resentment or redress. Mobs were also the order of the day, and the poor colored people were the sufferers.

In the northwest part of the city was a place called Addison Hollow, but was nick-named Hardscrabble. A great many colored people purchased land there, because it was some distance from town, and hence quite cheap. They put up small houses for themselves, and earned their living in various ways. They could be seen almost any time, with their saw-horse, standing, some on the Great Bridge, some on Shingle Bridge, and some on Mill Bridge, waiting for work. As hard coal was not known at that time, (except Liverpool coal,) everybody used wood. Some men did jobs of gardening and farming.

A man named Addison built houses, and rented to any one who would give him his price. As he rented cheap, people of bad character hired of him, and these drew a class of bad men and women, so that the good were continually being molested, having no protection. At last disturbances became so common that they raised a mob, and drove many from their houses, then tore them down, took their furniture—what little they had—carried it to Pawtucket, and sold it at auction. This was done late in the fall. One colored man named Christopher Hall, a widower with three or four children, a pious man, bearing a good character, and supported himself and family by sawing wood, had his house torn down by the roughs and stripped of its contents. He drew the roof over the cellar, and lived in it all winter. The people tried in vain to coax him out, and offered him a house to live in. Many went up to see the ruins, among them some white ladies, who offered to take his children and bring them up, but he would not let them go. In the spring following he went to Liberia, on the western coast of Africa. Not long after this there was another mob, commenced at the west end of Olney street. Here were a number of houses built and owned by white men, and rented to any one, white or colored, who wanted to hire one or more rooms, rent payable weekly. Some of these places had bar-rooms, where liquors were dealt out, and places where they sold cakes, pies, doughnuts, &c. These they called cooky stands. In some houses dancing and fiddling was the order of the day. It soon became dangerous for one to pass through there in the day time that did not belong to their gang, or patronize them. Most all sailors who came into port would be introduced into Olney street by some one who had an interest that way. I remember when a boy, passing up one day to my father's garden, which was on that street, in company with two other boys, looking at the people as we passed along. Some were sitting at the windows, some in their doorway, some singing, some laughing, some gossiping, some had their clay furnaces in front of their houses, cooking, and seeing us looking at them, said, "What are you gawking at, you brats?" hurling a huge stone at the same time, and we were obliged to run for our lives. This street had a correspondence with all the sailor boarding houses in town, and was sustained by their patronage. Vessels of every description were constantly entering our port, and sailing crafts were seen from the south side of the Great Bridge to India Point. It was the great shipping port of New England in those days, and although the smallest of all the States, Rhode Island was regarded as among the wealthiest, the Quakers occupying a large portion of the State.

CHAPTER V.

In my last chapter, I had much to say about the condition of the colored people of this State, and the bitter prejudice they were subjected to, and the mobs by which they were surrounded. I will say more in this chapter about sailors, and the influence brought to bear upon them while in port.

There was a sailor boarding house in Power street, kept by a man from Virginia by the name of Jimmie Axum. He was a sailor, every inch of him, and his wife, Hannah, was an Indian woman of the Narrgansett tribe. Uncle Jimmie was a shipping master and a fiddler, and when he failed to entertain sailors, they all knew where to go—Olney street was their next port of entry.

When a ship's crew of sailors came ashore they would all go to Uncle Jimmie's to board, and Uncle Jimmie, with his household, would entertain them with fiddle and tamborine. There would be drinking and dancing throughout the day and evening, and every half hour some one would take a pitcher and go after liquor, which they purchased by the quart or pint. The best of Jamaica rum then sold for nine pence a quart; gin at the same price. Brandy was twenty-five cents a quart.

In those days it was common to drink liquor; everybody used it. Ministers drank and Christians drank. If you were passing on Main or Water street in the morning the common salutation was: "Good morning, Mr. A. or B., won't you walk in and take a glass of brandy or gin?" If men were at work on the wharf, at eleven in the morning and four in the afternoon grog was passed around, consisting of a jug of rum and a pail of water. Each one would help himself to as much as he wanted. Even the people that went out washing must be treated at eleven and four o'clock, and people were considered mean who would not furnish these supplies to those whom they employed. If a person went out to make a call or spend the evening and was not treated to something to drink, they would feel insulted. You might as well tell a man in plain words not to come again, for he surely would go off and spread it, how mean they were treated—not even so much as to ask them to have something to drink ; and you would not again be troubled with their company.

The sailors often drank to excess. You could frequently see them on South Water street lying at full length or seated against a building intoxicated.

After sailors had stayed at Uncle Jimmie's boarding-house long enough to be stripped of nearly all their money by Uncle Jimmie and his wife, and the females which hung around there, they would be suffered to stroll up to Olney street to spend the rest of their money.

One night a number of sailors boarding at Uncle Jimmie's went up to Olney street to attend a dance. It was about nine o'clock when they left the house, expecting to dance all night and have what they called a sailor's reel and breakdown. About ten o'clock there came to Uncle Jim's a large, tall and powerful looking black man to the door. He said, "Uncle Jimmie, where is the boys?" He answered, "You will find them up in Olney street; they went up to a dance to-night." He replied, "I am going up there, and if anybody comes here and inquires for me tell them I am gone up to the dance in Olney street." Uncle Jimmy said, "Who are you and what is your name?" The man replied, "I am the Rattler." Thus saying, he departed. A little past ten o'clock while they were on the floor dancing, a tall man came in and as he entered the door he said, "I am the Rattler." No one took notice of him. Those that were on the floor continued their dancing. This man seeing no one noticed him went in amongst them and commenced dancing, running against one man and pushing against another, just as his fancy led him. There being at that time five or six large men calling themselves fighting men or bullies, came to the conclusion that they would not have their dance broke up in that shape by a stranger that nobody knew. One of the men by the name of James Treadwell, and known to be a great fighter, said to another large double-jointed man, so considered, by the name of Augustus Williams, "This fellow calls himself the Rattler, let's rattle his box." So they gathered three or four other men who would come to their assistance if needed. They approached the stranger and addressed him saying, "Who are you, stranger, and what do you want here?" He replied, "I am the Rattler." They said to him, "If you don't clear out we will rattle your box" He replied, "That you can do as soon as you have a mind to." Without further ceremony they all pitched into him. The Rattler threw one man into the bar, another he threw across the room, some he slammed against the sides of the house, and in a few minutes he cleared the house, and as they had no power to resist him, they very wisely concluded that he was the devil in fine clothing. This story was told me by Augustus Williams, who was present and witnessed the whole affair and declared it to be the truth. The next visitation in Olney street was made by two crews of sailors, one white and the other colored, consequently a fight was the order of the day, in which the blacks were the conquerors, and drove the whites out of the street. The white sailors not relishing this kind of treatment, doubled their forces the next night and paid Olney street another visit, and had a general time of knocking down and dragging out. This mob conduct lasted for nearly a week. They greatly discomforted the saloon keepers, drinking their liquors, smashing up the decanters and other furniture. One of their number was shot dead by a bar tender, which so enraged them that they began to tear down houses, threatening to destroy every house occupied by colored people. Their destructive work extended through Olney street, Gaspee street and a place called the Hollow, neither of which bore a very good reputation. They warned the better class of colored people to move out and then went on with their work of destruction, calling on men of like principles, from other towns, to help, promising to share with them in the plunder, or take their pay from the banks. Governor Arnold hearing of this ordered out the military, thinking that their presence would quell the mob. They were not so easily frightened, and continued their work of ruin until the governor was compelled to order his men to fire. This had the desired effect; broke up the riot and dispersed the mob; but Olney street had fallen to rise no more as a place of resort for rum shops, sailors and lewd women.

During this time I was attending school in order to finish my studies and learn a trade. I found plenty of work to do nights and mornings among my neighbors, often being engaged in waiting at evening parties, by which I earned enough to pay for my schooling and clothe myself. This was easier than sawing, wood. Several young ladies attended our school, and as I was somewhat noted for my graceful appearance, I liked to display my gallantry among them. One afternoon two of our young girls got into a dispute about some trifling matter, which aroused the teacher's anger, and he told them to stop. They had been twitting each other about having white fathers, and in his passion he told them that they both looked as if their fathers were white. I was much displeased at this remark, and waited upon one of them home after school, and learned the cause of the dispute. I waited upon her several times until it became rumored about that I was waiting upon her. I often met her at parties where we were often invited. My means were not sufficient to allow me to dress as fashionable as I wished, and went coasting, concerning which I shall speak more fully in another chapter.

CHAPTER VI.

I promised in the last chapter to say something about my life as a sailor. I went coasting on board of the sloop Venus, commanded by Capt. Childs, in whose familyI had lived some years previous. He offered me ten dollars a month to go before the mast. I accepted the position and went to work. We numbered six in all: the captain, mate, cook, steward, and two foremastmen. His sloop was the largest in the line but the dullest sailer, unless she was under a stiff breeze. We came out of New York one day heavily laden with cotton, and one hundred carboys of vitriol on deck, bound for Providence, intending to stop at Bristol to land freight; there were thirty-three passengers on board. We started with a light wind which increased during the night, and became so powerful by ten in the morning, that it carried away our topsail, which we afterwards secured. The sea ran so high, and we shipped such heavy seas, that we lost the blocking from two casks, catching uncle Tom, the cook, between them. I did not see the danger he was in until the captain coming out called all hands to rescue him from the danger he was in; we did so, John and myself blocking and securing the casks. I was securing the main boom when the ship came about; she shipped another sea and down went the forecastle and half a dozen casks of water. We were sent down to bail out the water; uncle Jack dipped it up, and I passed it over to John, and he threw it overboard. We had not been long at work when she shipped a second sea, and sent down more water ; it seemed to be about a foot deep. Uncle Jack said; "hold on Bill, it is no use bailing, we must go and shorten sail"; saying this he left me at the foot of the steps, went on deck, and said to the captain, "hadn't we better shorten sail ?" he said, "no, we will drive her through; " to which uncle Jack replied, "well drive her through if we go to the bottom." I kept at my post at the foot of the steps, waiting for uncle Jack's return, when she shipped another sea, filling the scuttle. I felt for the steps, for I thought she was sinking; soon I heard the captain's voice. I jumped around trying to get up the steps, when the hatch came down over me. It was dark, and the water was nearly up to my arms. I was getting out of the water, but reaching the hatchway, could go no farther. I put the top of my head against the hatch, but could not move it; all was still on deck; not a step or a voice was heard. I was determined to come out, and stooping down, raised myself with all the power possible against the hatch; Capt. Childs was sitting on the top of it to keep it down ; a sea struck him in the back at the same time I was butting the hatch and knocked him completely off; he would have gone overboard, carried by the force of the wind, had he not fetched up in time in the shrouds. When I came on deck a sad spectacle presented itself; her gunwales were even with the water, the men were trying to move about on deck and the water was up to their middle. Uncle Jack let go the jib and flying jib halyards, settled the peak, throttled the mainsails, lowered the sternsails, and she came up. It seemed by appearances that in one minute more she would have sunk, never to rise again. I took a handspike and knocked a board of the railing, letting the water off, and relieving the deck. I went aft to the pump, rigged it and went to pumping. The clattering of the pumps aroused the captain, and he said, "that's right, Bill, pump away." I kept watching the mate, thinking that if he got the boat which was hanging on the davits, I would grasp an oar and follow him. I asked a man who came on to work his passage to spell me at the pumps; he said he couldn't pump. There was a minister on board standing by, who said to him, "What kind of a man are you; here this boy is doing all he can to save the ship, which seems to be in danger of going to the bottom, and you refuse to help him." When the minister said that, I was frightened, for I was not fit to die, and if the vessel sunk, I saw no possible way of escaping hell. I began to pray within myself, for I never intended to go to hell, but I knew I must go there unless I repented; still I had confidence to believe that I must read the bible, and go according to its directions to be saved. I never thought of being taken by surprise before. I now felt that something must be done, and I promised if the Lord would spare my life, I would seek him in earnest, and not suffer myself to be caught in such a state again. We soon got through the race and came to anchor; as I came out of the forecastle a sea struck me, and knocked my hat off, my shoes were in the chain box, and my jacket lay in the berth. Uncle Jack asked me to take something to drink, as I was wet and cold; I told him I would; he handed it to me and I took a tumbler full of rum, and drank it, not knowing its power. I took two biscuits and got into my berth, and knew no more until ten o'clock the next morning. The sloop got under way, and they called for me but I was nowhere to be found; they found my hat and shoes and came to the conclusion that I was washed overboard; no one could recollect when I was last seen; they knew I was pumping, and that was the last they knew about me. The sloop arrived in Newport at twelve o'clock that night. He entered his vessel in the morning and reported the rough time he had on on the sound and the loss of one man; after breakfast they began discharging their freight, Uncle Jack had to work in the hold as they were one man short. I was awoke by hearing the words, "back down your tackle, hoist away." I could not imagine where I was. I lay some time thinking that we must be in Newport, for we had to stop there to leave freight. I got up, eat my breakfast, and went on deck; they had hoisted a barrel of flour up, and were just landing it, when I put my hand on John's shoulder; turning around he saw me, and jumped from me with a shriek; the man below asked, "What's the matter?" John said, "Here is Bill." They came out of the hold, to see if it was me. The captain hearing the sound came quickly into the sloop, They were all anxious to know where I had been. 1 told them I had struck my head against the hatchway, trying to get out of scuttle, then got into my berth and knew no more until morning. They were all very glad that I was safe; saying, they thought they had looked everywhere, but never once thought about my berth. When we arrived in Providence, and discharged our cargo, we found our sheet iron damaged. We had five hundred bundles in the bottom of the sloop. I felt as if I had been a sailor long enough, and now desired to turn my attention to business of a different kind; so I left the vessel and entered school again.

CHAPTER VII.

I now thought it time for me to look for a place to learn a trade, and my readers will at once see the hindrances I met with in every effort I made in that direction. My mother had just died, after a short illness; her burial occurring on the 3d of December, 1831, which caused a great change in our family. This change made me the more anxious to secure a good place to learn my trade.

My first call was on a Mr. Knowles, a first-class carpenter, to see if he would take me as an apprentice to the trade. His excuse was that he had but little work, and that he was going to close up business. I next applied to a Mr. Langley, a shoemaker, to see if he would learn me the shoe business; but he refused without giving me an excuse. I made application to several gentlemen doing business, for a chance to work, but all refused me, giving some very frivolous excuse. I could readily see that the people were determined not to instruct colored people in any art. I next called on Mr. Ira B. Winsor, a grocery man. Making known to him my wants I gained his sympathy, and a promise to do what he could for me. His promise to hire me as a clerk encouraged me very much. He had first to consult his uncle, who was his guardian, before he could give me a decided answer. His uncle bitterly opposed his hiring a black boy while there were so many white boys he could get. This objection of his uncle displeased him much, and he told him if he could not have me he would have none. So he never hired a clerk. I often went in and helped wait on customers. This, however, did not suit me. I wanted something permanent that I could depend on for future support, not to be shifting to various kinds of employ as I had been doing. Other boys of my acquaintance, with little or no education, jerked up instead of being brought up, were learning trades and getting employment, and I could get nothing. It seemed singular to me at first. I soon found it was a account of my color, for no colored men except barbers had trades, and that could hardly be called a trade. The white people seemed to be combined against giving us any thing to do which would elevate us to a free and independent position. The kindest feelings were manifested towards us in conversation, and that was all. I was now seventeen years old, and was at a loss to know what steps to take to get a living, for if I possessed the knowledge of a Demosthenes or Cicero, or Horace, or Virgil, it would not bring to me flattering prospects for the future. To drive carriage, carry a market basket after the boss, and brush his boots, or saw wood and run errands, was as high as a colored man could rise. This seemed to be the only prospect lying in my path. Some of my associates worked for eight or ten dollars a month, but what would that small pittance be to them, settled down in life with a family to support, if they should have long continued sickness to contend with. This wouldn't suit me; I must go somewhere else to find employ.

I now commenced the study of book-keeping, thinking it would be of use to me sometime. I continued my study one year, when I had a chance to get work with a wealthy lawyer, to take care of his office and bedroom, paying me five dollars a month, and extra pay for all extra work done. I was told that he was a very cross man, and difficult to please, and often very abusive. Several good men had tried him, but could not suit him and had left. I concluded to try him. My father thought it was useless for me to try, but still if I did I must give him half of my wages. I made no reply; but was willing to do so after clothing myself up. I made him no promise, knowing that if I did not promise I should not break my word. My father was very particular about people keeping their word. If they said yes, he expected it; if you said no, he would then be in doubt. Being suspicious that I would not give him the money, he called on Mr. Greene and told him to pay him part of the wages and the rest to me, but said nothing to me about what he had done. I commenced work Monday morning, and found Mr. Greene very pleasant, and soon learned that my work suited him. When my month was up I asked for my pay. He then told me what my father said about my wages being paid one half to him and the rest to me. I was much struck back, thinking that my game was blocked; however, I agreed that it was all right, and offered to carry my father's portion to him. He gave it to me, and now, says I to myself, if father gets this he will be smarter than I am. I purchased a nice little green broadcloth dress coat in Mr. H. Brown's store. This used up my month's wages, although I had taken great care to have it appear that I had a large roll of bills in my possession by getting my money changed into one-dollar bills, then rolling each bill in a separate piece of paper, it looked as if I had a large amount of money. I took my coat home and laid it where my father would see it. My sister who kept house asked where I got my coat; I told her. Soon my father came home to dinner, and seeing the coat asked whose it was. My sister told him I had just bought it. He asked her if my month was up. She told him it was, for I had no money before that day. She told him I had also bought a pair of shoes; he asked if I had left any money for him. She said no; I couldn't have much left after buying those things. Nothing more was said about the money or things. At the end of the second month I asked for my money. He told me he would pay me the next day, but that my father had been there and told him to pay me three dollars and keep the rest until he called for it. I then told him about spending my money to purchase a coat, which I had bought at a great bargain. As he paid me I told him that if it would be any accommodation to him, I would hand it to father and save him the trouble. "It will be no trouble for me to pay him," he said. Mr. Greene was much pleased with my work. After working for him three months his cousin, William C. Greene, hired the house and rented him a room in it. He had a large family; kept a cook, chamber maid and housekeeper, as his wife's health was very delicate. He said to me one morning, "William, I want to make a bargain with you to work for me. My chamber maid is going away on a visit and will be absent two months or more. I want you to do all the errands that my folks want done, and split some wood for them, (I believe they are now out,) and anything Miss Paris wants you to do, do it, and I will pay you. As soon as you have done Mr. Richard Greene's work in the morning, you can get your breakfast here, and then be in readiness to do the chores." I told him that I went to school, but would do what I could between school hours. This arrangement pleased him, and I commenced with him that day, doing whatever I was called upon to do. After working for six weeks I made out and presented my bill at his office; he being away, I left it on the office desk. I had been very careful in setting down my charges, as I was to be paid for going on errands a certain sum each time, never higher than twelve cents or lower than six. He was quite displeased with the bill, refusing to pay it. I was very calm, and told him I thought my charges were reasonable; but I did not wish to cherish hard feelings, one towards the other. I then submitted the prices of my work to his judgment; he seemed much pleased with my mild way of speaking, and said he would take my bil and fix the prices, and let me know when he was ready; and I could keep on doing his work as usual. In about three weeks he sent for me to come to his counting room. I went down and found my bill ready for settlement, but he had reduced the bill from six and a half to two dollars, allowing me three cents for every errand this side of the bridge, above Market Square, and ten cents an hour for cutting wood. As he was willing to be governed by these prices in the future, I receipted the bill and took my pay, which was $2.50. In two months and a half the maid returned, and as my services were no longer required, I went away, made out any bill and carried it to the office. Some two weeks passed, when his clerk, meeting me, said that Mr. Greene wanted to see me. I went to his office and found him fretting about my bill.

I asked him if he could find any charge on the bill which did not correspond with the dates on the books where the purchases were made. If he did I would alter the bill; but if he found it to be of the same date the purchases were made, I could make no change in the bill. Finding nothing to justify his belief, he paid me and I left him.

I was without work some three months. I then applied to Enos Freeman, a colored man who had just opened a shop to repair shoes. He said he was unable to keep a man; he could hardly take care of himself by his trade, as he had just commenced business. I told him I wanted to learn the trade and if he would learn me I would board myself. He told me to come and he would learn me all he knew about it. I went home and told father; he was much pleased about it and said if I would go there and learn my trade he would board me. He said if he had learned the trade he could have made four or five dollars a day where he had been in foreign countries. I commenced and learned very fast. At the close of that year Mr. Freeman was taken sick and after a short illness died. I purchased all his tools of his half brother, Geo. Peters, determined to work until I could raise means to go away, which would take about eighteen months. My custom increased and promised great success. I had the waiters' work from the City Hotel, Franklin and Mansion House, besides waiters that lived in private families; and the prospect was that if my business continued good, I would have a sufficient amount of money at the appointed time to travel with, to some place where I could make a permanent living, for I was determined to go to some place where my prospects would be more encouraging. I also began to think that if I could be more successful in business, I would like to get married. But old people would say that it is very difficult to keep the pot a-boiling; so I concluded to make an effort to test my powers to do extra work. Then if I should be compelled to resort to that method to support a family, it would not be a new thing to me. And if I succeeded in performing extra labors I would get married, and if not I would remain single a while longer. I commenced working nights until 12 o'clock, then replenish the fire and rest while it was kindling. Then it would be warm enough to commence work again. I followed it up one week, but the last night the fire did not burn very fast, and in waiting for it to kindle I fell asleep, and being near the stove I began to make one of my graceful bows until my head gently touched the stove, and to my great discomfort burnt my forehead, nose and chin, which speedily aroused me, as the pain was quite severe, taking a portion of skin off my forehead so that I could not work for an hour or two. I continued working for two weeks to see if I could endure the extra task. One night while resting I fell asleep and dreamed that a man entered the shop to kill me. I awoke, looked round, saw nothing, fell asleep and dreamed it again;

and again the third time dreamed the same over again. Being startled by the dream I awoke and found my shop on fire, all in a bright flame. I looked to see where the fire originated; learning the cause I soon put it out with my shoe tub of water. A piece of canvas belonging to father was hanging up in the shop; he had used it a few days before when he spun oakum for Captain Bullock's ship which was under repair, intending to take it home in a few days. One end of it got unrolled and fell to the floor, and moving my bench it got dragged out; the room was very warm and the candle melted and falling on the floor set it on fire and nearly consumed it. After putting the fire out I went home and spent the rest of the night. I felt that I had been working at night long enough to warrant success in supporting a family. Another important matter I must settle was to leave the company I had been with so long, and break off from the Tuesday night Society. Many had watched me from the time I joined the church and I had to be reserved in my deportment, for they well knew how I used to be; I allowed no one to insult me or make useless threats. I found much difficulty in this respect.

In the summer time work was very scarce, and I did any work I could get to do. In the winter season I had a plenty to do; as customers must have dry feet. In the summer I was without work half of the time. I could not stay at home and wait for work to come in, so I went out and looked for any thing I could find. I found several persons at the water-side below the great bridge waiting for work. I stopped there awhile, until James Johnson, one of our members, drove up on his dray and asked what I was doing there. I told him I was looking for a job, as I had no shoes to mend. He said jump on my dray and go with me to get a load of cotton. I went, but told him I did not know how to handle cotton but would do the best I could. He got me a hook to use, but had most of the work to do himself. He gave me twelve cents for my work. Finding nothing to do during the next three or four hours, I went home; spending the money I got for groceries. Passing Mrs. Helme's on George street, I saw in front of her door a cord of wood; I called in and engaged to saw and put it in the wood-shed. I put it in the yard and sawed the most of it that night, finishing it the next morning—using Bro. Gorham's saw and horse, which I took without asking for it, thinking no harm to use it at the time, as I lived in his house. I had scarcely gone up stairs, when I heard Bro. Gorham asking for his saw, saying to his wife I cannot see what has become of my saw and horse; where did you put it, she asked; he said somewhere in the yard. Mrs. Gorham came to the door, and said to him, there is your saw, just where you left it; you never know where you put your things. He took his saw and horse and went to work. Some three months after, I told him I had his saw and horse at the time he was looking for it, for I knew he would not be offended. I was out of work and knew I must find something to do to get us some food. I took some soap and a bucket of clothes, and with my sleeves rolled up went toward the college, inquiring for work as I went along, finding none. At the college I rapped on a student's room door and asked for work, also at a door where a young man wanted his bedstead cleaned and floor washed, which I did; he then wanted some painting done, that I also did; earning four dollars and a half for the job. I was again out of work, and went out to look for more, but did not find any; on returning home my wife asked me what luck I had, I answered none; she said she had found a job at the Boston and Providence R. R. depot; a man had called that afternoon and engaged her to go to work in the morning. I said I would go and help her; we went, taking such things as we needed. I asked the gentleman what he wanted done. He said the ceiling, sides and floor of the office cleaned; overhead and the sides of the office was cased. I got some hot water and we went to work, and worked until night, finishing that room. We were told to come in the morning, as there was more work to be done, but my wife was not able to do any more cleaning, so I hired my brother-in-law and went to work the next day; he got sick after working one day, and said it was too hard for him to clean. I continued and finished every room in the building in eleven days, which, at $1.50 a day, amounted to sixteen dollars and a half. I asked how they liked the work? They replied very well. I made out and presented my bill to Mr. Humphreys the next week; he read it and said it was too much, and said he would not pay it. I said I had not charged no more than the common price, $1.50 a day; he said he would have got the work done for four dollars, but would give me five, and that was all; I must take that or nothing. I went away and told my brother-in-law what he said respecting the bill; he said I ought to have taken it, for now I wouldn't get any pay. These railroad and steamboat men do as they please about paying bills; paying what they see fit. I have seen men working on steamboats grumbling about their pay, and would be kicked ashore with nothing. I said I would make them give me my money, I will not work for nothing. I hear that Mr. Moses Ives is president of the company, and if they won't pay it I will go to him, for he will see me righted. Some three weeks after I went again on the fourth of July, saw Capt. Comstock, master of transportation, and said to him, I have a bill of sixteen and a half dollars for cleaning your depot, and want some money to-day, and would like to have you settle it, if you please. He looked at the bill and read it, saying, I suppose it is all right, William; I said, yes, sir; he handed it back, saying come down at nine o'clock and Mr. Humphreys will pay it; tell him I say he must pay it. I went to the office at 9 o'clock, Mr. Humphreys said, so you have concluded to take five dollars? I said no, sir, I have concluded to take sixteen dollars and a half. Mr. H. said, I told you

before that I would not pay the bill. I said, Mr. Comstock told me to bring
it down and you must pay it. When did you see him? he said. I replied, this
morning. Did he say I must pay it? I said, yes, sir; he said, I shall not pay it;
I said well, and will tell Mr. Comstock you won't pay it, and started for the
door. He said, come back, I didn't say I wouldn't pay it, but said I didn't
want to pay it until I saw Mr. Comstock. My movements affected him. I
said, let me have three dollars, I want to use some to-day, and handed the
bill to him; he took it and credited the amount. I took the bill as it was
receipted and went away, feeling safe that he had acknowledged the bill. A
week afterwards I went again and finding Mr. Comstock in the office, I
said, I had had a great deal of trouble in coming three times for my money.
He told Mr. Humphreys to pay the bill. Mr. H. said, he has charged sixteen
dollars and a half, and it is too much for the work. Mr. Comstock said,
William, do you make two days work out of one, or charge two days work
in one? I said, I do as much work as any man can do, and charge only the
common price, one dollar and fifty cents a day. He said, Mr. Humphreys,
pay that bill; and he was obliged to pay it, although he was much displeased. Mr. H. was not aware how intimate Mr. Comstock and myself
were, and that we were boys together.

I found that other jobs kept coming in, from sources I little expected, yet
I had not been able to get a sufficient sum to meet my arrears. I lived in a
house belonging to a widow lady, and was back in rent fourteen dollars; she
told me she had concluded to occupy the tenement herself, and as soon as I
could to give it up; she lived up stairs. I soon learned that Barker & Wheaton wanted a man to dress new work. I made application for the place,
telling them I heard they wanted a man; they said they did, and asked if I
understood dressing new shoes with gum; I said I was a shoemaker by
trade, but had never used any gum; they asked for recommendations; I said
I had none, I had never worked for anybody to get one; they said they
wanted a man that didn't have a lot of company coming into the shop, and
one that would give no back talk when spoken to; I told them I never had
anyone loafing around me, but if any one had business with me I expected
to see them wherever I was, and as for back talk I never have any, and if I
did not suit a man I left him; one asked if I knew his barbers, James Scott
and Charles Burrell; I said I was well acquainted with them; he said I will
see them, and if they speak well of you, you come next Monday and I will
let you know. The next Monday I went to the store and Mr. Barker said to
me, Messrs. Burrell and Scott spoke well of you, and said you was just the
man we wanted; we want you to come mornings and open the store, make
the fire and sweep the room; for that we will pay one dollar a week; we
want you to dress shoes with gum, and we will allow you twenty-five cents

a case; when you assist in rolling leather, we will allow you one cent a boll; you need not close the store at night, we attend to that; we pay out money but once in three months for work; we sell and receive on three months' credit; if you can serve us on those terms you can begin next Monday morning; we want you to look out for the shop, let no one trouble our books; you must be dressed clean, for you will have to be in the front part of the shop. Very good, sir, I will commence next Monday morning, I said. Mr. B. said, when you come go up stairs to Mr. Wheaton's room, rap on the door, and he will give you the key; the shop must be opened by half past seven o'clock. Now, I wondered how I should get along for three months without any pay, as I had no means to sustain myself and family during the time; however, I thought I would trust the Lord and do the best I could, and if I got into straightened circumstances I might get some money of them, to keep me along until the three months were up. I told my wife if any work came in during the day to keep it and I would do it in the evening. I went to the store Monday morning, got the key and opened the store, made up a fire and put the store in order, as my employers would be in at half pas eight o'clock; I then went around to see how everything was placed, as I was very near sighted, and did not wish them to know it for some time; as it was generally the case as soon as a person found I was near sighted, the next opinion would be that I was about blind. After learning the places of the different articles they would use during the day I sat down and waited for them to come in. Mr. Barker soon came in, walked around the store, and said, William, you have every thing in first rate order, I think you will suit us. I thanked him, saying I should endeavor to. Mr. Barker was a smaller man than myself, very large in feeling, quick in motion, sharp in perception and would try to make one think he knew everything. Mr. Wheaton, his partner, was very tall and large in proportion; slow and easy in motion, dull in perception and moderate in appearance; you would think he knew but little; he did the business in the store, and Mr. Barker did the travelling business. Mr. Barker told me to go to breakfast and return as soon as possible, as they had a great deal of work on hand. When I returned the first thing called for was a hammer, saw and chisel; I brought them, and when he finished put them back in their places. He opened two cases of shoes, and set me to work dressing them; he had two bottles, one of gum arabic to dress the bottoms to give them a lively red color, the other was gum tragacanth to dress the upper leather, making it look fresh and smooth; after having been shown how to dress the shoes I commenced doing precisely as I had been shown, and worked all day on that one case, and got only about two-thirds of it done. I thought if I made no better progress than that during the week I should leave off. The next day I finished that case and another one besides, and at the close of the week I was able to dress three cases a day; being particular to have him examine each case before they were repacked. When I went home nights I would find some work to be done to sustain myself the coming day. I now found that I was obliged to put in practice that which I was once trying as an experiment, working nights. Some nights I would work until eleven o'clock, and other nights until after midnight; by this means I was enabled to keep along nearly two months. One morning while waiting I felt drowsy, and when Mr. Barker came in he suddenly opened the door, and said what is the matter, William, are you sick? I said, no, sir; He said, what makes you so dull, did you not have sleep enough last night? I said, no, sir. He asked what time I retired? I answered three o'clock this morning. He said what was you doing that you did not go to bed before, as you ought to? I said, I am obliged to work nights to support myself and family, as you could pay me no money for three months. He said that is too bad, we cannot get our money until it is due, but if you or any of your friends want shoes, we will let you have them at wholesale prices and credit them to your account, and you can receive the money. When the three months expired I made out my bill, setting down each day's work, the number of cases of shoes I had dressed each day, and presented it for settlement. It was examined by my employers and they wanted to know who made it out for me? I said I always kept my own accounts and made out my own bills. They said they had no idea I could write such a fine band, for neither of them could begin to write like it. My work came to over eighty dollars, and they settled it, lacking ten dollars I then could settle up some of my back debts; the first was my rent, amounting to twenty-one dollars. My landlady was much pleased at receiving her rent in full, and said I need not move as she had concluded to remain up stairs, and had concluded that she should never tell me to move the second time, and as soon as I could better myself, to do so. I was soon able to dress six cases a day. I commenced the second quarter by putting down the balance due, ten dollars, and the charges underneath. I sold twelve pair of shoes, which I took out of the store, to my neighbors, and with the balance due on the last quarter I sustained myself until the second quarter was up. I carried in my bill, which was over eighty dollars, that was paid, (keeping out a balance of eight dollars); the sum enabled me to meet all my back debts so that I was not compelled to sit up nights to work. After commencing on the third quarter, one day while dressing shoes, Mr. Barker came on one side of me and Mr. Wheeler on the other; Mr. B. said, William, how long have you been working for us? I said nearly nine months. He said, I think you are a very honest person. That is what I always try to be, I said. Mr. B. said, if some men were working here and trusted as we trust you, they would carry off a great many dollars worth of boots and shoes. I said I have no doubt of it, some people are just so foolish; you would certainly know if they took away any of your property. He said, how would we know it unless we saw them? I said, don't you have an invoice of every thing that comes into your shop on your books, and every article you sell is on your sales book, and when you post your books and take an inventory of your effects, every article that has not been sold must be in your store, and if they are not found in your store somebody must have taken them, and who would be accused but me? it would fall on my shoulders; you have given me liberty to take any shoes that I wanted and charge them to myself, and I have done so, charging them to my account, and when I presented my bill you have seen the credit given of what I had drawn. He asked me where I got this knowledge of doing business? I said, I attended school and studied book-keeping. He asked, how long I went to school? I replied, until I was twenty years old. He said, no wonder you are so well posted; you ought to know something about business. I want to ask you, Billy, if you have ever taken any change out of the drawer and forgot to tell Mr. Wheaton about it, or made change for any one and made a mistake, as you cannot see very well. I answered, I had not troubled his drawer, either to get change for my own use or any one; I had no business with your drawer, and if I wanted any money I should ask you for it. Mr. Wheaton said, I told you that I didn't think William had taken any money out of the drawer; the mistake has come by me, I have not been particular enough in setting down the postage I paid out. Mr. Barker said we have found a little discrepancy in our accounts in posting up our books; we can't strike a balance of four dollars and a half, and thought we would mention it to you, thinking you might have taken some change out of the drawer and forgot to mention it to Mr. Wheaton. I worked there fifteen months, when the firm failed and made an assignment. Thinking business was closed with them, I made out my bill and presented it to Mr. Barker, who said he had closed up business, but to leave my bill and he would settle it in a week or so; (the amount was seventy-one dollars). When I called to settle with them, Mr. B. said, I have got your bill made out from the time you commenced until you closed, embracing fifteen months; you have made a great mistake in your bill; we owe you a balance of twenty-two dollars, and if you receipt the bill you can get your money now. That made a reduction on my account of forty-nine dollars. I said I didn't think I had made any mistake. I examined his bill, and well knew there was something about it. I asked him to let me have ten dollars and I would go home and look over my accounts and see what the difficulty was. He said he would not pay a cent until he paid the whole, and that would be when I receipted the bill. I asked him for the bill to take home for examination and would return it the next day. He said if I would do that I could take it. I promised I would and took it and went home, there copied the bill and returned it to him the next morning, and said I would see him the latter part of the week; I having a copy of his bill, and from my account, I saw that he had altered the charges I made; when I dressed six cases, I put down four, and when I dressed four, he put down two and three, and proceeded on, carrying out the bill fifteen months. I took the amount I had received and substracted it from the amount due, and it came to seventy-one dollars, just like the balance on my former bill; I took the amount of credit he had allowed for fifteen months, added my account with it, which increased it forty-two dollars; for he copied his credit from my former bills— he just cited the amount due me on his account and went on with the bill, without noticing that I had reckoned the money, and by this means I trapped him. I called again and told him I was ready to settle, and explained to him what he had done to deceive me. When he found himself trapped, he said, well, Billy, I will settle it to suit you and give you seventy-one dollars; he was glad to back out in that way. I was again without any work; I had stopped repairing shoes so long that my customers had gone elsewhere; I went about to see what I could find to do, when Royal Farnum met me and said, your people have failed. I said yes, sir; he inquired what I was doing now? I told him I was trying to find something to do. He kept shop on South Main, above Planet street, and was connected with a Philadelphia line of packets; kept ship stores and seamen's clothing. I went into his store and he showed me a large number of small size boots and shoes he could not sell (having sold his larger sizes); he said, if you will oil, dress and sell these shoes I will give you half you make. I accepted the offer, went to work on them, and was kept very busy some three months.

CHAPTER VIII.

Among the varied causes which came up for consideration, and in which the colored people became interested was the temperance cause. Meetings were held and a temperance society was formed, with G.C. Willis as President; and the more respectable young people who were anxious to sustain a good reputation became members of it. We commenced having lectures and addresses to keep up the interest. Three of its members were appointed very month to deliver address. The first three that were appointed were Geo. C. Willis, C.M. Cozzens, and myself. I would gladly have backed out when my turn came to speak, but was not allowed to do so. The President gave the first address, followed by Chas. H. Cozzens, and my address came last, but was said to be the best and won the praise of the audience. Mr. Waterman came to me with a paper, saying, "Brother Brown, we are in need of six new lamps, three on a side. Now you have more time than I have; will you circulate this paper and see what you can get. We will need $24." I consented, took the paper, and soon collected sixteen dollars, and the night before the committee were to meet I called and paid Mrs. Waterman the money ($16), as Mr. Waterman was not in. She was pleased, and said she would give it to her husband, but I had better attend the meeting myself. I did so, and when the papers were called up no one had anything on their papers but Bro. Waterman, who after counting out sixteen dollars gave up his paper. The names of the contributors were read and the amount proved correct by the paper. Mr. Waterman was commended for his praiseworthy exertions in raising so much money; he arose and said the praise belonged to William J. Brown, for he collected the money. Then it was moved that I should have a vote of thanks, which was passed. Mr. Anthony Cozzens then arose and addressing the president, (Edward Barnes,) said that we ought to have some of these young men on the committee to take our places, for we are growing old and will soon pass away, and I move that William J. Brown, Geo. C. Willis, Jr., and Charles H. Cozzens, be added to the committee on the meeting house. Someone one inquired if we owned a pew, as a man must be a pew holder to be appointed on the committee. The secretary, Anthony Cozzens, arose and said, that Mr. Willis and Mr. Cozzens

owned pews, but he didn't know whether William J. Brown owned one or
not. I informed them that I did not own one; but my mother owned a quarter
of a pew. Mr. Cozzens arose and said that Mr. Brown was too valuable a
young man to lose, and he made a motion that the committee make him a
present of a pew. There was a pew, No. 47, that belonged to a man named
William Brown who went to Hayti, and died, and the pew became the
property of the committee according to the statute book; he moved that the
committee make it a present to William J. Brown, that he may be a pew-
holder; which was seconded and passed unanimously. Now I move, Mr.
President, that George C. Willis, Jr., Charles Cozzens and Wm. J. Brown be
added to our committee; this was seconded and passed. Mr. Cozzens then
moved that the committee be discharged, which were appointed to collect
money to buy lamps, and that William J. Brown be appointed to collect the
amount for the lamps; the motion was seconded and passed unanimously.
At the next meeting of the Board I made my report, and having collected
enough to procure the lamps my report was received and a vote of thanks
given me.

It was now time to elect officers. Mr. A Cozzens resigned as secretary,
which was received; and I was made secretary for the ensuing year, and the
books were passed over to me. I now began to feel the responsibility of my
position; and pledged myself to perform my duties to the best of my abili-
ties, and endeavor to always be in my proper place at proper times.

Among other incidents of the past which was very unpleasant to bear,
was an instance of terrible abuse, which if it had occurred at any other time
would have received a richly merited rebuke. It occurred shortly after I
experienced religion. It was on a Sabbath afternoon after church, I waited
upon two ladies to their homes. I escorted the first lady over on the west
side of the bridge, and leaving her at her home, I returned with the other
lady going down South Main street. In passing Market Square, two young
men followed us, using improper language and were very insulting; we
passed on taking no notice of them, supposing they would keep down South
Main street; we turned up Hopkins street, walking on up through George
street. They turned up the street following close behind us, using the most
abusive and vulgar language, till at length, one of them threatened to kick
the lady I was waiting upon; hearing that expression, I released my arm
from the lady's and turning around requested them to cease such vile talk as
we had not troubled them. This only increased their insults; but seeing me
release my arm they anticipated an attack and fell back a few feet, but kept
following up at a respectable distance. I did not want it to be said that I was
fighting the same day after I had taken Communion; but had made up my
mind that if they had carried that threat into execution and broke the peace

by striking or kicking to knock the first man down, and give them a good beating. If the insult had occurred a week or two sooner, they never would have been able to follow me up the hill, using such disgraceful and abusive language. After reaching the head of George street, we turned into Brown, hoping soon to reach our destination on Benevolent street. Just then a colored man came through Brown street, and seeing these fellows in our rear, making motions as if to kick us, he hailed them asking, what they were disturbing those peaceable people for? They said they were only in fun. He told them he had been watching them since they turned into Brown street, and said, if you want to kick any one come and kick me. He then said to them, clear out, if I catch you troubling those people again I will pitch into you. They hurried away, and we were glad to get rid of their company. Who they were I do not know, but think they must have been fellows who had heard of me, and as I had had frequent skirmishes on the street they wanted to test my religion. It was a common thing for colored people to be disturbed on the street, especially on the Sabbath. On the north side of Market Square, in front of the Granite Building, were generally found afternoons and evenings, a row of men stretched along in the doorways of the stores, looking at the people as they passed, insulting them, knocking off men's hats and pulling off ladies' shawls and often following them as they passed to and from church. That corner bore the name of "Scamps Corner."

Colored people had little or no protection from the law at those times, unless they resided with some white gentleman that would take up their case for them. If you were well dressed they would insult you for that, and if you were ragged you would surely be insulted for being so; be as peaceable as you could there was no shield for you. One day I was going in company with another young man to an evening school, carrying our lamps with us which we used in school. Two colored ladies were close behind us followed by two white men, who ordered them off the sidewalk, or they would kick them off. The females fearing they would do so, went out into the street and walked until they came on the walk near us. The men then ordered us off. My companion gave me the lamp and grappled with one of the men, who being a tall strong man, threw him into the gangway, where he fell striking on a joint bone of an ox. He seized the bone in one hand and leaped at the man like a tiger, clenched him by the shirt collar and dealt him three or four blows in his face in rapid succession. The man cried murder, which drew around a large crowd of people. The blood was streaming from his face and the man who was in company with him said that we assaulted them.

One tall well dressed man said to the people that surrounded us, take these niggers to jail, for I have seen enough of their actions to-day. Without further information we were seized, and would have been dragged off to prison and locked up, had it not been for the timely appearance of Mr. Joseph Balch, who came out of his apothecary shop, being well acquainted with us both. He exclaimed, hold on, "what are you going to do with those boys?" and this would-be-somebody, said "we are going take them to prison, I have seen enough of their actions today." Mr. Balch replied, "no you won't, I know both of them, they are nice boys." He said, "where are you going boys?" We told him to evening school. He said, "go on, and nobody shall trouble you." The man said, "why, he is beating a white man." Mr. Balch said "well. he had no business troubling them, and if the white man let's a boy like him beat him he ought to be beat." We went on and the crowd dispersed.

I will now speak of our Society, which was called the Young Men's Union Friendly Association. It continued to grow and become very prosperous. I became a very active member in it being called upon to fill many prominent offices, and although all our members were married men, they still kept up the organization, proposing to get incorporated. Some opposed it, saying it had been tried but without success. I did not believe any one had tried it, and knew no reason why it should not succeed. I continued to agitate it, until finally the opposition was overcome and a committee were appointed to draw up a petition. I was appointed chairman. When the time arrived for them to meet, not one of the committee came. I then went to Mr. Hamlin's store to get paper, when one of the committee, Mr. Cozzens, said to me, "what are you doing here? you are a pretty fellow, get a meeting appointed at your house and you in the street." I said, I waited until the hour we were to meet, and no one came, so I came down to get some paper and am going right back. When I get home I am going to write a petition for a charter for our society, and if you have a mind to come, all right, but if not you can remain here. He went with me to the meeting. I wrote the petition and gave it to him, and he gave it to Mr. Wingate Hayes to carry into the general assembly, and was noticed in the papers. The society expressed great surprise at our next meeting to find that our petition had gone into the general assembly, and at the next meeting I had the pleasure of informing them that our charter was granted. It was the first charter ever granted to a colored society of Rhode Island. The society were proud that they had made such an advancement, and proposed having a banner and paying a visit to some place where we could show ourselves. Some of our members went to a man on Westminster street who did that kind of painting, and asked that he would charge to paint a banner for our society. He inquired about the society, and was told that we had just been chartered. He wanted to see our constitution. We let him see it, and after examining our charter he said that he would get us up a banner for fifteen dollars, but did not wish to have it known as he would paint one for any one for less than fifty dollars. He got us up one with a house and a weeping willow on one side, over which was a star and the letters Y. M. U. F. Society, instituted 1828, and on the other side was a white and colored man joined hands with a flag staff between them, bearing the American flag and encircled by a wreath, having at the bottom the word Union, and above the wreath in a semi-circle form were the words Young Men's Union Friend Society, incorporated January, 1844.

Our uniform was black caps, with glazed tops. On the left breast was a gilt star with a blue ribbon attached, and cream colored patent leather belts with a brass clasp in front, and white pants, dress coats, and white gloves. They made a contract with Mr. Comstock, master of transportation, to carry us at half price. On the morning of the first we started with a large company. It was quite foggy, and rained hard before we reached New Bedford. They had postponed the celebration until the next day. The committee were in waiting for us at the depot, as the rain had ceased, and escorted us up, our banner being covered. The day was clear and bright, and at half-past nine we marched to the place where the line was to be formed. The procession moved at ten a. m., having a cavalcade of one hundred mounted men in front, followed by the Anti-slavery societies, then our society, making a fine appearance. We marched to the Town Hall, escorted in and welcomed by the citizens. After being addressed by some of the officials the line was again formed and made a parade through some of the principal streets. We then repaired to the grove. A stage was prepared for the speakers and music. The society appointed me as the orator. It was a warm day and we had had a long march. I said to Mr. Cozzens, let us find some retired place when we could sit in the shade for awhile. We started to look for some comfortable place, and seeing an empty buggy near by we stepped into it and soon fell asleep. I don't know how long we slept, but the gentleman and lady who owned the buggy came and woke us, saying, gentlemen: "if you have no objections we will take our carriage." We excused ourselves for taking so much liberty, saying "we were tired and had fallen asleep." On seeing us we were told that they had been looking for us; that they had been looking for the orator from Providence, but he could not be found. I went with them to the stand, ready to take my turn in speaking. The band struck up as I was going on the platform. Just then the stage broke; as dinner was ready, and the day far advanced, they concluded not put the stage up again, but finish speaking in the hall, in the evening. The next morning we went home well pleased with our visit. After we got our charter, the Young Men's Friendly Assistant Society, and the Seaman's Friend Society, applied for an act of incorporation and received charters. We then had three incorporated Societies in our city, besides The Mutual Relief, The Young Men's Morning Star, The Temperance Society and the Anti-Slavery Societies, making in all seven active societies, ready to unite on any occasion requiring their services. They were called out every year on the first of August, as we generally had a grand demonstration on that day, with a procession which paraded the principal streets of the city, and retired to a grove and spent the day in speaking and partaking of refreshments.

The young men of our city were trying to get up a band, and were very anxious to have me to be their leader; I partly made up my mind to join it. Several had bought their instruments and were waiting for me to practice with them. They sent a man to my shop with a bugle to sell; he called and exhibited the bugle, telling me the price. I told him I would send him word the next week, and if I concluded to take it, I would send him the money with the man carrying the word. After he left, I went to Leonard Brown's shop, the man that told me, when at the anxious seat, that if I came with a sincere purpose they would all pray for me. On entering, I said, Bro. Brown, I want to ask you something, and I want you to tell me the truth. He asked me what I wanted to know. I said, "Is there any harm for a Christian belonging to a band and playing on an instrument." He said, "no harm at all, if you can serve God on it." I said "is there any sin in it?" He said, "no sin in anything you can do, if you can praise God by it, that is the point you must decide. Now you know whether you can praise God by it or not." I said that I did not know us I could particularly praise God by it. Then he said, "Brown, if you join that band you are going to play for anybody that hires you, and if your band is hired out to play you have got to play songs, nobody wants hymns." If you belong to a band you have to spend an hour or two every day to practice, and you practice on songs not hymns. Now if the Lord called on you when you were practicing songs you wouldn't be in a fit state to receive him, would you?" I told him, "No, sir." He then said, "don't meddle with anything that you should be ashamed to answer the Lord for, if he should call on you." I thanked him for his advice, and told him I had my doubts about it, and that was the reason I came to him. But now I am perfectly satisfied and I will have nothing to do with it. I then told the bandmen that I had been converted and united with the church, and that as a christian, felt it my duty to tell them that as a christian I had no right to belong to a band, and that as they did not profess to be christians, and if they felt disposed to form a band they had a perfect right to do so, and I wished them success. But if I joined them I would be a hindrance to them and their prosperity; instead of a blessing, I would be to them to a curse. They said they didn't know but what I was right, and they would release me. Having got rid of the band, I went to the society and told them that I could not be with them and I had formerly, for my church duties demanded my services and attention, especially on Tuesday evening, but at any other time when I could meet with them and not infringe on my church obligations and duties, I would be with them, and serve them according to the best of my ability. The society was well satisfied, saying they would not have me interfere with my Christian duties. Thus I freed myself from the various causes which had entangled me in the past.

CHAPTER IX.

I often thought when a mere youth that I would like to be a christian and belong to a church, and fill some important position of usefulness, but I had little or no idea of the responsibility of such a position. My mind at times had been very deeply impressed with a sense of my sinfulness and the importance of trying to save my soul, but I liked to keep such things to myself, and I did not like to have any one continually asking me why I did not try to pray? At one time when recovering from a severe illness, feeling my health improving, I called on my sister who inquired very particularly after my health; after I told her what I had undergone, she told me I had better prepare myself to die, for everybody said I would go off in one of those attacks, and if the Lord took me off in one of those attacks I should be lost. This made me very angry, and I told her that people had better mind their own business and not be telling about me; I did not meddle with other people's business. I used some profane language in this remark, which shocked my sister much, for she had never heard me make use of such language before. She said, go on, young man; if you will not take advice the devil will soon have you; you are making your way down to destruction. I arose and left the house, intending to go home, but the words of my sister rang in my ears, for I knew they were too true; it was high time for me to alter my course; then came to me the promises I had made when on board the Venus, that if I lived to get home, I would attend to the saving of my soul. I knew that God would not be trifled with, and every attack of sickness told me plainly that there would be the last attack. In a few days I had another attack much more severe than the last one, so severe that my folks despaired of keeping life in me; my father and brother left off work and came home in the afternoon, thinking it impossible for me to live; when I recovered from this attack I said, live or die, I would spend my time striving to get right before God. There had been a protracted meeting carried on in our meeting house by Rev. John W. Lewis, who had recently organized a Free Will Baptist Church in our house of worship; I attended the meetings and abandoned the idea of going away, thinking that I would first attend to the welfare of my soul. I tried to look into my case and see what my life had been that I was so awful sinful. I was not aware that I had been very bad; I tried to keep the Sabbath by going to meeting when it was convenient, and that was generally every Sabbath, and I thought my conduct was as good as the common run of christians; it was true I liked to tell big stories for amusement, and found that christians liked to hear stories told and sometimes tell them themselves; I never intended to lie unless I was obliged to, and that christian people would do; I tried to be honest and not to steal; and did not fight unless I was abused, and that christian people would do; and on the whole, I did not think that I was much worse than people belonging to meeting; but after all, reasoning in this manner did not calm my feelings or bring peace to my mind. I thought if I should die in one of my attacks, according to the word of God, which I had read, that manner of reasoning would not stand, and if all the church acted bad, it would not excuse me. I knew I was not righteous but wicked, and the word of God declared that the wicked shall be turned into hell and all the nations that forget God. Now I could not perceive any possible way of shunning hell; my case was liable to be decided on any attack of sickness I had, and if that decided my fate, my doom was fixed and my only escape was the short intervals between the attacks. I concluded that I had no time to lose, so I fully made up my mind that I would attend the meetings and make every effort that lay in my power to save my soul. I went in company with some boys to the meeting house, and there heard the pastor preach a discourse, after which the meeting was turned into a prayer and conference meeting; three or four pews were cleared for the anxious to be seated in, and the invitation was given, that all those who wanted to get religion to take those seats and the members would pray for them. Several persons went forward to be prayed for. I felt inclined to go, but could not move; the members commenced singing, "Turn to the Lord and seek salvation;" I said to myself that after they had finished singing I would go up for needed prayers. The people ceased singing, then the minister said, I want every one that can pray to come to these pews and pray for these people that their sins may be forgiven, for the scriptures saith, "that the effectual, fervent prayer of the righteous availeth much." Some three or four prayers were made by the brethren in their behalf, after which two or three verses were sung; during the singing, Wm. Bowen, who was sitting beside me, said, let us go up. I said you start and I will follow. He arose and I followed. The young men sitting at the head of the pew flung the door back with such force that it aroused every one's attention to us standing. We walked out and toward the anxious seats; my struggle was so great to get up that reeled to and fro like a man intoxicated; we took seats prepared for us, and the brethren united in prayer in our behalf; the anxious were weeping and praying when the service closed. Several of the brethren came and talked with the anxious; one Leonard Brown, a licensed preacher, came to me and said: "Mr. Brown, you have got good learning, and you can read the Bible for yourself, and if you have come here to get these brethren to pray for you in order to make fun, it will be the means of sinking you into perdition. But if you want these brethren to pray for you for the Lord to forgive you your sins, they will do it cheerfully and God will have mercy on you." I told him I did not come there for the sake of making sport, I was in earnest. Then he said, we will remember your case in our prayers.

After the close of the meeting I returned home, feeling that I needed the prayers of christians. I resorted to my bible, and turning over to a chapter in Matthew, my eye fell upon these words, "Ask and it shall be given, seek and ye shall find, knock and it shall be opened: for every one that asketh receiveth, and he that seeketh, findeth, and to him that knocks, it shall be opened to him." There was no passage in the chapter that I could realize the meaning of except that. I then fell on my knees and asked God to forgive me of my sins, and retired to my bed, but lay awake a part of the night trying to pray and thinking of the right way to ask God. In the morning when I awoke my anxiety had all left me, and a thought arose in my mind that I had made a complete fool of myself by going to the anxious seat, as they called it, and having the people there to pray for me; and the only thing I could do now was to keep away from the meetings and not go near them any more. Scarcely had those thoughts entered my mind than they were followed by another; by that I knew I was a sinner, and had never offered one prayer to God acknowledging that I was a sinner and asking for his forgiveness; and as I had already made a beginning I had better go on and have the case settled at once, and I would not be in a safe situation until I did. I arose and dressed myself, fell on my knees and asked God to show me my sins, that I might realize the nature of them and might better know how to get free from them. After which I went to my work as I had a great deal to do that day, but soon found myself unfit for work, for God showed me just what I was, a miserable sinner, having no claims upon him for his mercy; all I had ever done was against God, and that I had no real love for him or his people, and was unworthy to take his name with my sinful lips. I tried to read and I tried to pray, but could not get a feeling that God would forgive me. That evening I went to the meeting and to the anxious seat; several brethren came to talk with me, asking me how I felt. I told them that I was a miserable sinner, and could find no relief. Some told me to keep on and not give up the struggle and I would find relief; some told me I must have faith, and some told me I must pray for myself. The next man that talked with me was Winsor Gardiner, the oldest Deacon and the oldest man in the church, who feigned to know the most of them all about church governments. When the brethren talked with me I would rise up to see who they were, but when Bro. Gardiner spoke to me of the way, he would always drop his eyes down, as though he did not wish to look me in the face, and assumed an appearance of being absent-minded or indifferent about the subject. Mr. James Johnson also talked with me; he seemed as deeply interested as if carrying a part of my burden. After the pastor had finished his remarks, the brethren and sisters engaged in a prayer and conference meeting, interspersed with singing; before closing, an inquiry meeting was held, commencing at four o'clock, in the school-room. I went home that evening determined to keep on striving. The next morning I arose and went down to pray anew, hoping to find the Saviour. I gave up all work and spent my time in reading, meditation and prayer. I did not care to see any company nor take any nourishment; I remained at the shop until time to go to the inquiry meeting; when I reached the meeting many brethren inquired if I had found any peace yet. I answered, no. When the meeting opened the pastor came and spent some ten or fifteen minutes endeavoring to instruct me. Some who had been seeking, had found peace to their souls, and testified to the happiness they enjoyed. After the meeting closed I went home; mother seemed quite alarmed because I would not take any nourishment, saying I had better try to eat a little of something; I must have something to sustain me. I took a little tea and bread, more to satisfy her than my appetite, for I had none; after praying, I retired. The next morning I continued in prayer. The scripture I first read, and which rested on my mind, was "Seek and ye shall find." I believed that passage to be true, and that I should find, if I had not committed some unpardonable sin; I tried to think what awful sin that I had committed; I knew I had not killed any one, but falsehoods I had told a good many; falsehoods, however, I did not consider to be unpardonable. Whenever I was attacked, which frequently happened, I would defend myself—I was seldom the aggressor—and I did not think that was unpardonable, for every one would defend themselves; still, I believed that something was wrong, and until that wrong was removed, whatever it might be, I might go on day after day and make no advancement. I spent that day looking over my past life, and praying and reading. I went to the inquiry meeting in the afternoon, thinking I might pick up something that would bring peace to my troubled soul. I had conversation with the pastor and some of the brethren, but found no relief. I went home and found mother troubled again, because I did not eat—I was troubled about the sin and guilt I was carrying. The next morning I determined to make greater effort to ascertain why my prayers were not heard; I knew they were not heard, otherwise I would have some relief; I thought, perhaps the reason was I did not pray aright, so I endeavored to change my

mode of praying, but that did not bring relief to my mind. In the afternoon I
went to the inquiry meeting, and two young ladies, about twelve and fourteen years of age, got up and testified that God had removed their sins and
they were happy. I then thought there was no chance for me, every one
could get religion but me. I could find no peace, but the brethren encouraged me to persevere, and not give up; I told them I would keep on praying.
On my way home an elderly brother met me, took my hand and asked if I
had found peace yet? I told him I had been striving several days, but found
no peace. He said, I pray to God you never will until He sets you free, for
he will give you the right kind of place. I did not understand this, for I
expected every one would speak to encourage me, but he was an old member and I believed what he said was true, although I did not understand what
he meant. I tried to thing while on my way home, what could be the cause
of this delay. I had tried everything that I knew of and given up everything,
and was willing to do anything I could to bring peace to my mind; I was not
afraid to tell any one my feelings who would give me instructions. Just then
a thought ran across my mind like some one whispering in my ear, saying,
do you want religion enough to go down on Market square and pray, if by
so doing you could get it. I could not say yes to this thought. I at once saw
that there was pride in my heart yet, and I could not find peace while it
remained; so turning my eyes toward heaven I said, Lord I am willing to do
anything I can to have my sins forgiven. When I said that, a light as large as
the full moon shone in my face, and a voice spoke within me, saying, thy
sins, which are many, are all forgiven. I looked around in amazement for a
few minutes, for it seemed as if everything was changed; the fields and the
trees looked delightful and seemed to be praising God; for a while I could
not tell whether I was dreaming or awake; my heaviness was gone, and my
soul was filled with joy; everything seemed lovely and beautiful; I had
never enjoyed or had any conception of such a feeling before; it was inde-
scribable. I hastened home and as I entered the house I was so changed in
appearance from what I had been for several days, mother noticed it, and
she said, inquisitively, William, how happy you look. I said I am, soul and
body, and I thank the Lord for his goodness to me. She said now you will
set down and eat something, won't you? I told her I would try, but didn't
feel much like eating, for I was happy. I felt as if I would go to the church
and tell every body how happy I felt. I could then see the reason why I
couldn't get the blessing before. Instead of giving myself into the hands of
the Lord, as I ought to have done, I was too reserved in my efforts, and
thought I was doing something when I was doing nothing. I started on my
way to the church, feeling anxious to tell my feelings to the brethren, but,
before reaching the church, a thought came in mind that I had better not be

too fast and sure, for I might, probably, be deceived; my change of feelings might arise from being convicted and not converted. I paused for a while and tried to sum up my feelings of heaviness, which had separated from me but a short time before. But that despondent feeling could not be found. Joy had taken its place, and I loved every one, and was anxious to tell them how I felt, and how suddenly the change came upon me, when I was on my way home. When I arrived at the meeting-house I was met by the brethren who grasped my hand and said, you have met with a change? I asked how they knew? they said by the looks of your countenance. I told them how I had found the Saviour. I was on Prospect street between Lloyd and Jenckes streets, when he spoke peace to my soul and my burden left me. The countenances of the brethren were lit up with cheerfulness, and the very atmosphere seemed to indicate love. The same evening many others also told what the Lord had done for their souls.

After the close of the protracted meetings we were all invited to the church meeting; there we related our experience, telling what first caused us to seek religion. After hearing our experience we were all received into the church as candidates for baptism; that ordinance was administered on the second Sunday in April, 1835, and the same afternoon, for the first time, I partook of the Lord's Supper with the church.

CHAPTER X.

Soon after this my pastor called to see me, and wanted that I should study for the ministry, saying that a gentleman requested him to get two colored young men who were advanced in education to study. He promised to clothe and board them, and give them a thorough education at his own expense; and he wanted two white young men, as nearly equally qualified as he could find them, and he was going to do the same by them; for he wanted to see if the colored young men were susceptible of attaining to as high a degree of intellectual culture as the white young men, as it was stated by some that they were not, and as he was a wealthy man he meant to solve this question and know for himself if nature was any more defective in the colored race. Now I notice that you are well advanced in literature; I have tried several of the brethren of our church, and know that some of you must have had a call to preach. Have you never felt, Bro. Brown, that you could do more good in extending our Saviour's kingdom by preaching the gospel and laboring for the good of souls, than you can by setting here in your shop working. I told him that I had, and sometimes felt that I ought to give up working and go round talking and laboring for the good of souls, but I have never heard any one call me to preach, and nothing like a call, that I must leave off as a duty involved on me, as I could read the Bible and explain it to those who could not read. People would get the Bible wrong and think it was right, and would put such construction on it that it would do more harm than good. He said, "now for the past six months I have spoken about it, at the church meetings and round about, and you have heard me, and never told how your mind was." I have heard you several times speak about it, you spoke about a call; I didn't know what you meant; supposing that a call meant an audible voice, and that I knew I had never heard. He said, "no; an impression of the mind is what we term a call and now if you will go I will write to-morrow." I told him if had known it six months ago I would have went; but I have made up my mind to get married in three months' time, and can't alter it. He said, I am very sorry, but won't the lady change the time if you would go and state the case to her. I said that, I didn't think she would. He said, "Bro. Brown, suppose you go and try; if you don't want to go for four years go for two years, which will be all the better for you when you once get through." By continually persuading me I finally agreed. I would make the statement to her, and if she would agree to postpone the time I would let him know the next day. That evening I visited my intended, and told her a proposition had been made to me. She asked me what it was. I told her that Mr. Rollins wanted me to work for him a couple of years, give up my shop, and he would learn me so that I would be such a workman that no man in this town could beat me; and he is considered to be the best workman in the town. I told him I expected to be married in three months; and he told me to ask you if you would put it off a couple of years, so that I could finish my trade and I make a good workman. I told him if you would agree to it I would come and work for that length of time. Miss Slain asked, "Do you not have plenty of work at your shop?" I said "yes, as much as I can do." "Then," she said, "as we have set the time, I think we had better not put if off." I said "very well, it shall be as you say, we won't put it off, and I won't go." I had been and made a false statement to her, so fixed that I could have an answer to give to the people and to my pastor. If I had asked the question right, as I should have done, no doubt but that she would have agreed to it. I knew, however, that in the way I had stated it, he would not. I thought that if I went to study two or four years some one might cut me out, and then my studying would do me no good, for I had a very exalted opinion of her accomplishments, and I believed in the old saying, "that a bird in the hand is worth two in the bush," so I concluded not to accept his offer. The next day the pastor called, and I told him I could not accept his very generous offer; my lady was not willing, so I felt it my duty to fulfill my engagement. He received this news with regret and went away. After I had made this decision I became gloomy, followed by a low depression of spirits which hung over me wherever I went. The happiness I once enjoyed had fled. I felt condemned. I could not talk about religion with any comfort or joy. If I staid away from church I was miserable, and if I attended I could not enjoy the meetings. Nor was this all, my work fell off, some customers left me, others wouldn't pay, and I became so straightened in circumstances that I was compelled to give up my shop and move to the house, for I could not pay my rent; still, my affairs did not change for the better, work disappeared. I became so involved in debt for rent and groceries, that I nearly lost my credit, nor for two years after we were married was my wife able to obtain any work, and we knew not what to do to remedy the case. I was satisfied that these adverse circumstances was the result of trying to deceive others regarding my convictions of duty. To change the matter now was out of my power; however, I resolved with myself with the help of the Lord, if he would forgive my wrong doings to follow the teachings of his Spirit. For two years, I was unable to take up my cross as a Christian, but now I resolved to neglect my duty no longer. The next Sunday I went to church, determined to do my duty. After the meeting was opened by our pastor, who spoke some twenty minutes, he gave way for any one who felt a desire to pray or give an exhortation to do so. I immediately engaged in prayer, and continued praying for some time, and many were affected by that prayer; the pastor remarked that that was the first time he had heard me in prayer for more than two years. "I knew Brother Brown was a christian, because he said he was; but now I know he is a christian because I have gained him as a brother, and there are many in this church at present that I have not gained as brethren. I only know you are christians because you say so."

The interest of the church had been dwindling until it was very low, and the membership had decreased from sixty to forty, and an average attendance on the Sabbath was about two thirds that number; our weekly attendance was from five to seven. I attended the meetings regularly, and took up my cross, speaking and praying for the space of three weeks, when a thought came across my mind that I had better cease speaking, for there was such a thing as a person being too forward, and I had already satisfied the minds of the brethren that I was alive, and with them in labor, and now I could slacken my exertions. If I continued on I might run myself out. I was reflecting upon these thoughts when another thought came to me, which was, if God had kept me all this time he was able to keep me all the time, and I need not entertain any fears or doubts, for God will attend to his own work. Upon this my doubts and fears were dismissed, and I continued in the discharge of my duty. My sickness, which was severe, attacking me every three weeks, had entirely gone. This surprised me, and I believed God had used this method to prevent my straying away in answer to the prayers and labors of my mother. Just before her death some of the church members told her to take her mind off of her family and place it on Jesus, and give her children into the hands of the Lord. So she, calling brother and myself to her bedside, said, obey father and be good children for she was going to die and would leave us in God's care; and I believe if I had not been afflicted so often I should have left home, wandered abroad, formed new acquaintance and exposed myself to the various snares which entraps young men. But my afflictions kept me from wandering and impressed upon me the necessity of being prepared for death. The interest of our church seemed to weaken, notwithstanding the increasing efforts of our pastor, with a few brethren to keep it up. At last he got discouraged and left the church, saying the church could not prosper in that house, there was something wrong about it, but if we would hire another place he would preach for us. Many of the brethren were of the same opinion, but made no charge. We were now without a pastor, and we were obliged to depend sometimes upon the students, the ministry in Brown University, and sometimes on our own resources. At last the Lord sent Jeremiah Asher among us, a licientiate Baptist preacher, belonging to a church in Hartford, Conn., whose pastor was Rev. Henry Jackson, formerly of Providence, to get an education that would fit him for his ministerial duties. He came and commenced his studies. The church procured his services during the time he was to remain here. He charged nothing for his labors, knowing their means were limited; but advised them to get the colored brethren belonging to the several white churches to unite with them that they might be able to support the gospel and get a good minister to labor among them. The church followed his advice, calling a meeting of the colored brethren for that purpose. They agreed to unite together, become a regular Baptist Church, and have a public recognition. When the time came for the service to take place, a large portion of the number did not come, but hired a place to hold their meetings, and continued their service as a Free Will Baptist Church, thus having two churches in existence at the same time, a Calvinist, and Freewill Baptist Church of color. The number who responded to the call were George C. Willis, Robert A. Lincoln, Charles Gorham, William Howard, James Johnson, George Waterman, William J. Brown, Betsey Hammond and Esther Tabor, nine in all, and they were recognized by the council at the Meeting street Baptist Church. Mr. Jeremiah Asher having previously accepted the call of the church, was by request of the council presented and related his christian experience, call to the ministry, and views of Bible doctrine, all of which were satisfactory to the council. He was ordained and installed in the evening of the same day. The church was recognized December 8th, 1840. The Methodist people tried to form a church and build a house for worship, but could not agree where to locate the house, some wishing to build on Gaspee Street, where many poor people lived and some of bad reputation; those opposed to that location bought and built them a house on Meeting street. The Episcopal people leased a lot on the north end of Union street, and built them a very handsome place of worship, making three colored churches in our city. Our church was flourishing and rapidly increased in numbers ; our officers were Jeremiah Asher, pastor; George C. Willis, Zadi Jones and George Waterman, deacons; Willliam J. Brown, clerk. Our committee were Charles Gorham, James Johnson, William Howard, Robert A. Landers and William J. Brown; our Treasurer, George C. Wiillis. We enjoyed peace and harmony in the church. I was changed for the better, both spiritually and temporally.

CHAPTER XII.

My present subject is rather a delicate one, and yet those of my readers who are acquainted with the diversified movements in this pathway of expectant joy will have some realizing sense of the seeming hinderance, that of times checks the progress of the delighted aspirants.

I have previously remarked that the colored people have but very little chance to elevate themselves to a position of influence and wealth, and I determined to travel until I could find a brighter prospect for the future than Providence. I found, however, that there was a very formidable hindrance blocking up my pathway. I had made the acquaintance of a young lady schoolmate while attending school. This acquaintance was not formed for any special purpose, but simply to have some one to spend my leisure hours with. I made it a practice to call twice a week, as I was remarkably fond of being in the society of ladies. The reason I did not want to make a wife of her then was, because I was not able to support her, having no permanent business that would warrant me a living, and thought it better for one to be miserable than two. I had been waiting upon her some two years, and thought I would break off the easiest way I could. I commenced by making short visits when I called, saying I could not stay long, as I had some engagement that called me away, at the same time watching to see the effect it would produce. I found it created a worriment of mind, making her very inquisitive. The next step was to omit a visit at the regular time. This brought forth questions I could not answer satisfactorily without telling a falsehood; finally I knew not what to do, for my visits had aroused a passion in my heart and mind I could not smother. I was also satisfied that if I wished to make a companion of her for life I could find no one with more attractions in personal appearances, qualifications or ability, than she possessed in my weak judgment. The question was, however, soon decided with me, for the time was fast approaching when I must settle on the subject of my departure. I was taken suddenly ill, suffering much from pain, which I could not account for. I had eaten nothing to cause it. It continued increasing until I was compelled to shut up my shop and go home. This was before my mother's death, and she was an excellent nurse, and at once continued to all do she could for my relief. I had repeated attacks, each one becoming more severe, until I was compelled to give up the idea of going away, and I was fearful that I would be attacked with the same complaint, and if were among strangers who knew not what to do, I might lose my life, so I contented myself to stay at home. I had said nothing to my intended or any one else about going away, but had merely said that if people could not prosper in one place they had better move to another; the world was large enough to make a selection, which would be the most favorable to our interest. I have previously remarked that I made this young lady's acquaintance while attending Mr. Anthony's school. She was one of the two Mr. Anthony spoke so disrespectful about when trying to quell a disturbance between them. At the close of the afternoon session of the school that day, I waited upon her home for the first time, and wished Mr. Anthony to see that I was escorting her, so that if he used such language to her again I would show myself interested in her behalf, for I considered it an honor to defend the ladies in any respectable case, and they in turn always paid me a distinguished respect for my kindness and politeness Now the question to be settled was, would she accept me for a husband. I could not boast of any beauty and was near-sighted. Uniting in wedlock was no small thing to consider; its conditions extended through life. In making up her mind these defects might make her change her opinion of me. She might think it for her interest to marry a man blessed with good eyesight; if anything happened after marriage it would be something out of her power to obviate. I prized my good education highly, for it was in my favor; it excelled that of my associates at this time and if anything, present or future, could be accomplished by it, the means were in my posession. I also prized the good character I bore, for I was held in esteem by the elderly people for industry and politeness The young people had a good opinion of me, because I was well spoken of by the aged; having a knowledge of the estimate placed upon my character, I thought my defects would not be noticed. I now felt that the time had come for me to settle this question, for it had long been a source of trouble to me. I had made her frequent visits and enjoyed myself much in her society. Now I desired to know something of her personal appearance during the day, when engaged in her domestic affairs. To accomplish this I would drop something during the evening, which would cause me to call after during the next day. I would go at different hours for the things. It was common for ladies to be prepared for company during the evening; then one could find no fault with their appearance; but to my satisfaction I always found her in trim, dressed according to her work. I considered her every way qualified, so far as domestic affairs were concerned, to make a suitable companion for any one, whether in high or low degree, and every one spoke well of her character. Her temper was mild, and there was but few who could equal her in looks, besides she enjoyed the best of health, having a carriage and appearance well calculated to sustain it. Thus having the matter settled in my own mind, I found no just cause to prevent us from getting married. I went and brought matters to a close respecting our union in just three months from that day. The varied incidents which had been thrown in my way had made its impression upon my mind, and my views in regard to the future were entirely changed. Instead of making preparations to go out and see the world, I decided to settle down at home; my business was good and increasing every day, everything seemed to warrant my success in supporting a family if I had one.

CHAPTER XIII.

In this chapter I propose to speak of the excitement which often prevailed on the subject of politics, which would occasionally arise to disturb the quiet of our city, and increase hard feeling between the whites and colored, and between the whites themselves. Party spirit oftentimes arisies to so great a height that it becomes necessary at times to call out the military to quell disturbances and protect the participants in their struggles for right. The time of which I now speak was when there arose a strong contention between the Free Soil party and the Suffrage party which lasted for some time after much excitement. The Suffrages party became very quiet and resorted to other means to carry out their projects. Some united with the Free Soil party, claiming to be Abolitionist, others fell back to the Democratic ranks, and made preperations to attack and break up the law and order party. The colored voters numbering three or four hundred were the balance of power between the two parties, but as the colored voters helped them through their struggles the party brought them into the Constitution as legal voters, and held a claim upon them for assistance, but the colored people began to loose their interest in voting. The law was that all tickets should be enclosed in an envelope and the name of the voter placed on the outside before being deposited. Many colored voters were not able to write their names, and disliked getting some one at the town house to write for them; and so refused to vote on that account, the Law and Order party became weakened thereby. Mr. Henry L. Bowen, chairman of the central committee, learning the cause of the colored votes falling of, by the advice of some colored voters hired a room opposite the town house where they had their tickets prepared without being exposed to the public. The committee hired James Hazzard to look after them. Mr. Hazzard was a man who liked to have people think he was worth twice as much as he really was. He undertook to bring the colored voters to the polls and got Charles Cozzens and Charles Gorham, men of influence, to help him. Mr. Gorham asked how many in my society I could get to vote for the Law and Order party. I said I could not tell, but would see. He said the party were falling off, and the Democratic party were increasing. I found I could get the greater part of our society to sustain the party. I informed Mr. Gorham of my success. He said if I could get all their votes on election day I would be paid for it. I went to work and on election morning I went to the room we hired for the voters to meet in. Mr. Balch was there to do the writing, and I was there to see that my men voted right. Messrs. Gorham and Cozzens were present to attend to the part assigned them. James Hazzard asked Mr. Gorham if our voters would come up strong. Mr. Gorham said yes. This question was asked by several, when Cozzens said, if Brown says they will come, they will. I spent the whole day in this work, and was successful. I was paid two dollars for my work. The next year, just before election, Mr. Bowen called and wanted me to do what I could the coming election. Mr. Cozzens told him I was an excellent hand for that purpose, and wished me to write for those who could not write, and see that their tickets were right; he had hired the same room he had last year, and would ask Deacon Willis to assist. I agreed to serve them and commenced looking for voters. On election day I was on hand, and when the polls opened Mr Bowen brought me some tickets and envelopes and we were prepared for business. We were getting along finely, when Henry Bibb, from Tennessee, came in. He had taken an excursion from home and had never seen fit to go back again. He saw the Free Soil ticket spread out, which gentlemen of that party left for distribution. Mr. Bibb was nearly white, and knew well what slavery was. Taking up a liberty ticket he said, "I hope the colored people will sustain this ticket." Several of our people being present and knowing that the ticket was nothing more than Democratic bait to draw off the colored voters, came down with vengeance on the tickets, much to the great surprise of Bibb. The discussion drew many people both white and colored, and during the discussion the Democrats threw hot shot at us, saying that we voted for crackers and cheese. When any colored man came to lecture they would say the same. When Frederick Douglass paid us a visit, I met him, in company with several brethren, and he was introduced to me as a Methodist preacher. He said he had heard we were bought up on election day on crackers and cheese. He received his information from an Abolitionist in the Democratic party. It came about in this way: When the colored people were first called upon to vote to see whether the people wanted a constitution or not, the Suffrage party threatened to mob any colored person daring to vote that day. We proposed to meet at the old artillery gun house the day before. We had a meeting that evening and thought it best to get the people together and keep them over night, so they would be ready for the polls in the morning. In order to keep them we must have something to eat, for if the Democrats got hold of them we could not get them to vote, for they would get them filled up with rum so that we could not do a thing with them; so in order to to secure them we had to hunt them up, bring them to the armory, and keep men there to entertain them. I met with them in the afternoon and found men of all sorts, from all parts of the city, and all associating together. They had coffee, crackers, cheese and shaved beef. During the time a lot of muskets were brought in, and put in a rack. It is said they were brought in to use in case of a disturbance; some said good enough, let them come. They scraped the hollow and every place, getting all the men they could find; then coffee, crackers and cheese were plenty, and no one disturbed them. When the polls were opened, those in the first ward went to vote in a body, headed by two powerful men. They voted in the Benefit street school house; the officers went ahead to open the way. They all voted and then went home, that ended the crackers and cheese. Mr. Bibb tried hard to get the colored voters to vote the Liberty ticket. We made him understand it was not all gold that glitters. He left our quarters and went about his business, and the Law and Order party elected their candidates. I received six dollars for my work. Mr. Bowen employed me after election to go around and see if there were strangers that had been here long enough to vote, and see that their names were registered, and at the next election he would pay me. I collected quite a number who had never taken the trouble to register their names. The Law and Order party broke up, the colored voters went over to the Whig party, the most of the Law and Order party being Whigs, still claiming our support. Their candidate for President was a slaveholder, Zachary Taylor. We did not like the idea of voting for a slaveholder, and called a meeting on South Main street to see what we should do. I opposed the meeting being held in that part of the city, fearing it would prove injurious to my interest. I was in that part of the city working at shoe making, my custom was good, and I knew that if I attended that meeting and spoke in favor of the Whig candidate, I should lose their custom and perhaps get hurt. I could not speak in favor of the Democratic candidate for I was opposed to that party. I was obliged to attend the meeting in the third ward. I was at my wit's ends to know what to do. I attended the meeting and found the place packed with people, and about one hundred and fifty people filled out to the hall door. The meeting was opened when I arrived, Mr. Thomas Howland presiding as chairman. I went in and took the farthest corner of the room. George C. Willis was called, and took his position in front of the stage ; addressing the chairman, he remarked, that we were in a very curious position ; we must be decided in favor of one party or the other, and his opinion was of the two evils, we must choose the least ; and his choice was in favor of Zachary Taylor, the Whig candidate. Several others spoke, and in harsh terms denounced the Democratic party. I was then called, and tried to decline, but the call came from every one, Brown,

Brown. I was compelled to speak. I arose, addressed the president, and told the audience we were called together to settle a very grave question, which as citizens, it was our duty to decide which of the two parties we were to support. We were not to decide upon the man, but the party. If we were to decide on the candidate, it would be not to cast a vote for Taylor, for he is a slaveholder; and this I presume is the feeling of every colored voter, but we are identified with the Whig party, and it is the duty of every colored person to cast his vote for the Whig party, shutting his eyes against the candidate; as he is nothing more than a servant for the party ; but I wish it understood that I am not opposed to either party as such ; because I believe there are good and bad men in both parties. I have warm friends in the Democratic party, which I highly esteem, and who would take pleasure at any time in doing me a favor. Some of them are my best customers; but in speaking of the party, those men know well the duty demanded of them by their party, and would not neglect it for the sake of accommodating me. I blame no man for carrying out the principles of his party. He has a perfect right to do sof, or this is a free country, and we all have a right alike to enjoy our own opinion; there being two parties we are stirred up to action. It makes lively times, and I hope the times will continue to be lively, and our meetings to increase in numbers, for the more we have, and the larger the attendance upon them, the more my business will increase, for the more shoes that are worn out in attending these meetings, the more custom I shall have. I sat down amid loud cheering. It was a bitter pill for us to vote for a man who was a slaveholder; but placing him in the light of a servant for the party, and we identified with that party, we managed to swallow it down whole. After voting to sustain Zachary Taylor as a candidate for the next Presidential election, we closed the meeting.

Now having changed my residence, I could not well work at shoemaking in my new quarters, and finding a shop empty in this part of the city, with cheap rent, I hired it for a month, with a privilege to occupy it as long as I saw fit. I did not know how my custom would be, as many suffrage people resided there, and they were not overburdened with love for the colored people, for they held them responsible for their defeat in a great measure. They said if it were not for the colored people, they would have whipped the Algerines, for their fortifications were so strong that they never could have been taken by them. Their guns commanded every road for the distance of five miles. Why then did you surrender your fort, I asked, if you had eleven hundred men to defend it? They said, "Who do you suppose was going to stay there when the Algerines were coming up with four hundred bull niggers?" This excitement, however, gradually died out, and for a time everything in political matters seemed to move along very quietly, and peace and harmony reigned.

CHAPTER XIV.

I now thought it best to get a place to carry on my work. As I could not do it very well at the house, I hired a shop down in the third ward, where there was a fine shoemaker's shop. I got no work except what came from Benevolent street and from the members of our church. I concluded to give up the shop, as so many shoemakers were there of which I did not know when I took the shop. They of course took all the custom, and all the work I had I brought from home, and I thought I might as well stay at home and do the work, and save the money that I was paying for rent. When the landlord came in I told him that I could get no work, and just as soon as my month was up, I was going to move. He told me not to be discouraged; that the people had not found me out; and if I would stay another month, he would give me a pair of boots to bottom, which might go towards the rent. With that promise I concluded to stay another month.

After he left my shop, I discovered my boot sign moving, and I saw a hand unfastening it from the stick, and rising up I saw a boy standing on the fence unfastening the boot. I took my shoe strap and commenced amusing myself by putting it on him. The boy not fancying such a warm reception, tumbled off the fence and ran away. Soon after my landlord came in and I told him what I had done. He said I had done a very wrong thing, for the boys would club together and give me a beating. He said they gave him an awful flogging at one time. I did not the boys or their sticks. On the evening before fear Thanksgiving, on going home I stepped into Mr. Hall's grocery to get some groceries; opening the door to go, Mr. Hall said, "here, Mr. Brown, is something left for you." He went to the back part of his store and brought me a fine pair of chickens. I asked who sent them. He said "Uncle Zach. Taylor." I said, "give my compliments to Uncle Zach. and tell him, with pleasure I receive them."

Soon after, I went to father's house on Sunday afternoon, as I was accustomed to do. Father asked me what great speech I had been making. I said I had not made any speech that I knew of. He said he had been down town with his wagon, and coming up some one hallowed after him; he stopped and Mr. Earl, the expressman, came to the wagon with a large

turkey in his hand, saying, "Noah, I was at a meeting not long since, and
heard William make a speech; I had not seen him before for some years. He
made a first-rate speech; I couldn't have made a better one if I had tried
myself, and I am going to give you this turkey for having such a son." He,
father, took the turkey, and thanking him, said he hoped he would make
some more such speeches. My landlord, according to promise, brought me
his boots to mend. They were a light French calf boot. As soon as he went
out I began to work on them. I bottomed and dressed them off, making
them look as nice as I could. I put one in the window, and at 12 o'clock a
squad of workmen passed by, when one of them stopped to see the boot in
the window. "Ain't that done nice," he said ; they answered "Yes." "Do you
suppose that nigger done them?" "No, he never could do work like that,"
they said. And drawing close to the window, he said, "Yes, he did, for he's
working on the other one now; let's go in and have a close look at them."
They came in and giving me the time of day asked me if that boot was some
of my work. I said, "Yes." "May I look at it?" I said, "Yes." After examining it, they said, "There ain't a man on this street that can do work like that.
You are a first class workman, sir." I said, "I try to do my work satisfactory." "Whose boots are they?" I replied, "Mr. Morgan's." They all promised to give me work, and left. They were as good as their word, for my
work daily increased, so that in order to meet the demand I was compelled
to rise very early in the morning and commence work, and work until very
late at night. A man that works at shoemaking needs but two meals a day ;
being seated all day he has but little exercise. I followed the practice of
working late at night for several weeks. My landlord frequently called on
me, and spoke of visiting the different shoemakers, and learned that their
customers were leaving them and coming to me. Mr. Colby, who worked at
the corner of John and Hope streets, and had previously employed five
hands, now employed only two. He came in one day and asked me who I
was going to vote for, for Governor, I said I could not tell at present, for I
was not troubled about politics ; but as the Law and Order party is broken
up, the colored people fell in with the Whig party, which was the only party
we could conscientiously support. I made this remark because I was aware
he had heard of the speech I made at the the third ward mass meeting, from
the Suffrage people who were present, and more than probable was there
himself, which was one reason why I opposed the mass meeting being held
in the third ward, for almost every one knew me, and Mr. Morgan was
aware that I was a member of the church, and he held me strictly responsible for the faithful discharge of all the duties of a christian. He then said, "I
have used every possible means in my power to get custom for you; I told
the people that you was the best workman in the vicinity, and the other

shoemakers are losing their custom, so that some of them were obliged to discharge some of their hands. You now have as much, if not more, work than you can do; now I have some choice in the election of our next Governor, for I want an office under him during his administration; and I wish you to work a little for my interest." I said I knew he had been laboring for my interest, and I was very grateful for the kindness he had shown towards me, and was willing to do what lay in my power to help him in his contemplated intentions. "But we are identified with the whig party, who, under the name of the law and order party, had given the colored people the power of elective franchise. I am thereby brought under deeper obligations to sustain that class of our community, no matter by what name they might be identified, in preference to all others, and that class composes the Whig party in our State. I cannot conscientiously vote for any other Governor than the regular candidate for that party. Now, if you are identified with that party I shall do all that lays in my power to secure their candidate ; but if you are opposed to that party and their candidate, with regret, I must tell you, it will be entirely out of my power to tender my aid in assisting you to elect your Governor or procure you an office." I expected he had some plan in view, by visiting different shoemaker's shops, they being suffrage people as well as himself; and in order to break me up they had put him up to force me to vote for the Democratic candidate, knowing that the colored people had tried to unite with the suffrage people and had been refused. It would now be impossible to get them to vote for a Democratic Governor, and I would be compelled to refuse to vote, and that would make a division between the landlord and myself, and by that means I would be ejected from his premises. I was hurting their custom, and the only remedy was to get me out of the neighborhood. I had expected the attack and therefore was prepared for it, and when I opened my arguments the shock was so great that he hardly knew how to receive it. But gathering himself up he said, "I must look out for my interest as other people do their own; and all there is to it is, if you want to stay in this shop, you must vote for the man who is going to help me. So I want you to consider on it, and make up your mind." Having said this he went away. I hurried to get my work all done because I would have to move, although I hated to give up my shop and lose my custom, which bid fair to place me in a better position than I had enjoyed since working at my trade. Yet I could not aid a party who would not receive or aid us on an equality with themselves, when they declared they were struggling for the very rights they denied us when we appealed to them for aid. The two parties were now obliged to show their strength and contend for victory. The Democrats were anxious to obtain it and hired money to get it, and promised to pay it back when they got the government in their hands. The Whig party knew what they had promised and were determined to beat them if possible. The strength of both parties was about equal in regard to numbers, and the colored people were the balance of power, but did not like the idea of voting for a slave-holder, although we voted to sustain him at the mass meeting, yet we couldn't speak for all the colored voters. The Democratic party, knowing the obstacle which would prevent many colored persons from voting for Taylor, sent a detachment to join their party with the free soil party, pretending to be abolition men, and demanded the aid of the colored voters for their respective candidate. This was intended to draw off the voters of the Whig party. The Democrats would then elect the candidate of their party. I called on Henry L. Bowen, chairman of the committee for the Whig party, and told him: "We couldn't expect the strength of the colored people now as when they were with the law and order party. Then our voters felt it their duty to act together in order to restore peace between the two parties. Now that party is done away and we are called to act with the party whose candidate is a slave-holder, and we cannot conscientiously vote for such a man. The Democrats are running a liberty and free soil ticket, and calling on the colored voters as abolitionists to sustain them. You make a distinction between your white and colored voters by placing a star against the names of the colored voters. You say you cannot do without them ; they are the balance of power, and you want to know how to get them again. Now, hire a room to meet in, then hire men qualified for the business and set them at work; have them attend the mass meetings ; work day and night until the election is over, then pay them enough to satisfy them for their time; and in this way only you will elect your candidate." Mr. Bowen said, "Hire as many men as you want, have as many meetings as you want, and get the best men you can find to help you, and when the election is over make out a bill of all your expenses and I will settle it." I went to work, hired a room, and hired Charles Gorham and Charles Cozzens to help. We elected our Governor. After the election was over I made out the bill of all the expenses attending the election, including rent, and carried it to Mr. Bowen, chairman of the committee, and he paid it, at the same time requesting me to keep in readiness for the next election, which was for President. We got through with the State election very well, but it was going to be a bitter pill for our people to swallow to vote for a slave-holder for President, but we voted to sustain the party and not the man. Mr. Bowen hired the same room he had before; I drummed up the colored voters, while Mr. Gorham and Cozzens entertained them night after night until the election was over. We were successful and carried the election; Mr. Bowen was praised for his skilful management, and I beat the bush while he carried off the bird. The political fever was now over and quiet again reigned. After we had enjoyed a season of quiet from political disturbances and harangues, we were brought into another conflict, extensive and severe, but of comparatively short duration. For a time we were much stirred on the subject of free suffrage, and mass meeting were being held to discuss the question. It was suggested by some that the colored people hold mass meetings among themselves and discuss the matter. The suggestion met with their approval and a meeting was called, and I was appointed secretary. The question was discussed by several who approved of the movement, as it was thought to be a good time to get our rights in common with the rest of the people, and a committee of five were appointed to confer with the suffrage party and tell them if they felt oppressed we were more so, and we would unite with them for free suffrage if we could share equally with them when they obtained it. The committee conferred with their leaders, made our request known to them, and by invitation attended their next meeting, and laid the case before the party. One of their leaders made a long speech in our behalf. Many opposed our immediate equal union with them, but wanted us to unite and help get their rights and then they would see about ours. Our committee reported at our next meeting, and were instructed to tell them we could not agree to those terms. Then the man who made the long speech said to our committee, "Report to your people that we leave you just where we found you," and we decided to have nothing to do with them. The Suffrage party said they were fully able to control the State, have their own constitution and elect their own officers. They said the other party was in the minority, and they would not be ruled by them. They attempted to carry out their object by making and adopting a constitution, and the Law and Order party also took measures to get a constitution, submitting the question for the citizens to vote whether they should or should not have one. The colored people asked in common with other citizens to express their views by voting, whether we should have a written constitution or remain under the old charters. The vote of the colored people was unanimous for a new constitution. This act very much enraged them. One day I was in Mr. Crocker's store when one of their number (who had taken a great interest in their party, and had loaned them twelve thousand dollars to carry out their object) came in and said: "Crocker, I have concluded to fight; them Algerines have got the niggers to help them out, and I will not stand it. I think it the duty of every man to come up and help, when niggers are allowed to vote against us." One of the finest men in the city, as I supposed, came to me and said, "I suppose you voted?" I answered, "Yes, sir." He said, "Do you suppose you are ever going to vote again?" I said, "That is so far in the future I cannot tell." He said, "Your wool will grow closer to your skull than it does now before you vote again." I took no notice of this, but went out, for I did not know how things would turn.

The Suffrage party continued their preparations to carry out their object, but the Law and Order party would not yield, saying they had one constitution, and it was the peoples, and they were the sovereigns. They tried hard but in vain to put the suffrage party down and put in force their constitution, but they fortified themselves at Chepachet, and reported eleven hundred men in fort with cannon to defend it. Every possible measure was taken by the Law and Order party to capture and take them prisoners. Many turned out in defence of their party; soldiers were drilling to be in readiness, and the colored people organized two companies to assist in carrying out Law and Order in this State. Two hundred men came forward and joined these companies. The next week they met to elect officers. On that evening three men were present, each wanting to be head. One was Thomas Howland, a stevedore, and a man of some influence and considerable money, but very little education. He thought his position would sustain him. The next man wanting the office was James Hazzard, dealer in new and second hand clothing. He was the richest colored man in the city; he thought the command belonged to him. The third man was Peterson, the barber. He could not boast of money or influence, but had a good education, and thought that he should have the place on that account. He soon found that that would not sustain him, and that others were getting the advantage. He said to the assembly, they had better understand what they were about to do, and not be too fast, for colored people had often been deceived. When they were needed, great promises would be made, and when they were through with them, they would be forgotten. He referred to the speech of General Jackson on the banks of Mobile to his colored soldiers. This created such a sensation that they closed without proceeding any farther, and the company broke up, saying they would not organize a separate company, but would offer themselves to the different companies, which they did, and were received. Companies were formed in each ward, and the chief officers took up their quarters at the Tockwotton House. Mr. Hall, the quartermaster, called on me to come and help, stating that he wanted to hire two men, for the two that he had hired were gone, and there were five hundred men that wanted supper that night, and there was no one to get it for them. He said if I would come and bring another man to help, he would pay me my price, for these men must be fed. My neighbor, William Gorham, agreed to go, so we both started for Quartermaster Hall's. We went to work cooking for the soldiers, and remained eleven weeks, during which time the soldiers took the fort at Chepachet, which they found vacated, gathered up a quantity of stores and prisoners, and returned to the city. So the Suffrage party was defeated, and peace and harmony were restored by the Law and Order party. This was in 1842.The command was disbanded, Gorham and myself were discharged and paid, being allowed one dollar a day. This ended the great contention which had existed so long in this State in political matters.

CHAPTER XV.

My eye sight now began to trouble me very much, until I became entirely blind in my left eye. Feeling better one day, I went up to Mr. Ives's to collect some money he had subscribed. He gave me the sum of twenty dollars, and told me to count it over and see that it was correct. As I was counting it, I held my head so close to it, that he asked me why I did so ? I told him I had lost the sight of one eye, and the other was very weak. He asked if I had been to see Dr. Rivers? I told him I had not, as I was told that he charged five dollars for an examination, and I had no money to spare. He told me to go to Dr. Rivers, and ask him to examine my eyes and see what could be done for them, and tell him "I sent you." Soon after, he went to Europe to visit a relative who was sick. I did so, and after one application, he told me that he could not help me; but go to the Eye Infirmary in Boston, and perhaps they could help me. I told him Mr. Ives was away, and I could not go until he returned. After his return from Europe he called at the Episcopal mission rooms, and, in conversation with the proprietor, my case was brought up, and Mr. Ives promised to attend to me and send me to Boston. Some two weeks passed, when, returning from church service Sunday morning, I met him; he bid me good morning, and asked if I knew him. I did not recognize his voice at first, as I was not expecting to meet him. He told me to get ready to go to Boston the next Tuesday morning. I told him I could not get ready to go until Thursday. He said that will do, but call on me to-morrow morning at ten o'clock; and he gave me a letter, and asked if I was ever in Boston? I told him I had never been there. He gave me a roll of bills, and told me to "take the early train to Boston, which leaves at half-past seven o'clock, and when you arrive there take a hack and tell them to take you to the Boston eye and ear infirmary on Charles street, and stay there as long as the doctors want you." I thanked him for his kindness, and returned home and got ready to go. I was on time at the cars and purchased my tickets, and seeing that my letter was not sealed, opened and read as follows: "This is the colored man I spoke of last week. He is a very respectable man, and I want you to retain him at your Institution as long as you can do him any good, and I will be responsible for all his expenses.

Robert H. Ives." This was the purport of his letter. When I arrived at the Institution, I took my seat in the hall, where all the patients were, and remained there until one o'clock, when I was called into the office by a man who waited on the doctors, and presented to Dr. Bethune; that being the day he attended to the patients. Two doctors attended the patients and one put up medicines. After Dr. Bethune examined my eyes through his different glasses for an hour, he committed me to the hands of Dr. Hooper; after he had spent an hour over me, I was passed over to Dr. Hayes for an hour, then the three doctors came together, and expressed their views in writing. Dr. Bethune said, "Mr. Ives, it appears by his note, called at the Infirmary last week, and spoke about this man's coming here. Mr. Ives is a millionaire of Providence, and wishes us to retain him here as long as we can do him any good, and he will be responsible for his expenses." He said to me, "You are Mr. Ives' servant, I suppose?" I replied, "No, sir. I am not the servant of Mr. Ives nor any one else." The doctor started, and said, "Ah, you are not?" I said, "No, sir." The doctor then gave me a card with my name on it and told me to hang it up at the head of my bedstead. He gave me another card with some numbers on it, which I was to keep always by me, to use when I went to the table. On my first arrival, I felt lonesome, and were it not for the kindness of Mr. Ives in sending me there, and paying my expenses, I would have taken the next train home, but I thought it best to content myself, and make the best of everything. One day one of the men came to me and said, "Mr. Brown, you are lonesome; come up among the men and unite with them in conversation." I told him I would come presently, but I preferred to be alone for awhile. I went up, soon after, and joined them in the conversation. I made myself sociable with all the inmates at the Institution, and had many discussions, which often caused some exciting talk and much enthusiasm, but always resulted in good. At one time we had a warm discussion on the subject of dividing the wealth of the rich among all classes, so that all would have an equal amount of money. I convinced them that such a course would prove were injurious to the poor themselves; for then they would refuse to work, there would be nothing to encourage the farmer, mechanic, manufacturer and tradesman to do anything besides supplying their own wants, and increasing their own comfort. There would be an end to all industrial pursuits, commerce would cease, and disgraceful conduct, waste and ruin would follow in the wake. At the time President Lincoln was about to take his seat, much anxiety was expressed by the patients for his safety; some felt that danger surrounded him on every side, but all expressed themselves in his welfare. A very exciting discussion took place one day concerning the conduct of the Mayor of Boston at a time his services were needed to protect the citizens. The Abolitionists were going to have a public meeting, and Fred. Douglass was to address them on the subject of slavery. The merchants and proslavery men of Boston did not want such a demonstration in their city, as many favored the system; so they induced a large party of men to go in and break up the meeting. Many blamed the Mayor for not quelling the disturbance, and protecting the citizens in the enjoyment of their rights, and thought that he favored the movers of the disturbance, and shonld be turned out of office, and lose all his salary; but in a short time things quieted down and there was nothing done about it. I received a call one day from Mr. Ives, who was in the city on business. He wanted to know how I fared, and what my accommodations were, and if the doctors thought they could help me. I could answer all the questions satisfactorily except the last one. I did not know what the doctors thought of my case. I learned that Dr. Bethune was a very curious man, and that if he said my case was favorable, he could help me, but if he said it was unfavorable, there was no help for me. I remarked that I was treated very well. Dr. Bethune was out of town, and Mr. Ives did not see him; He asked me if I had any message to send to any of my folks, or anything that I wanted? if so, he would attend to it for me. He then bid me good bye, saying he would be down shortly to see me. After he left, the inmates wanted to know if that was the millionaire that sent me there. I told them it was. They were surprised to see him sit down beside me and be so sociable. I told them the rich white people of Providence associate with all respectable colored people; and we associate with them, because from them comes our support. We also are in harmony with the poorer class of white people, and treat them well.

I found people of all persuasions in the hospital; and some were much displeased to think that they were compelled to go into the chapel and attend service Sunday afternoons, saying it was a perfect shame that a man was compelled to attend; because he was poor he must submit or be discharged from the infirmary; they did not like to sit a whole hour and hear a man preach doctrines they did not believe. I took no notice of their conversation, for I was pleased to go to church, and enjoyed the services much. After closing the services one Sabbath afternoon, the minister desired to speak with me. I went up to the pulpit, and he said, "Do you belong in this city?" I told him I belonged in Providence, and was there to have my eyes doctored. He said he had noticed me sitting and listening very attentively, and asked me if I was a Christian? I told him I was, and a preacher too. He said, "I am glad you are; I have preached here for some fifteen years; I know that I am not much of a preacher, but do the best I can and charge nothing for preaching; I know that some of these people don't like to hear me by their actions." I told him I liked his preaching very much. We came down together, shook hands and parted. The men in the ward wanted to know what he said. I told them what he said, and that I liked his preaching. They said, "Mr. Brown, you are a man of intelligence and education, and can you, of a truth, say you like that man?" I replied, "Yes, for he tells the truth." Mr. Oakes said, "I have been in this institution six years, and I never heard but one man before you say that they liked that man, and he was a Methodist preacher." I said, "I like to hear him, and I am a Baptist preacher." Mr. Oakes exclaimed, "The mystery is solved, we have been thinking how you came here, and was boarded and sustained by that millionaire of Providence. When the Doctor asked you if you wasn't his servant, you said No, sir; you was no one's servant, and then we could not imagine what caused him to sustain you here. The cat has been let out of the bag. You preachers can have some one to send you around and dress you too." I found that being obliged to associate with so many different classes of people, that unless a person has Divine aid, it will be impossible to enjoy religion here, especially when it is known that he is a professor of religion. Had I not made the advancement in religion that I did at the time I was attacked with sickness thirteen years before I went to the infirmary, and had been obliged to associate with the same class of people that I was at this time, I don't think I would have been able to sustain a religious character; but having settled in my mind, beyond a doubt, that I had been changed from nature to grace, or, in the language of our Saviour, been born again, I should have fell into the same belief that others had; that is, to think I was deceived, and never had met with a change; for as we are in a sinful world, we are more or less subject to its influence, and were it not for the aid of divine Providence, would fall victims to it. But we are held by the power of that influence which protects every soul by its spiritual light, so that nature loses its influence over us, and we are safe; and if we are called to die before that time arrived, it will be well with us. But after that time, being subject to its power, if we do not embrace Christ in the new birth, we fall victims to Satan's influence. Hence the wise man tells us to remember our Creator in the days of our youth, before the evil day comes, for the influence of Satan is turned against us, and we are responsible for every digression from God's ways, and continue so until the Spirit of God brings us to realize our situation, and we are brought to the knowledge of the truth as it is in Christ Jesus. Then the words of the Apostles comes to our assistance saying, As we have received the Lord Jesus, so walk in Him. We all know how we receive in joy and love, and how we feel towards those who have not been changed. We desire to see them brought to the light, and honor God in body and spirit, which is His. We are commanded to walk on in love after the Saviour." Here I made a stop, and had I been in the company then that I was at present, I should have felt that I had never been changed, and was deceived; but by the mercy and goodness of God I was enabled to see my situation and re-dedicate my life anew to His service, and regaining my health, I laid aside the various weights and the sins which so easily beset me, and run the race before me, looking unto Jesus, the author and finisher of my faith; and the Lord came to my assistance by the manifestation of His holy spirit, and I gained a knowledge of my sanctification, not in the light some view it, thinking they cannot sin any more, but knowing that if I sin I have an advocate with our Father, Jesus Christ, the righteous. Hence, I flee to the advocate, and I can withstand the influence by which I am surrounded, and thereby gain the respect and esteem of all.

I remained through the winter at the hospital, and in the spring, Dr. Bethune told me that they had done all they could for me, and discharged me, and I went home. I regretted leaving the hospital, as I had many friends there, and had spent the time very pleasantly. The sight of my right eye was somewhat improved, but I had received no benefit to my left eye. I was now at a loss to know what to do to support myself and family. Soap making and shoe making were both injurious to my sight. I therefore assisted the Rev. George W. Hamblin in printing a monthly paper called the *L' Ouverture,* but was induced by the white people to stop its publication for fear it might have a bad effect. This closed up my work in this direction.

CHAPTER XVI.

The long talked of war had at last begun, and men from every State were going forth to put down the rebellion. I was satisfied that the citizens of this State had become a unit in feeling on the subject. In a few days the Governor issued a call for colored troops, and Mr. George Henry called on me to know if I had read the call, and what I thought of it. I told him I had, and I believed that the colored people would be called on to help them before they got through with the war. He said they propose to hold a meeting at eleven o'clock, at Charles Brown's, on College street, and wanted me to attend. I went and found a large number of colored people had assembled, and Mr. John Waugh, holding a copy of the Journal, read the call of Governor Sprague for colored troops, which was as follows:

"The Sixth Regiment Rhode Island Volunteers, to be composed of colored citizens, under General Orders No. 36, from the Adjutant General's Department, will, if organized, be formed under the order of the Secretary of War, under the date of October 22d, 1861. The Regiment to be subject to the same service, and the officers and men drawing same pay and rations as other regiments now in the service of the United States.   C. S. ROBBINS,
Brigadier General R. I. M.
Providence, Aug. 13, 1862"

Mr. Dennis Laws asked if the Governor was in earnest in the call, or whether he wished to deceive them. I arose and said I once knew a man who said that if he could have the privilege of taking his spite out of the slaveholders of the South, he would bring his own arms and ammunition and travel all the way South to do so. Now you have an offer to be supplied with arms and ammunition, and all necessary expenses paid, and repay those slaveholders for their wicked conduct toward our brethren. If that man were living he would rejoice at this opportunity. "Who was that man?" cried out a dozen voices. I said it was Charles Gorham; there would be no hesitation on his part if he was living. A motion was made and passed unanimously, that we accept the call, and a committee of three, viz.: Wm. J. Brown, John R. Creighton, and John T. Waugh were appointed to wait upon the Governor and inquire into the particulars of the call. The meeting adjourned, and the Committee went to call upon the Governor, and learning that he had gone to New York, we called on Major Robbins. He asked who sent us to him? We replied that we were appointed at a meeting of the colored citizens. He said, "then I will talk with you. He said, "more than twenty men have called to see me to-day and wanted an appointment to raise the regiment, but I would have nothing to do with them. You come by the appointment of the people. I will telegraph to the Governor, and you can increase your committee to the number of seven, and bring their names to me in writing this afternoon, and to-morrow, at eleven o'clock, call at my office and I will give you your appointments." We sent the names of seven men to General Robbins, and the next day received our commission to enroll one thousand men, and report to the Governor. I was appointed Chairman of the Committee, and John R. Creighton, Secretary. We completed the number, took a copy of the roll and delivered it to the Governor, and told him that the men were anxious to go into camp, and he requested me to tell the regiment to hold themselves in readiness until he called for them. But there was some law in existence that the Governor was not aware of which prevented colored men from being enlisted equally with white; that the regiment could not be legally organized until that law was annulled, which took place soon after. When President Lincoln had issued his proclamation to emancipate the slaves, if the Confederates did not lay down their arms at a set time, many people thought he was only scaring them, but when the time drew near, and they did not comply, the colored people called a meeting to make preparations to receive intelligence of the proclamation; and Rev. Samuel White, William J. Brown, George Henry, John T. Waugh, John Banks, Jared Morris and George W. Hamblin were appointed. The Committee met at the Rev. Mr. White's resident on Benevolent street, and passed several resolutions, which were to be printed in the Providence Journal, and voted to procure Pratt's Hall for the day and evening. I was then appointed President of the day. Twenty-four Vice Presidents and five Secretaries were also appointed, after which they adjourned to the first day of January, 1863, at ten o'clock. When that day and hour arrived, a respectable number was present, but not the proclamation. The meeting adjourned and re-assembled at two o'clock; the proclamation had not yet come. The meeting adjourned to meet at seven in the evening. The proclamation not having made its appearance, the people were getting doubtful, the hall was packed, and at the hour of nine, when the bell was tolling, a man rushed into the room with a telegram from the President that the proclamation was issued. No one that was at that meeting can ever forget the sensation it produced. God was praised in the highest, and every heart swelled with gratitude. The meeting then closed, and thousands rejoiced that our prayers were heard and our country was free.

CHAPTER XVII.

I will now turn my attention to the interest of the Church, assisting in the prayer-meetings, and the singing and Sunday schools. I was well spoken of by all the members of the Church, as being always ready to attend to its interest whenever I was needed. All were satisfied with my Christian character, and spoke of me in the highest terms, but I was not altogether satisfied with myself. I felt very anxious to lay my case before the Lord, and know of a certainty how the case stood between the Lord and my own soul, and felt the necessity pressing on my mind to understand if I had been born again, for I had the clear statement of our Saviour to Nicodemus, in the third chapter of John, declaring that unless a man is born again, he shall never see the kingdom of heaven. It matters not what the minister, or deacons or church had to say of me, and though backed up by the community, if I had not passed through a new birth, I should be lost, and his word can not fail. Now this is comprehensive language, and every person can see for themselves the necessity of having a positive assurance of being born again in the way described by our Saviour. I looked at the state I was in before I had passed through the second birth; and the motive that prompted me to act under the circumstances, and discovered that all of my actions were based on selfishness. If I did anything, it was done for self, to make a grand appearance. God was out of the question altogether. He had no part nor lot in the matter. If I told lies it was to please self and elicit praise and admiration from my fellow men, and no part went to praise God for his goodness and admire him for his greatness, and Satan laid at the bottom of all my movements. I had no relish for God nor his word, and was each day hardening my heart and turning my mind away from God, nor did I realize it until I was brought into a place where five minutes would decide my fate. That was when I was going through the race on Long Island Sound. I heard a minister on board say that five minutes would decide whether we would remain above or sink below the waves. I well knew if the latter should be the case, my fate would be sealed, and I lost forever. I then said if I was spared, my first business would be to secure my salvation. This thought remained on my mind until I felt satisfied that through the blessings of God

I had accomplished the work. I found it to be directly reverse to the feeling which I had previously possessed, which was love and praise to God, recognizing that all things come from Him, and that He was the creator and owner of all things, and it was our first great duty to acknowledge His power, which would bring peace to our minds and fill our hearts with light and joy.

Our church was much reduced in numbers by so many enlisting in the service as soldiers. Our house was out of repair and our means limited and we concluded to issue a subscription paper and raise means to repair the house, which the committee estimated would cost eight hundred dollars. They asked me to circulate the paper, promising to give me twenty-five per cent. After much persuasion, knowing that they could procure no one for that purpose, I consented, and drew up a paper and circulated it. Many promised to give something, but would not head the paper. I labored several days without success, and then went to Mr. Robert H. Ives. After examining the paper, he said to me, "Why don't you get some one to sign your paper, recommending you to the public? People don't want to stop their business to read your paper; if they can see one or two responsible men recommending your object, that would be satisfaction enough for them to give." I told him we had a Committee of Seven, who were responsible men, and he was acquainted with the whole of them. He said, "Your Committee are no ones for that purpose." I said, "Who do you wish for—ministers?" He said, "No; they are not the ones for that purpose." I asked him what he thought of Prof. Caswell, also Dr. Wood and Dr. Wayland. He said, are they good men; those names would be satisfactory to any one who wanted to give help. Now get their names, and I will do something for you." I went and procured their names. Then calling on Mr. Ives I showed him what I had done. He said, "Now your book is in good shape; now then go to your Baptist brethren and let them open your list. I am an Episcopalian, but will do something for you."

I commenced trying to get some one to head my paper, each one excusing himself, and all saying they didn't know how much they would do, but would not head that paper, and what they intended to do would be but very little. After spending a week working without success, I called on Mr. George Hail. He examined my book and said, "How would you like to swap lots with me?" I asked him where his lot was located? He said, "It is a lot with a cellar dug in it, between Meeting and Congdon streets, and facing on Congdon street" I said, "That depends on how you want to swap, and what boot you want to give?' He said, "I think that the boot belongs on the other foot, for my lot is worth three or four of your lot." I said, "That may be in some respects, and perhaps to some persons, but not to me. Our house and lot is free from debt, and if we should trade with you, it would cost a great deal to move our house down there, and we have no money to do it with, and if we do it without money we will involve ourselves, and if we continue in our old house we will be free from all embarrassments, and a great deal better off than to be involved." Mr. Hail said, "It will not cost you a great deal to move your house on the lot, and if I should give you my lot for yours, I think you would make a very good bargain." I told him I would mention it to my people, but you can put your name down on my paper and help us out with our enterprise. Mr. Hail said, "If your friends trade with me, they won't want to repair the house." I didn't know he was in a hurry about trading. I thought any time would do for that, but if that be the case, I will stop right here about repairing and inform the corporation of your proposals, for they are the ones to do the trading. So I left, promising to let him know as soon as possible. I then called upon the treasurer of the corporation, Charles T. Cozzens, and told him Mr. Hail wanted the lot that our meeting house was standing on. He said he would swap with us for his lot on Congdon street. He said he would like to change very well, but he would want a great deal to boot, and we had no money to give. I told him that Mr. Hail did not say anything to me about any boot, so I suppose he wants to change even. Mr. Cozzens said it is not likely he is going to give his lot for ours, standing behind two or three others. If Mr. Hail was willing to trade even, would you trade? I asked. He replied, "Certainly!" I then said, "That is what I understood Mr. Hail to say, and I told him I would call a meeting to-night to consider it." He said, "Give notice of a meeting of the corporation to-night at eight o'clock, to be held at my house." I notified a meeting at that hour, and the corporation was in session. I laid the case before them, and told them I wanted an answer as soon as possible. They said if Mr. Hail wanted to trade even, they would; but if he wanted anything to boot, they could not trade, for they had nothing to give. I told the corporation that I wanted some one to go with me so that whatever was agreed upon I would have witness to hold it, and I invited the Rev. Charles Williams to accompany me if his services would be agreeable. The corporation said it would be acceptable. The next by Mr. Williams and myself waited on Mr. Hail and told him that the corporation held a meeting the night before, and appointed Mr. Charles Williams and myself to see him and make an agreement to exchange lots. 'And now how much boot will you give us in trade; for rather than involve ourselves, we will remain as we are." Mr. Hail said, "I want to do what is right with you, William, and any one that sees the lots will tell you that mine is worth three times more than yours, and your lot is not worth anything scarcely to any one, except to me. Now this I will do with you: if you can give me a warrantee deed of your lot

I will give you my lot and a warrantee deed, and one thousand dollars to move your house on it." I said "that is a good offer, and seems like business, but I think we can do a little better than that yet. Now suppose we move the house down there, and should need five hundred dollars to put it in order, would you give that?" He said, "William, I don't suppose you have got any money, but if you are lacking that amount, I will agree to fetch it up." "Well, that seems something like it, Mr. Hail; I knew you would do things right. It racks old buildings more or less to move them; we have no means to do it with; if we fail to meet whatever expense occurs in completing it, even to the amount of fifteen hundred dollars or more, will you agree to give us five hundred dollars more, making the whole two thousand dollars." He said, "Yes, I will, William ; I won't see you suffer," I then said, "That is a good promise, Mr. Hail; now you put two thousand dollars down on my book, and the bargain is made; that will head my book." Mr. Hail said, "I won't do any such thing; I will head your book with one thousand dollars; then, in case five hundred or a thousand should be needed, I will give it to you to help you out." I asked Mr. Williams, if it was the opinion that we should close the bargain with him. He said that Mr. Hail made us a good offer, and we had better close with him, as we had been invested with that power by the corporation. I told Mr. Hail that we, being appointed by the corporation, would close the bargain, when he had received the warrantee deed of our lot, and we had received the same of his lot. I went to the corporation meeting the next evening, and informed them of the interview we had with Mr. Hail, and the contract entered into by both parties They were highly pleased with the agreement, and desired me to carry out the project by appointing me sole agent with power to call whoever I saw fit to assist me, and voted to build a new house, providing the old one cannot be removed, and that I should collect all moneys needed in building a house, and other expenses, and receive a commission of eight per cent. on what I collected. With this agreement, the entire business was left in my hands to complete. The first thing I did was to consult the brethren of the church to ascertain their opinion respecting the change of lots. So I called on the Rev. Mr. Caldwell, pastor of the First Baptist church. I rang the bell, and his wife opened the door, and learning what I wanted told the Doctor that a colored man wanted to see him. He came to the door with a hasty step. I raised my hat and said, "Good morning, Doctor." He replied, "Good morning." I said, "I would like to see you a few moments, if you are at leisure." He said, "Walk in and take a seat." I did so, and said to him, "I have called to ask your advice concerning our Congdon street Baptist church. We have a very generous offer from Mr. George Hail, residing in that street; in the rear of his residence is our meeting-house and lot. He wants to make an exchange with us for his lot situated on Congdon street between Meeting and Angell streets, and will give one thousand dollars to boot, to remove our meeting-house on to the lot, for our lot, and our brethren thought it a good bargain for us; but we wanted to take the advice of our brethren before we completed the bargain" He said he thought it would be a very good bargain for us. I told him we were going to get the advice of all the pastors and deacons of the Baptist churches in the city, and to hold a meeting four weeks from that day, to consider the subject, and as his house was the most central of any, if he had no objections we would appoint it at his vestry, and would be pleased to have him attend the meeting when held. He said as far as he was concerned, we could have the vestry, but I would have to consult Deacon Read as he had control of the vestry when no legal meeting was appointed there, but when and wherever the meeting was called he would attend it. I told him I would call again before the time arrived, and tell him when it would be. Then bidding him good morning, I left and visited Deacon Read at his store, and informed him of my proposed meeting and time and said that his house being the most central, would like to have the meeting called there; and as the Doctor had promised to be present at the meeting, I should also be pleased to have his attendance on the occasion. The deacon replied that I could have the house and that he should endeavor to be present. I then called on Rev. Mr. Graves, Secretary of the Rhode Island State Baptist Convention, telling him the same. He immediately fell in with it. Then I visited every Baptist church in the city, and secured their approval and the promise of their attendance.

Now I had so much of my work completed. I had not mentioned a word to any of the brethren, what I intended to do; for I well knew that if I informed them of my intentions it would be carried from east to west, and north to south, and everybody would know it; and would have their different views on the subject and a way to execute them. I thought it would be time enough to tell them after I had accomplished my object, then I should not be bothered with them. The next week after I had laid my plans, I was attacked with rheumatism, and it continued for three weeks, with no prospects of being relieved, so I despatched a messenger to my invited auditors, telling them I had been afflicted with rheumatism for the last three weeks, and the prospect was that I should not be relieved for some time to come, and should be obliged to postpone the contemplated meeting until my recovery, and I would give them due notice. Four months elapsed before I was able to gain my feet. I then found that all my past labor was in vain, and I had got to begin entirely anew. The question arose in my mind, whether I was going to be successful or not; if had committed sin by using deception in laying the plans for my first meeting, it would be useless for me to try the same over again; but if I had not used deception, I could reasonably expect success. True, I had twisted points a little in my favor by telling Deacon Read that I had talked with Dr. Caldwell, conveying the idea that Dr. Caldwell was anxious to have the meeting in his vestry, when I was the one who was anxious, and the Doctor concurred in my views. As I could perceive nothing criminal in that act, I ooncluded to make the second attempt; so I called on Deacon Read first, but found that I could not hold our meeting in the vestry, nor could the Deacon himself attend, as they were going to have a four weeks' meeting. I also found that the same reason would prevent Dr. Caldwell from attending. But the Doctor said this to me: "I will tell you what to do, Mr. Brown, and I think it will be all for the best. The quarterly meeting of the Rhode Island State Baptist Convention will be held four weeks from next Tuesday, at Rev. Mr. Graves' church, on Brown street. The meeting will close about twelve o'clock, or a little after. Now if you will see Brother Graves and get his consent to have the meeting at his church at two o'clock, I will invite the Convention to remain back and join us in considering your offer. The house will be all warm and comfortable." I told the Doctor I highly approved of his proposals, and would call on Brother Graves and obtain his permission and let him know.

I called on Brother Graves and found him perfectly willing. I extended an invitation to all the pastors and deacons of the Baptist churches in the city, telling them that Dr. Caldwell was going to extend an invitation to the Convention to remain and unite with us. Having now established my plans, I thought it prudent to have some of our brethren present to hear what would be said in regard to the object. I soon learned that our church had put upon me a heavy task to perform, which would make me appear in the eyes of the brethren a very foolish man and a disgrace to the church in allowing me to represent them; or a very wise man in their estimation of the church for their selection, as the church and society's business was placed in my hands to accomplish. I invited Deacon George Waterman, and Brethren Charles Johnson and Charles H. Williams, telling them the meeting would commence at two o'clock, and I wished them to be there before that time. They promised to be punctual. I called at Brother Johnson's house on the day of the meeting and found him at work, holding conversation with those present. I said, "Come, come, Brother Johnson. It is time for you to be at that meeting." "Hold on, Brown. I will be ready in a few minutes." I told him I would be there soon, and went after Mr. Williams, and on my way up met with Deacon Varnum J. Bates, of the First Baptist church, and he said, "Halloa, Brown! Where are you going right away from the meeting? You have invited brethren from every part of the State, detaining them from their time and business, and you ought to be there to receive them." I said, "I am just going to Mr. Robinson's store to notify a brother who I am afraid will be belated. I will be at the meeting some minutes before the time." He said, "See that you do; and don't make fools of those people." I found Brother Williams, and told him to come, and soon got him ready, and stopping at Johnson's, took him and went to the church. I said, "Now, brethren, I have got a task to perform, and want you to stand by me and help me out. If you see I am about to break down, come to my rescue. As for deacon Waterman, we have no time to bother about him." We reached the church, and went in and took our seats in the centre of the house. A large number was present, conversing among themselves. It was then five minutes of two. When the clock struck two, one of the brethren asked, "What are we detained for?" Some one said that Brother Brown, a member of Congdon street church, has got some business with us, and turning around to me, said, "What is it, Brother Brown, you have got to say to us, for these brethren are anxious to go home." I arose and said, "Brethren, I have important business to submit to your judgment. It is necessary that we should organize in a proper way to receive it. If any of the brethren will make a selection by a motion, I will submit the same to the house for approval." Some one moved that the paster of Central church be appointed chairman, which was seconded and received unanimously. I then asked the Brother to come forward and take the chair, and he came; after which the house appointed a secretary. The chairman then called on some one to open the meeting by prayer; and announcing the meeting legally opened, I was called on to state the object for which the meeting was called.

I arose and told them that our church was a member of the Rhode Island Baptist State Convention, and we deemed it obligatory upon us, being connected with that honorable body, before making any final movement in any matter whatever, to hold a consultation, directly or indirectly, in regard to the merits of the same. Mr. George Hail, a highly esteemed member of the First Baptist Church, has made our church and society a proposal, which is, that he will exchange with us his lot for ours on which our house is located, it being in the rear of his house, with only one way of access to it, ten feet wide and ninety-three feet long, situate in the rear of Congdon and Meeting streets, whilst his lot is situated on the east side of Congdon street, bounded by Angell court on the south, and larger than the lot on which our house is located. This lot he will exchange for our lot, and give one thousand dollars to remove our house on it or to build a new church. Our church and society look upon it as a profitable exchange in our favor; but as we are liable to be mistaken, we felt it our duty to apply to you, brethren, for advice, knowing that we cannot be too particular in procuring the best information and from the highest source, before closing the bargain for an exchange. This is the reason we have called upon you for advice and assistance. The chairman said, "Brother Brown has stated the object which has brought us together, to ask your advice in relation to the proposed exchange of lots made by Mr. George Hail. Now, brethren, you are at liberty to ask Brother Brown any questions that may be on your minds pertaining to the exchange." The brethren then questioaed me respecting the lot we occupied and its advantages and the lot owned by Mr. Hail. After being questioned for an hour, a committee was appointed, with Prof. Greene as chairman, to draw up resolutions in reference to the statements they had heard, and submit them to the meeting for their consideration. The committee, after an absence of twenty minutes, reported a number of resolutions, concurring with the exchange of lots. The committee then asked if I had any objections to having three brethren appointed to advise with me. I told them none in the least. They appointed Deacons Hartwell and Daniels and Brother F. Miller as an advisory committee. The meeting then adjourned. The secretary, Rev. Mr. Graves, requested me to call on him in a few days and he would have my papers fitted out for me. In a few days afterwards I met Mr. Graves in front of Mrs. Rogers' house. He said, "Brother Brown, here is your book, all fixed for you. You can proceed on your mission, and I hope you will be successful." I thanked him for his good wishes, and went directly to Mr. Ives' counting room. Mr. Ives said, "Well, William, how do you succeed?" I said, very well; relating to him Mr. Hail's proposal to exchange lots and his gift to the object; the meeting of the Rhode Island Baptist Convention, their advice and cooperation, and the good feeling of the people generally in our favor, and what as a church we proposed to do; the situation being very different from what it was when I saw him last. He said, "Different, in what respect?" I then said, "When I last saw you, I had added to my list the names of Dr. Woods and Professor Caswell, recommending me to the public. I then called on Mr. George Hail to get him to head my list. After reading it he asked me if my folks would like to exchange lots with him. I asked him where his lot was situated? He said on Angell court, a lot that has a cellar dug in it. I told him I did not know, but I would ascertain. He said if we would give him a warrantee deed, he would exchange and give us one thousand dollars to remove our house on it, or towards building another. I told him that I would call a corporation meeting and let him know. I then called a meeting of the corporation and laid the case before them, and as far as they could see they were perfectly willing; but to have the advice of our friends, we invited the pastors and deacons of the several Baptist churches in the city, and obtained the permission of Mr. Graves to hold the meeting at his church at that time, and to invite the members at the meeting to remain and unite with us." I handed the book to Mr. Ives. He examined it, and said, "You have gone the right way to work; now I hope you will be successful; go among your brethren, and I will give you something. I suppose you have got the deed of your lot recorded?" My deed? I have not got it yet." "Your paper says you have made an exchange; and how can you make an exchange without receiving your deed? Now stop just where you are, and go tell Mr. Graves that his papers are not got up right and you must not deceive the public this way, feigning to have what you have not." I thanked him for his advice, and went to rectify the mistake. I saw Mr. Graves just going from Mrs. Roger's house, and delivered the message sent by Mr. Ives. He examined the book, and said, "This is a great mistake of mine, and I am glad that Mr. Ives discovered it. I would not on any account go with this book and thereby deceive the public. I will take this book home and correct it, and when I get it right I will leave it for you at Mrs. Rogers' house."

CHAPTER XVIII.

Our church had been in a very low state. It commenced to decrease in 1855, directly after our pastor, Rev. Chauncey Leonard, left us. He had been with us some two years, when he united with us. He had come directly from a Theological institution. His education was good, and his oratory surpassed any paster that ever graced our pulpit since the organization of our church. He was receiving from us four hundred dollars a year, which was all we were able to give, and a portion of that came from the Rhode Island Baptist State Convention. But our paster was greatly in debt for his education, and if he did not go as a missionary to Liberia, he must repay them. As soon as they learned that he had settled over our church, they demanded their pay, and this brought him into such straitened circumstances that he could not remain here and support his family ; and having an offer from the people in Baltimore, Md., to take charge of a select school, and supply a church, with a salary of six hundred dollars, he tendered his resignation to our church and accepted the call to Baltimore. That left us without any pastor, and the church fell into a despondent state. Remembering the remark that the council made at the time of his examination for the ministry, stating that this brother has got a good education, and if the church cannot flourish under his labors, they cannot prosper under any one. And some of the brethren, it appears, had come to that conclusion. Brother Waterman remarked that we had better disband, as we were all paupers, our paster had gone and we could not do anything. But the majority proposed to continue together and trust in the Lord. For the convenience of the committee, we removed their regular monthly meeting down to Brother Gorham's house. When the meeting had commenced, Brother Waterman was absent. The committee requested me to go after him and tell him he was wanted. I found him seated by the fireside. I informed him that the Committee had sent me after him. He replied that he had got his shoes off, and it was no use for him to go over there, for we couldn't do anything. I told him if he was not going to be with us to come and get his letter, and not leave us in that kind of style. His wife told him to put his shoes on and go along to meeting, and that he was a pretty deacon; he had ought to be ashamed of himself. He got up and went over to the meeting with me. The committee had but very little business to transact, and were very much depressed in spirit. Deacon Willis inquired if any one knew of any business that ought to come before the house. Some of them said they knew of none. I stated that I knew of some, and I suppose it was as good a time to present it as any. I informed them that directly after I was brought to a knowledge of the truth, I had a call to the ministry. I kept my feelings suppressed as much as I possibly could, and strove to do all that laid in my power among my unconverted friends, both in walk and conversation. I continued for months striving to smother my convictions, until I was brought to a stand to make a decision, and then I explained my call in full, after which the striving of the spirit seemed to cease. But when I was brought down with sickness in 1847, the only thing that troubled me was I had refused to obey a call from God to the gospel ministry. I made a solemn promise to the Lord that if I was spared, whatever duty devolved on me to do, I would strive by his help to discharge that duty. But if I was not spared, I believed that the Lord would forgive me and take me home. I am coming to that conclusion. God gave me knowledge that my prayer was heard, for something seems to speak within me like a voice saying, "You will not die this time." I immediately began to amend, and after I got well so that I could go abroad, I went to the house of God. Now, brethren, I have been with you, always striving to discharge my duty, and as we are not left without any pastor, I would tender my services if they can be of any use to you, and you see fit to give me a trial sermon or two. I am ready to appear before you whenever you are ready to hear me." The committee, then asked me some questions, and vote that I should attend the church meeting, and there relate my call. I attended the church meeting and related my call, and they voted that I should have a trial sermon on the evening of the following Thursday. When the evening arrived for my trial, as it was noised about, we had a large congregation. I preached my sermon, and they all seemed to be satisfied, and when the next church meeting came around, my case was called up, and it was voted that the church would license me to preach for them during the absence of a pastor, and when they had procured one they would empower him to give me license to preach abroad. I continued preaching for the church Sunday afternoons and evenings. In the morning we held a prayer-meeting. Our members became very much scattered when the different colored churches had commenced their protracted meetings, but still there were a number hung together. One Sunday morning we went to the church ; it was snowing lightly. When we went in the forenoon, we generally remained to afternoon services, especially those who lived some distance from the church, taking with them a lunch to partake of during the day. It had been snowing gently during the day, and when we closed our afternoon services, it began to fall very fast. I said, "Shall we have services this evening, or shall we close?" Some answered, "Just as you say about it, Brother Brown; if you have a meeting we will come." I replied, "If you leave it to me, we will have a meeting." When I returned to the church in the evening, and was preparing to hold our services in the hall, the number was small. Soon a couple of young men came in. I had got the hall prepared for our meeting and was waiting for the members to assemble. I said to the young men. "We shall not have any preaching here this evening as the weather is very inclement, and there will be but a few out. I thought I would tell you of it, for if you want to hear preaching you can go elsewhere, and you won't be disappointed." They said they would remain there. I then asked if they had been to the different meetings? They said they had. I then said a great many have embraced religion, and have you not been affected by those meetings? They said they had not. Soon after the members began to come, and we commenced our meeting; and in my first prayer, those young men pressed heavily on my mind. I presented their case to the Lord, and every one that addressed the meeting that evening carried their case to the Throne of Grace. Before closing the meeting, I notified a prayer and conference meeting at Mr. George Haskins' house on Tuesday, and a meeting on Thursday evening at Sister Prudy Jackson's house, she having a sick daughter at the time, extending an invitation to any one who wished to attend either of the meetings. And on Friday night our regular prayer meetings at the meeting house. When we met on Tuesday evening for prayer those two young men were present; also on Thursday and Friday evenings. We continued our meetings for three weeks, and these young men continued their visits, when Edward Perry arose at our Friday evening meeting and stated that he had found the Saviour. He said he once thought he had embraced religion before when he resided at Newport, but after some length of time concluded he must have been mistaken; but now he felt for a truth that the Lord had changed his heart, and he commenced laboring for the other young man, whose name was Edward Terrance. He shruggled for a space of two weeks seeking peace, but could not find any. We appointed a meeting at Sister Terrance's house on the following Monday evening for the purpose of helping him find the Saviour. The evening was very tempestuous, but news had gone abroad concerning Perry's conversion, and a good number attended the meeting that evening. The Rev. James E. Crawford arrived from Nantucket that day, and I had the good fortune to meet him, and invited him to attend the meeting. He promised to come and help us, and was present and the Lord was there, and not only helped Brother Terrence through, but brought down his younger brother to ask for prayers. After the conversion of those two young men, it brought our members together, and we had several seeking the Saviour, and were forced to open our meeting-house to hold our meetings, for we could not get any house large enough to hold them. And we soon had seventeen or eighteen waiting for baptism, and the church was obliged to seek for some one to baptize them, and on learning that Brother William Thompson, of Boston, was not laboring anywhere, our church wrote to ascertain what they could procure his services for one month, as they had quite a number of candidates waiting to be baptised. He informed us that he would serve us for one month for twenty-five dollars and board. We engaged his services, and he labored for us a month, baptising some seventeen or eighteen candidates; and still having more candidates, we secured him for another month; and as the interest seemed to demand it, the church hired him for a year, agreeing to give him $350 per year. The church then brought my case up again, and vote that Brother Thopmson give me a full license to preach the gospel. He accordingly prepared a document for that purpose. And on the Communion Sabbath, immediately after the sermon closed, they requested my presence in front of the pulpit, and read to me in the presence of the church and congregation, the document empowering me to preach the Gospel wherever in Divine providence might lot may be cast. By his request I responded to it, and he extended to me the right hand of fellowship. I remained assisting him whenever called upon. As I was preparing to commence my agency our numbers increased rapidly, and the church seemed to be inspired with new zeal, and their desire increased for the exchange of lots that their new edifice might be erected.

CHAPTER XIX.

After receiving my book, which Mr. Graves had corrected, I called upon Samuel Currey, Esq., to draw up a deed conveying our lot to Mr. Hail, telling him it was the request of the Meeting street Baptist Society. Mr. Currey said he wished to see the deed, which I carried to him. After examining it, he said the proper parties to convey the lot were the pew-holders, and the only way the Meeting street Baptist Society could convey the lot, was to have the pew-holders convey their right and title to the Society, then they could convey it to Mr. Hail. I then, by order of the society, drew up an agreement, stating to the pew-holders that if they would convey their right and title to the Meeting street Baptist Society, they could then exchange their lot for Mr. Hail's, and the society build a house of worship thereon; that when said house was built and finished, they should have their pews reconveyed to them in the new house as pleasantly situated as in the old one. This agreement I read to each pew-holder, and obtained their consent to exchange. I informed Mr. Currey, and he drew up a warrantee deed, conveying the lot that our house of worship stood on in the rear of Meeting and Congdon streets, to Mr. George Hail. He also drew up another deed, conveying the right, title and interest of the pew-holders to the Meeting street Baptist Society. I then took the latter deed, and accompanied by Mr. Mowry, visited each pew-holder and obtained the acknowledgment of their signatures, being their free and voluntary act, and for the attorney's services I paid fifty cents per signature, drawing the money from the treasurer, Brother Charles H. Williams, the money that belonged to the church which has been previously collected by sister Mary A. Cone, for the purpose of repairing the old meeting house. The former deed, by order of the Society, was presented to Mr. George Hail to complete the exchange of lots. Mr. Hail took the deed to his attorney for examination, who informed him that the Meeting street Baptist Society's title to the land they wished to convey was not in his opinion according to law, and would advise him to obtain the opinion of the Supreme Court on the same. Mr. Hail was not satisfied with the deed, according to the advice of his counsel, so the Society voted to refer the same to the consideration of the court. The matter was brought up at the next session of the court as a case in equity, and decided that the title was not valid. Mr. Hail's attorney, J. G. Markland, Esq., stated to the society that the obstacles which prevented our deed from being valid could be removed by having the law amended, and if we would put the case into his hands he would file a petition for that purpose to the General Assembly of this State. The society accepted his proposals, and voted to employ Mr. Markland for that purpose. The petition was presented to the General Assembly and granted. The next petition was to the Supreme Court, to ascertain the lawful feoffees in trust, according to the provisions of Moses Brown's deed, and was declared by the court to be the City Council, which duties they assume. The next petition was by the Meeting street Baptist Society, for the City Council to accept as feoffees William J. Brown, George W. Hambliu, and Charles Gorham of the deed of Moses Brown, which, according to its provisions, and the decision of the Supreme Court, devolved on that body. The petition was received by them and they voted to comply with the request of the Meeting street Baptist Society. Another petition was filed in the Supreme Court, praying for the appointment of William J. Brown, George W. Hamblin and Charles Gorham, as feoffees in trust to the deed of Moses Brown, in place of the City Council, and for the acceptance of the resignation of said body, of the duties imposed upon them by assuming the office of feoffees in trust, which the deed of Moses Brown imposed. The petition was received, and a decree issued, appointing William J. Brown, George W. Hamblin, an Charles Gorham, as feoffees of the deed of Moses Brown.

Mr. Charles Gorham was taken sick and died before we had an opportunity of making an exchange of lots, and we were obliged to file another petition to the Supreme Court, praying them to confer the power that devolved on Charles Gorham as trustee to the deed of Moses Brown, on the other trustees, William J. Brown and George W. Hamblin, Charles Gorham having been removed by death since his appointment by their honorable body. The petition was received and the requisition complied with by the court, having the powers then invested by the court to the two feoffees in trust, namely William J. Brown, and Geo. W. Hamblin. A title deed was drawn up by J. G. Markland, Esq., at the request of the Meeting street Baptist Society, conveying the lot of land whereon the African meeting and school house was located, in the rear of Meeting and Congdon streets, to George Hail, in consideration of a lot of land situated on Congdon street, between Meeting street and Angell court, deeded to William J. Brown and George W. Hamblin, feoffers for the Meeting street Baptist Society. Both deeds having been prepared for exchange, I appointed Mr. Joseph Rogers to receive the amount which Mr. Hail agreed to pay, the sum of one thousand dollars and the lot he owned on Congdon street, for the lot which the Meeting street Baptist Society conveyed to him. The deeds were duly signed and delivered to the parties to which they were assigned, and one thousand dollars paid over to Joseph Rogers, Esq., to hold in trust, until it was legally drawn to cancel the debts of the Society, and for the house to be removed off the premises on or before the first day of April, on the conditions that if the house, or any of its foundation, remained over the specified time, it should be forfeited. Having obtained the lot, we were in readiness to receive collections for our new house of worship. I accordingly issued eighteen books for collecting subscriptions among such members as wished to collect, having a card placed in each book containing rules and regulations for collecting and making returns. After such members had received their books for collecting, I took the book which I purposed to use, and after asking Divine aid on my labors in collecting and directing me in the course I should pursue, I went to the residence of Mrs. Cornelia Greene, and inquired for her, and she requested me to send up my message. I sent to her my subscription book. After retaining it a few moments she sent down to know if I was willing to leave my book that night with her, so she could have ample time to look it over and she would leave it at Mrs. Rogers' house the next day for me. I replied that I was perfectly willing. The next forenoon I called on Mrs. Rogers and received my book, and two hundred dollars in cash, one hundred with the name of Mrs. Cornelia Greene, and one hundred to Miss Fanny Greene, her daughter. Mrs. Rogers then put down one hundred and fifty dollars, and Mr. Joseph Rogers, one hundred and fifty dollars. The next day I obtained of Mrs. Pardon Miller three hundred dollars, and Mrs. _____, two hundred dollars in cash. Those were my two first days' work. After obtaining three hundred dollars more from sundry individuals, I came to a standstill, as people were loth to subscribe. I called a meeting of the collectors to ascertain the full amount we had subscribed out of the eighteen books I had issued among the members. There was only six that had subscriptions, and the amount subscribed was sixty-two dollars. Some of the members were very anxious to commence building, and making the same known to Mr. Frederick Miller, who was chairman of the Advisory Committee, he procured the draft of a house which Messrs. J. F. And T. Hull would build for the sum of fifteen thousand dollars. The Society seeing the draft, thought the cost too much, and preferred having a cheaper one. After striving for six months without succeeding to build a cheaper house, without they were able to pay for it when the house was completed, they concluded to engage Mr. Hull as the contractor. I then inquired of Mr. Hull how small amount he should need to commence to build. He replied that he wanted eight thousand dollars, and if I could not obtain that amount, he did not know but what he could begin with six thousand dollars. After striving a whole year, traveling throughout the city, meeting with no success, comparatively speaking, I took an account for the subscriptions from the church, and found that they amounted to three thousand dollars. Then adding the subscriptions that I had on my book, which were thirteen hundred dollars, making a sum of four thousand, three hundred dollars, I requested Mr. Miller to state to the contractors how much I had, and asked them if they would not commence building with that amount? He returned an answer that they could not commence short of six thousand dollars.

I commenced to travel among the members of the different Baptist churches, and for three months I labored day after day, but nobody was ready to subscribe, and those who had subscribed at first, said if we were not going to commence we had better refund the money. Finally, I took the subject to the Lord, and asked him to touch the hearts of the contractors, that they might respond to my wishes. I then waited on the contractors, and told them that if they would commence our building so as to have it in readiness to lay the corner stone on the third day of October, 1871, I would pay them on the second day of October, one thousand dollars, and when they had got it raised and covered, I would pay them fifteen hundred dollars, and if I did not have the whole amount to pay them down, they might stop working until I obtained the amount; and so they could proceed on, as each thousand dollars worth of work was done, they could stop working until they received their pay. To this they agreed. We appointed our building committee, namely, Ebenezer P. Hallam, George Waterman, William J. Brown, Major W. Hamblin, and Levi H. Hamblin. The contract was signed, and the work was commenced on the second day of October, 1871. I paid to the Messrs. Hull one thousand dollars and received the receipt for the same. The next day the ceremony for laying the corner stone commenced at two o'clock, and after appropriate exercises, the stone was laid. The work went on, until it amounted to fifteen hundred dollars. I paid the contractors eight hundred dollars. Chicago had just suffered greatly by fire, and assistance was called for from citizens to aid the sufferers, and money was difficult to collect; so the contractors concluded it would be best to quit work during the winter and commence in the spring ; and that would give me time to collect the balance due of the fifteen hundred dollars. Having consented to the proposition, the contractors ceased working. I made every effort to raise money, but people would not give. The winter passed, and spring came, and the money was still held close by our people ; finally, I tried another method: I obtained consent to appoint a meeting in the vestry of the First Baptist Church, it being the most central, to be held in the afternoon of a certain day; I then visited the pastors of the several Baptist churches, and those whom I found at home I persuaded to attend the meeting, and those I could not find I left a note for them to attend. When the time arrived for the meeting, seven pastors out of twelve were present. I told them my object in calling them together, which was to recommence work on our meeting-house. The contractors were ready to commence work, when we were able to raise money to pay what was due on the last payment, seven hundred dollars. Those who had subscribed were backward in paying their subscriptions, and those who had not subscribed were unwilling to subscribe; and those who were not of our denomination said, "When your own denomination will come up and do as they ought with their subscriptions, we will help you; but if they are not able to do it, let them say so; we have to look out for our own denomination, and it is no more than right that your denomination should look out for you." The pastors present stated, that they had not done as they should have done; and as there was not a sufficient number present, they adjourned to meet one week from that date at the same place, and appointed me to notify the other five pastors that were absent, and some of the deacons from the different churches, and have my accounts present at the next meeting for examination.

At the time appointed they met, and my accounts being present, they spent the principal part of the time in examining them. Being satisfied with the accounts, they recommended to appoint one person from each church, which should be an advisory committee, and that Frederick Miller be their chairman; and that the committee meet one week from date, at the same place. When the time arrived, the committee being present, they selected from my account subscribers that belonged to the Baptist churches that had subscribed to any amount, and put it into the hands of the advisory committee, that they might be able to make an immediate payment, so that the contractors might resume their work, and the residue of the subscriptions for me to collect, together with such other subscriptions as I might be able to procure.

The committee proposed to have a union entertainment to raise funds to carry on the work, each committee to urge their respective churches to unite in getting up the entertainment, which proved a success, and the house was finished outside. Money again was wanted, and the contractors were about to stop work, and I became responsible for three thousand dollars, and they continued. I then wrote to Mr. Hail, as he had promised he would not see us want, and if we came within one thousand dollars of paying for our house, after it was finished, he would give us that amount. I told him in my letter that our house was paid for within one thousand dollars, and in all probability we should be in it worshiping, but now we were in debt three thousand

dollars, and could not get into it and get the house finished until we paid
that amount, and asked him if he would not help us out of this dilemma.
After submitting my letter to the Lord for his directions, I went to Mr. Wall,
a broker that attended to Mr. Hail's business, and he delivered the letter to
Mr. Hail. In two week's time Mr. Wall received a check for four thousand
dollars for the Meeting street Baptist Society. The contractors began on the
work inside the house, and finished the vestry. Then they proceeded to the
upper part of the house. Mr. Miller, the chairman of the advisory committee, informed me that he thought it would be better for the society to have
the Rhode Island Baptist State Convention appointed trustees, and Mr.Ham-
blin and myself had better resign. I told him that the pew-holders would
have something to say about that, as the society had to reconvey to them
their pew according to their agreement, and then if the pew holders and
society did not need my services I was ready to resign; but we were going
to have a meeting shortly, he could attend, and I would lay his proposals
before them. The meeting was called, and Mr. Miller was present. I laid his
proposals before them, and they rejected them unanimously. Mr. Miller
then suggested to me the propriety of my resigning, and Mr. Hamblin
would resign, and they would be compelled to have the Convention trustees. I informed him that the people had confidence in me, and had appointed me trustee, and I should never turn my back upon them. The house
now being finished, the contractors placed a lien upon it and waited on me,
and informed me that they were about closing up business, and wanted to
have a settlement on the meeting-house. I told them that the society had no
money to pay at present, and that Mr. Frederick Miller was appointed
executor on the estate of Jane Congdon, and had held the office for seven
years, and had not closed up the estate. The society was going to make an
effort to bring it to a close, thinking they would have means to pay whatever was due on the meeting-house, and if they would give us a suitable
time, we would be able to settle with them, and pay them interest for the
time they waited upon us. They said they would give us four years to pay
the debt in, and they were to receive it in four payments, at seven per cent.
per annum. I reported it to the society, and they agreed to accept of the
terms stated by the contractors. I told the contractors to draw up the mortgage deed, and I would present it to the society for approval.

In three months time, on the first of November, the mortgage deed was
complete, and I received it from the contractors. I presented it to the society,
and on examining it, I found we were to make four payments, and as each
payment came due, the principal and interest, of each note must be settled;
and if each note was not settled within six days after it was due, both
principal and interest, we would forfeit the house. I told the society the first

note would amount to seven hundred and eighty-four dollars, principal and interest, and we should not be able to collect any money until May. As a general thing, people could not get money to pay their debts, let alone to give the church, and if we signed that mortgage, it would bring us under obligations to pay the money or lose the house, and I deemed it best to hire the money, if possible, and pay the contractor and have a complete settlement. The society concurred in my opinion, and voted to hire the money on the house. After searching some time to get some one to accommodate us, I succeeded in finding a gentleman who had money belonging to a lady, to loan on interest, who said he would accommodate us with such an amount as we should need, providing there was no other claim on the house, and that the society had no note against them of any kind. I told them the society had one note of seven hundred dollars in favor of me, payable at a set time at seven percent per annum. He said if the society would bring all their accounts in one note he would let them have money to cancel the whole debt. The debts of the society were made up and found to be thirty-one hundred dollars. The mortgage debt was drawn up by the attorney of the gentlemen that loaned us the money. The society seeing the same, requested me to procure the money; after indorsing the deed I obtained the money, and by order of the society settled with the contractors, and received the receipt. Mr. Miller finding out that the settlement had been made with the contractors, and ascertained that I had hired some money for that purpose, wrote to Mr. George W. Hamblin, informing him that I was applying a portion of it for my own use, and advised him to resign as trustee. Mr. Hamblin supposing it was correct, wrote a statement to that effect. I was then waited upon by Deacon Lyon, with a written resignation for me to resign. I informed him that I would not resign, as I was of the same mind as heretofore. He told me I had better resign and sign the paper which he had and send it down to the school-room. I told him he might as well take the paper, as I should not resign; I should never turn my back upon my people. When my services were no use to them, I was at their disposal to dispose of. He left his paper and withdrew, and the next day I sent his paper to the school-room.

A few months after, I had served on me a summons by the sheriff, to appear at the supreme court, to answer the charges brought against me by William M. Greene and others; to show reasons why I should not be dismissed of the trust that I was empowered with, on account of my age, being blind, and other incompetencies.

Mr. Hamblin returning home to see his folks, fortunately, a few hours before the case was to come up, called on me to examine the society's books, and after being satisfied that everything was straight between the society and me and their books, he informed me what Mr. Miller had written him, and stated his intention to recant from his former decision, and in the presence of a magistrate, revoked his former statements. When my case was called up, the document held by Mr. Lyon, purporting to be my resignation as a trustee and signed by me, was read, which I frankly denied as my signature. The court then called Mr. Lyon to the stand and asked him if he knew that document; he answered in the affirmative. They asked him if he saw me sign my name to it, and he replied "No." He said he brought it to my house for me to sign, and left it there, requesting me to send it down the next day. Then they asked him who brought it down? He said he did not know; he saw it lying on his desk and it was signed and he supposed I had signed it. The document was then shown to lawyer Mowry. Mr. Mowry stated that he was acquainted with Mr. Brown's handwriting, and that was not his. Mr. Hamblin was next called to the stand, who stated to the court that he had signed a resignation, as he had been misinformed about the affairs of the meeting-house, but when he came here and examined the books, he found they were all right, so he wished to resume his former position as trustee. Mr. Hamblin was then asked if he was acquainted with Mr. Brown's handwriting. He replied that he was. They showed him the document and asked him if that was Mr. Brown's signature. He stated that it was not. The case was then closed up by the court stating, that there was no cause to remove Mr. Brown and Mr. Hamblin as trustees, and they could continue on discharging their duties that devolved upon them. The society then requested the church to assist them to pay the interest on the money that they had hired to pay the church debt. The church agreed to help to pay the church debt, if the society would help to sustain their minister and allow six members of the church to join the society. The society voted and received six members of the church, as members of the society in full, and by the request of the church a notice was written and published in the Journal, of the union that was entered into by the church and society, which was, that the society would unite in supporting the pastor, and the church unite with the society in paying the debt on the house. The act of the church in creating a union was signed by the pastor and clerk. The act of the society in affirming the union, was signed by the president and secretary. There was another plot formed to institute another lawsuit. As they had been deceived in removing the former trustees by some person or persons, they planned this second attack by proposing to create a union. After proceeding thus far successfully, another movement was made for the church committee to unite in examining the papers to see what the debt was on the house, so that the church might know how much rested on them to pay. The society set aside their ordinary course of business to accommodate the wishes of the church, appointed a meeting in the vestry of the meeting-house to examine the papers of the society, holding a meeting once a week for that purpose, they consumed five weeks, where all the papers of the society were examined concerning the money that had been received and the manner it had been expended, then the society made a second call on the church for aid, but instead of receiving aid, we received an answer, that they would have to consult the Rhode Island Baptist State Convention. The society concluded that they would not receive any aid from the church, and voted to hire some money to pay the interest, and empower me to make an effort to collect means to reduce the principal. Having procured a book for that purpose, I made an attempt to collect subscriptions. After laboring sometime I found that some person or persons had been circulating a rumor that I had been using the church funds for my own use. The rumor spread from house to house, and from church to church, and individuals who worked in private families carried the news to their employers, and frequently when I went to solicit subscriptions, if colored servants answered the call, I was refused admittance, or informed that the people were out. Every effort was made to prevent me from getting means towards the principal. In order to carry on more successfully another suit in law, and to have the church furnish them with means, they proposed a plan to remove my membership from the church. Accordingly they made some charges against my christian character, combined with embezzlement, and sent a summons for me to attend the committee meeting to answer to the charges contained in the summons, and the bearer who had the summons was told by my wife that I was sick in bed with rheumatism. He was not satisfied with the answer, but desired to see me. After being ushered to my bed room , and was satisfied that I was sick, he went away. In a short time another meeting was appointed by the committee, and a notice for me to attend was shoved under my door, and when the time came for the meeting to assemble, as I was not present, they voted to remove my membership. When the regular church meeting was held, they voted that I be removed from the church. After I got well, I visited the next church meeting, and was informed that I was not a member of the church. I inquired what I had done that they should turn me out, and asked them to read the charges that were made against me. The church clerk turned over his book to the last meeting that was held, and said there was no charge preferred against me, only that the church voted to have me turned out. I was advised by many people belonging to the different churches to sue those people who signed the warrant against me charging me of using the church's money, both, white and colored, but I told them I should not do any such thing, for christians are strictly forbidden going to law against one another, and if any person or persons goes to law against christians they go contrary to the teaching of the scripture, and as my brethren went contrary to the word of God to injure my character and reputation, I will not follow after them, but go according to the word of God, which is to pray for them, hoping they will repent of their sins, and before they die obtain grace enough to ask forgiveness which will by the help of God be cheerfully given. I told them it was against the Baptist rules to turn a person out of church without a cause. The church then referred the whole matter to the committee, and I was requested to meet them. When the regular committee meeting came around I attended, my case was brought up, and they could do nothing against me, and recommended to the church to revoke their vote which they passed to dismiss me from the church. At the next regular church meeting their report was received, and I was restored to the church. In the meantime another bill was filed against me in the Supreme Court, charging me of hiring money in the name of the church and using it for my own use, and also of disturbing religious meetings, when I had been requested to desist, but refused to do it, and other charges of similar character. I was summoned to appear to answer to the charges. When the case came up I was present, and a committee of five were appointed by the Rhode Island Baptist State Convention, and were present at the trial. They were, Dr. Johnson, Dr. Taylor, Rev. Mr. Everett, Deacon Mason and Deacon Lyon. The committee were examined by the court, first, Dr. Johnson, who stated that he was appointed by the convention to attend the court, and respecting the charges alleged against me, that he had received his information from Mr. F. Miller. The second was Dr. Taylor, who stated that he had received his information from the same source, and the residue of the committee's testimony was similar. The next was Mr. F. Miller, who stated that he had received his information from the colored people. In regard to what his letters contained which were sent to Mr. George Hamblin in Philadelphia, there was nothing he could vouch for, and as the knowledge that the colored people pretended to have, was nothing of which they had any proof, the charges were not sustained. After hearing all they had to say upon the subject, which occupied three days, the court continued me to discharge the duties as trustee. Mr. Hamblin taking up his residence in Pennsylvania, was removed from the trust, and the Rhode Island Baptist State Convention placed in his stead, and the vacancy of the their trustee, which was caused by the death of Charles Gorham, was filled by William Douglas, Esq. I had previously satisfied the court, when I had made my statement before them, occupying five hours on the stand, presenting to them a sketch of the affairs of the African meeting house, from the time that I was sixteen years old and was appointed secretary until the Congdon street Baptist Society had changed lots, and from that time until that suit was filed in court; also answering such questions that were put to me, showing when I was appointed by the society to hire money and reporting who I hired it of and the amount hired ; showing my appointment to pay out money, and the amount paid out, and to whom paid, which were all in accordance with the amount given in the Society's books, accompanied with the receipts of the same, which were all satisfactory to the court. After the case was dismissed from the court, the society held a meeting and voted to communicate with the Rhode Island Baptist State Convention, and inform them that if they would assume the debt of the meeting house, they would make them trustees of the property which was in their hands for the benefit of the Congdon street Baptist Church. The Convention agreed to assume the responsibilities, and requested the society to make up the account of all debts owned by them caused by the Congdon street Baptist Meeting House and all claims held against the society, and the Convention would be accountable and responsible for the same. The society accepting the statement of the convention, an agreement was drawn up, and the property, consisting of the real estate of Jane Congdon, together with the meeting-house was turned over to the Rhode Island Baptist State Convention as trustee for the Congdon street Baptist Meeting House. Not knowing that the Convention was satisfied that I was clear from the charges that was brought against me at the Supreme Court, and as their committee was present when the case was acted on, I then addressed a letter to the annual meeting of the Convention to ascertain their opinion respecting the rumors concerning me, and I received from them the following certificate:

"Concerning the charges against William J. Brown, President of the Congdon street Baptist Society, the Board of the R. I. Baptist State Convention puts on record its acceptance of the statement made by the Committee which has been concerned with the affairs of the Congdon street Church and Society that no reason has been found for suspecting that Mr. Brown used the funds of the Society for any but lawful purposes. And the Secretary is directed to send a copy of the minute to Mr. Brown."

Extract from the minutes of the First Quarterly Meeting of the Board of the R.I. Baptist State Convention.

W. W. EVARTS, Jr., Secretary.

Providence, Oct. 6th, 1880.

Now I close this eventful history of my life labors, and conflicts. Hoping the errors may be passed by, and its real merits duly appreciated, I commend this work to the favorable notice of the public.

LIFE

OF

GEORGE HENRY.

TOGETHER WITH

A BRIEF HISTORY

OF THE

COLORED PEOPLE IN AMERICA.

PUBLISHED BY GEORGE HENRY.

PROVIDENCE, R. I.:
H. I. GOULD & CO., PRINTERS
1894

Our volume concludes with chapters 14, 15, and 16 of George Henry's Life of George Henry: Together with a Brief History of the Colored People in America *first published in 1894. Henry worked at a variety of different occupations and as the narrative indicates was quite entrepreneurial. This narrative is especially valuable for its discussion of the efforts to integrate schools in Rhode Island and for Henry's discussion of jury service and the struggle against Rhode Island's anti-miscegenation statute in the 1870s.*

CHAPTER XIV.

ANOTHER VOYAGE AND OTHER OCCUPATIONS.

But yet onward, onward I still wandered over the dark blue sea, seeking for treasures, as all men do. Press forward! whispered the sweet voice. Such is the road to honor, virtue, righteousness and wealth.

I remember one of our voyages. We started from Providence at three o'clock in the morning, arriving in New York at eight p. m., a distance of nearly two hundred miles, which was considered one of the quickest voyages ever made by a sloop. The wind was blowing heavy to the eastward, and we carried a whole mainsail, squaresail and topsail. I must say with all my voyages, I never had a prettier run in all my life. Capt. McKinney was the most careful and safest man I ever sailed with, excepting Capt. Beymore. I should have staid with him longer, but I quit him upon principle. He took a stray boy on board from New York, and wanted me to wait for my meals till he got through, and I would'nt do it. So I quit him for good after that.

These voyages with this captain was about the winding up of my continued seafaring life. Although after settling down to shore life I made several voyages, at intervals, during the winter, and in summer took charge of St. Stephen's (Episcopal) Church, of which Rev. Henry Waterman was rector, corner of Benefit and Transit streets, in this city, where I remained upwards of twenty-five years. During this period the Society built a new and substantial edifice on George street, modeled after Dr. Waterman's own taste. He, together with his father, spent a fortune to carry out his designs. He continued their rector until a very short time previous to his decease. He was a man of ability and great power. He not only preached his religion, but lived it daily. I also worked for his father, and found him also a christian and a gentleman. I want his name to be honored and cherished, as a memorial, henceforth and forever, to all generations that shall come hereafter.

I found prejudice so great in the North that I was forced to come down from my high position as captain, and take my whitewash brush and wheelbarrow and get my living in that way. My first work on shore was at Mrs. Patrick Brown's, 45 Williams street, that of digging a well. When I got through with that she employed me to do all her work, until her death, twenty years afterwards. During that time I also worked for a colored man living on Benevelent street, named John Johnson, whose business was watering streets. He employed me at a dollar per day, to pump water to water the streets, which I pumped from daylight till dark, a very laborious work. That was considered great wages in those times. But I was determined to work, knowing it was my living, and I had to support a wife and two children out of that.

I worked thus one summer, and my attention was next called to the cheapness of land hereabouts, and I tried my best to get up a combination of colored men to buy up the land on east side of the bridge, which if they had listened to me then, they could have monopolized all the east side just as well as not. My attention was next called to a co-operative grocery store, which we did establish. Some five or six persons raised one hundred dollars, and with as fine a prospect before us (as we thought) as any set of men ever had, and was doing a flourishing business. We selected two as honest men to carry on the business, as we thought were in the city. That one hundred dollars turned over, according to the books, eleven hundred dollars. But I lost every cent of my enterprise, as did the others, excepting the two that we placed so much confidence in. Now I say if we had had honest men, as we supposed, we would have been as rich a firm as any in the city. So you see where confidence first began to weaken. So I say to all persons, when confidence is once betrayed, never trust them again under any circumstances.

My next enterprise was: I came in contact with a man who had nine lots, and houses on all except one. He was an aged man, having no family, and was anxious that the colored people should have the property. He would let me have the whole of the property for ten thousand dollars, part payment at first, and turn the rents all over into my hands. Not being able to take it myself at that time, which I knew was one of the best bargains that any man could offer to another. So I appealed to the colored men of this city, and more especially to the Society to which I belonged. I could'nt get a man to help to secure that property, but rather to the contrary. They did'nt want it, had no use for it. In twelve years time from that date the same property could'nt be bought for forty thousand dollars. Now I ask, in the name of Heaven, is it any wonder that we are such poor and degraded people as we are?

So I struggled on and never got discouraged, knowing what was in the grasp of man. After a lapse of time, through my ardent persuasion, I got six men besides myself, to put in eighty-four dollars apiece, to start another firm in the grocery line. We planked five hundred and eighty dollars cash, and selected two more men, whom we thought were as honest as the sun, to carry on our business, and it was carried on flourishingly for a year, and then that busted up, and I never got the sixteenth part of a cent, nor did either of the five who constituted the firm. Only the two that we placed there, who ran away with every cent, and every particle of the goods. Now where can confidence be established? I don't think with me it can ever be established again. Now I say sir, until confidence can be established amongst us, we must make up our minds to be hewers of wood and drawers of water for all generations to come.

My attention was next called to the caterer. I saw at a glance that the colored people could monopolize the whole city in the catering business. I never was nor ever wanted to be a caterer. But we had one here named Burrill, one of the finest in the world, and I saw it was necessary to sustain him and hold up his hands. So through my strong efforts I called a meeting in the lobby of the Old Baptist Meeting House, "on the hill," for the purpose of permanently establishing him in that position. My proposal was for him to select a half dozen of the best colored waiters in the city, and they should bind themselves to be ready at his call, to wait upon any party or gathering. And my idea was for each of those men to pick out four or five honest and upright men, and make them pledge themselves to be at their call, to wait at any gathering. I thought by doing this the catering machinery would be in perfect order. I still believe if that idea had been carried out, that the colored caterers would have been in the place of Humphrey and Ardoene today. So they may blame themselves for being in their present sad condition.

CHAPTER XV.

WATERING AND CLEANING STREETS.

My attention was next called very forcibly to the cleaning and watering of the streets, which at that day was a very profitable business. There were six or seven watering carts, all owned by colored people. We had one man here, very smart and energetic, named Joseph Gardner, who got up a small engine to pump water to save labor, and none of the other watering carts would patronize him, simply because there was no union. And here at this stage I interfered myself, and used all the influence I could bring to bear to unite those men in a body, so as to be able to build themselves up in the future, and they would have been able to monopolize that business forever. But I could'nt possibly get them to see the point, and so it failed, and threw all the business in their hands, and Mr. Gardner not being able to carry on the machinery it went down. Here was one of our great downfalls, through our own neglect. So they worked on in this hard way until water was introduced into the city. So I say now boldly that we have had the best chance of being the richest colored people in the New England States. But the great prejudice to one another has caused us to be as we are, and if it cannot be broken in any other way, let us pray God to send an angel from Heaven, that he may reveal unto every man's heart, to do away with this prejudice from amongst us. Then, and not till then, will we become a united and a thrifty people. confidence must be established.

In the year of our Lord 1855, I turn my attention to the subject of public school rights. I find myself paying a heavy tax, and my children debarred from attending the schools for which I was taxed. So a few of us got together and resolved to defend ourselves against such an outrage. Mr. George T. Downing was the leading man in the first part of the campaign.

The first petition was to break up the colored schools, and let the children go into the different ward schools. Upon that I bolted, and declared I would never sign my name to any such petition, because I did not believe we had any right to break up that school—told him so—and that upon that plank they would whip us, and they did. We were left with not a single plank to stand upon, and all said they would never agree to break up a school that their forefathers worked so hard to establish. So the next year my proposal was to petition the General Assembly that my child should go to school in my own ward, where I pay taxes and vote. So when that petition went in, our opponents had not a plank to stand upon, we swept every plank from under them, and I signed every petition after that until we gained the equal school rights eleven years afterwards. I made converts wherever I went by putting themselves in my place.

We had a very severe contest, but we were determined never to give the struggle over till victory was gained. When we started the battle, nine-tenths of the population was against us, ministers and deacons of churches, and what was more grinding to us, two-thirds of the colored population was against us. About the seventh year of the contest, Geo. Head opened his rum shop on South Main street, and invited all colored people who would remonstrate against the bill to come into his place and drink free rum. And the day the bill was to come up in the House he brought up over one hundred remonstrants against us. That day I lost my balance. I followed him and Davis out of the Court House, down the hill, and if he had opened his head I would have killed him dead on the spot. We were defeated, but we continued on year after year. John H. Clark, of Williams street, who went two or three times to Congress, was bitterly opposed to us. I pitched into him, handling him with "red-hot tongs," So we were at swords points two or three years. But when he saw the injustice he was doing us, he turned and was one of the warmest friends we had. Gen. Greene was also against me. Every place where I worked they were against me, and begged me to leave the field, and I could have everything I wanted. One said, "Henry, you had better leave the field or you will loose your bread and butter, and the d--d niggers 'wont thank you for it afterwards." I told him I was'nt fighting for the niggers, only fighting for principle, and when he heard I was dead, he might know I had quit the field. Every one that I worked for threw me out of employment except Mrs. Judge Ames, but that did'nt stop me. During this time John Waugh accidently got his son Fredrick into the district school, and there was such a time made about it that he was turned out in a little while. Then we were determined to try the law. So we begged Mr. Waugh to let us try his case. In laying the case before lawyer Blake, who said he would try the case for two hundred dollars, one hundred down, and if he lost the case he would'nt demand any more. We raised one hundred dollars and placed it in his hands for trial. When he came in court Judge Shaw non-suited us, upon some petty technical point, without giving us a hearing. That blow discouraged a great many of our men, but the women came up with fresh courage, namely Mrs. Mary Ames, wife of Judge Samuel Ames, Mrs. John E. Church and Mrs. Mary A. Waugh. The battle waxed hotter and hotter, till we finally won the day. So let the women have a name in history's fame. We finally triumphed on that glorious day of liberty, eleven years petition for Equal School Rights, April first.

In 1870 we petitioned the Honorable General Assembly to repeal that section relating to "Equal School Rights," and it was referred to the Judiciary Committee. They failed to report on it. In 1872 I published a pamphlet, which cost me forty dollars out of my own pocket, entitled the "Final Appeal," requesting the committee to report, favorable or not, a copy of which I laid before every member and clerk of the General Assembly. After that they reported every year promptly until the final triumph. This is one of the questions in my pamphlet which I asked Bishop Clark, Rhode Island, and he has'nt answered it yet, viz.: "Which seems the most like christianity and humanity, running the ignorant and down-trodden into heathenism, or gathering up the lost sheep of Israel and educating them, and adding them to the flock of Chrict? and as you stand at the head of the Church of Christ please answer that question." The Roman Catholic priests in the South gathered up the poor, weak, down-trodden slaves and educated them, to make useful citizens of them, and the Protestants, with Bishop Clark at the head, run them off to Africa and made slaves of them. This was the cause of my asking the question.

CHAPTER XVI.

SERVING ON THE JURY.

The colored American has ever been loyal and ready to die if need be at Freedom's shrine. The love of country has always burned vividly on the altar of his heart. He loves his "native land, its hills and mountains green."

In A.D. 1872, I was elected jurior in the Supreme Court, in Providence, R. I., and served thirty-three days, from April 22d to June 7th. When I was first called to act as a jurior, Mr. Burgess was my foreman. He rose and shook me by the hand and welcomed me to a seat by his side, and throughout the time I was with him treated me as a christian and a gentleman. During that time there were three sets of juriors discharged, and I alone was retained.

One of the most important cases that came up for trial, which I will mention here, was the noted case of Mr. Casey, a wealthy but elderly gentleman, and a blooming young lady as ever man laid eyes on—held the Court three days. During the time I watched the young lady closely to see if I could detect anything that I thought was unladylike and unworthy of due respect, and I saw nothing but the manners of a perfect lady. She sued in the lower court for $8000 damage, and it was decided in her favor, and he appealed to the Supreme Court. She then sued for $30,000. At this time I happened to be elected on the Grand Jury. When the court ended, and the Judge gave the case to the jury, the sheriff locked us up in a room, for every man to decide for himself how much she should or should not have. And there did'nt a man speak a word to each other but wrote the amount on a paper what they thought she should have, and ten out of twelve said she should have the whole amount of $30,000, and I feel proud that I was one of the ten, for it was the clearest and most just case that ever jury sat upon. So we bothered the second time, and there were ten out of twelve in her favor, the evidence being conclusive that she had been wrongfully treated, by having been to great expense in making preparations for the wedding. After a great controversy between us, we balloted the third time with the same result. Then we demanded to know of the two opposing ones, what was their reason, and neither could give any reason. We then agreed to compromise, and every man put down on a piece of paper what he thought

she ought to have, and the two would'nt agree to that. Then we dropped
down to $16,000, and one hung out to the bitter end. His only reason was,
that he thought it too much money for a poor girl to have at one time. So we
ten bore right square down on him, and he had to give in. We thought better
do that than to break the jury up, have another trial, and run the risk. We
then brought in a verdict for $16,000 for the deserving lady, and I as one
felt it to be one of the proudest acts of my life.

During the balance of my stay there we had some criticle cases to decide,
but in all cases I always cast my ballot with the affirmative, except in one
instance, the jury stood seven to five, and I was with the seven. My last
foreman was Mr. Stokes, of the firm of Stokes & Leonard, meat and produce dealers, and I served my time fully and got my honorable discharge,
and Mr. Stokes shook my hand and told the Clerk of the Court, that I made
one of the best juriors he ever knew.

The promises and obligations of marriage at the present day differ from
those of the past, because even in my day the slaves stood more upon the
principles and virtues of marriage, than the people of the latter days. The
marriage vow was held very sacred. Where there are now one hundred
divorce cases, there was not one among the people of those days. Why is
this? Moses said it was on account of ignorance that he gave them a writing
of divorcement then. Now we have the light of the gospel, which should
guide us in the path of righteousness. Let what may occur, a man should
love and respect his wife and family, and seek not for a separation except
for the crime mentioned in the Scriptures.

The first miracle performed by our Saviour was at Cana, in Galillee, at a
marriage. St. Paul then picks up the subject and says, "marriage is honorable among all men." Therefore about the year 1870, we struck that sacred
key-note, and commenced agitating the "intermarriage law," in the State of
Rhode Island, which we thought was unjust, and an outrage upon humanity.
When we looked over history, and found that law was placed on the Statute
Book in 1784, by such men as Capts. Gibbs, Scott, Townsend and others,
slaveholders of Rhode Island, we had a bitter contest against it, year after
year, for Rhode Island had at that time sixty-five slavers, running out of
Bristol, Newport and Providence, doing nothing but running slaves, on her
import and her exports, and thousands of our colored women's virtue was
sacrificed, and fell victims under that law. So we were determined to fight it
out till it was repealed. Year after year we were defeated, but kept on. Every
year when we came up with the petition, the question would arise on every
hand, Do you want your daughters to marry a negro? So in 1879 the Journal
came out in bitter tones against us. There was'nt a day but she had the
marriage law or the color line in her papers. The colored people were

roused to the utmost. I published a card in the paper, that it was'nt the color line or marriage question that had aroused the people, but it was the abuse in the House, that we had received from some of our Republicans. I made a little mistake in my card and the Journal refused to publish anything by way of rectifying my mistake, and I was forced to apply to the editor of the "Evening Telegram," and he was kind enough to open his column for a fair fight with the "Journal," and it was admitted by all that I whipped them fairly on race and color. I published a pamphlet entitled "An Address to the Hon. General Assembly and to the Editor of the 'Providence Journal,' " which cost forty dollars. I did'nt care if it cost one hundred, so as a black man could silence the editor of the "Journal." The marriage law was repealed March 17, 1881, by the following vote in the affirmative: Messrs. C. Anthony, J. Anthony, Bates, Bowen, Brownell, Burdick, Burrington, Carpenter, O. Chace, B. S. Chace, Chester, Chickering, Clark, Crandall, Davis, Eames, Freeman, Giles, Gregory, Jenckes, Lapham, Lee, Mason, Pendleton, Pendergast, Sanborn, Sheffield, Shove, Spooner, Stearns, Stone, Taft, Tallman, Thomas, Tounsend, Vincent, Stilman White, Daniel Wilkinson, Winsor—forty.

The following in the Senate: Ayes—Lieut. Gov. Fay, Senators Babcock, Bourn, Chase, Crandall, De Blois, Greene, Handy, Lyman, Maglone, Moies, E. C. Mowry, J. W. Mowry, Razee, Seabury, Smith, Tillinghast, Watson, B. F. Wilbur, G. A. Wilbur—twenty.

SELECT BIBLIOGRAPHY ON THE BLACK EXPERIENCE IN NEW ENGLAND

Cottrol, Robert J. *The Afro-Yankees: Providence's Black Community in the Antebellum Era*. Westport, CT: Greenwood Press, 1982.

Coughtry, Jay. *The Notorious Triangle: Rhode Island and the African Slave Trade, 1700–1807*. Philadelphia: Temple University Press, 1981.

Cromwell, Adelaide M. *The Other Brahmins: Boston's Black Upper Class, 1750–1950*. Fayetteville: University of Arkansas Press, 1994.

Daniels, John. *In Freedom's Birthplace: A Study of the Boston Negroes*. Boston: Houghton Mifflin, 1914.

Greene, Lorenzo Johnston. *The Negro in Colonial New England, 1620–1776*. New York: Columbia University Press, 1942.

Horton, James Oliver and Lois E. *Black Bostonians: Family Life and Community Struggle in the Antebellum North*. New York: Holmes and Meier, 1979.

Johnston, William Dawson. *Slavery in Rhode Island, 1775–1776*. Providence: Rhode Island Historical Society, 1894.

Kiven, Arline Ruth. *Then Why the Negroes: The Nature and Course of the Anti-slavery Movement in Rhode Island, 1637–1861*. Providence: Urban League of Rhode Island, 1973.

Moore, George Henry. *Notes on the History of Slavery in Massachusetts*. New York: D. Appleton, 1866.

Nell, William C. *The Colored Patriots of the American Revolution*. Boston: R. F. Wallcut, 1855.

Pierson, William D. *Black Yankees: The Development of an Afro-American Subculture in Eighteenth-Century New England*. Amherst: University of Massachusetts Press, 1988.

Pleck, Elizabeth Hafkin. *Black Migration and Poverty,. Boston, 1865–1900*. New York: Academic Press, c 1979.

Quarles, Benjamin. *The Negro in the American Revolution*. Chapel Hill: University of North Carolina Press, 1961.

Rider, Sidney S. (Sidney Smith). *An Historical Inquiry Concerning the Attempt to Raise a Regiment of Slaves by Rhode Island During the War of the Revolution*. Providence: S. S. Rider, 1880.

Robinson, William Henry, ed. *The Proceedings of the Free African Union Society and the African Benevolent Society: Newport, Rhode Island, 1780–1824*. Providence: Urban League of Rhode Island, 1976.

Salvador, George Arnold. *Paul Cuffe: The Black Yankee*. New Bedford, MA: Reynolds-Dewalt, 1969.

Steiner, Bernard Christian. *History of Slavery in Connecticut*. Baltimore: The Johns Hopkins Press, 1893.

Strother, Horatio T. *The Underground Rail Road in Connecticut*. Middletown, CT: Wesleyan University Press, 1962.

Thomas, Lamont Dominick. *Rise To Be A People: A Biography of Paul Cuffe*. Urbana: University of Illinois Press, c 1986.

Warner, Robert Austin. *New Haven Negroes, A Social History*. New Haven: Institute of Human Relations, Yale University Press, 1940.

Wiggins, Rosalind Cobb, ed. *Captain Paul Cuffe's Logs and Letters, 1808–1817: A Black Quaker's "Voice From Within The Veil."* Washington, DC: Howard University Press, 1996.

INDEX

Abolitionists, 145, 146, 161, 172–173
Africa
    occupations in, xiii, 5
    polygamy in, xiii, 4
    slave trade in, 9, 35
    warfare in, 6–9
African Governor's elections, xiv, xvi,
        xxii *n*.7, 44
African Greys, 119–120
Alcohol consumption
    of sailors, 124–25
    and temperance cause, 141–142,
        146
Ames, Mary, 209
Andrews, Wells C., 24
Anti-slavery societies, 145, 146
Aplin, William, 102
Apprentices, xii, 130, 133
Asher, Jeremiah, 157
Axum, James, 91, 124, 125

Baker, Elleanor, 39
Balch, Joseph, 144, 162
Banister, Henry, 103
Banks, John, 177
Baptist church, 96, 99, 148–157,
        178–201
Barnes, Edward, 121
Barrett, George, 120
Bates, Varnum J., 183–184
Benson, George, 100
Benson, Jerry, 101
Bethune, Dr., 172, 173, 175
Bevin, Mrs. Philo, 27
Bibb, Henry, 162, 163
Bingham, Abel, 20
Black Cloud, 120
Blacks in New England. *See* Free
        Negroes in New England; Slaves
        in New England

Book-keeping, 131, 139
Bowen, Henry L., 161, 163, 168
Bowen, Isaac B., Jr., 103
Bowen, Pardon, 76
Brainerd, Ansel, Sr., 26
Brown, Alice Greene, 76, 77
Brown, Cudgc, 76, 83, 88
Brown, George, 76
Brown, Jim, 101
Brown, Joseph George Washington,
        76, 96–97
Brown, Leonard, 150
Brown, Mary Alice, 76
Brown, Moses, xviii, xxi, 76–77,
        79–80, 83, 99–100, 192
Brown, Noah, 76, 77, 83–90
Brown, Obadiah, 100
Brown, Phillis, 76, 77, 79, 89
Brown, Samuel, 103, 118
Brown, William J., xvii–xx, 73–201
Brown University, 157
Brown v. Board of Education, xxiii *n. 15*
Burrell, Charles, 136
Burrill, Charles B., 103

Cady, Rev., 99
Caldwell, Rev., 181–182, 183
Caples, Dinah, 31
Catering business, 207
Chapman, Robert, 26
Chapman, Timothy, 20
Childs, George, 105–113, 127
Church, Charles, 19
Church, Mrs. John E., 209
Churches, 67, 78, 96, 99, 119–120,
        148–157, 173, 178–201
Civil rights
    and intermarriage law, 212–213
    and jury service, 211–212
    and legal protections, 143–144

ABOUT THE EDITOR

Robert J. Cottrol is the Harold Paul Green Research Professor of Law and Professor of Law and History at George Washington University. He is the author of *The Afro-Yankees: Providence's Black Community in the Antebellum Era* (1982) and has edited *Gun Control and the Constitution: Sources and Explorations on the Second Amendment* (1994). His articles and essays on law and history have appeared in the *New England Quarterly; Southern Studies;* the *American Journal of Legal History; Slavery and Abolition;* the *Law and Society Review;* the *Tulane Law Review;* the *Georgetown Law Journal;* the *Cardozo Law Review;* and the *Yale Law Journal* among others.